Gogol's *The Overcoat*

Gogol's

The Overcoat

Julian Graffy

Bristol Classical Press
Critical Studies in Russian Literature

First published in 2000 by
Bristol Classical Press
an imprint of
Gerald Duckworth & Co. Ltd
61 Frith Street
London W1V 5TA
e-mail: inquiries@duckworth-publishers.co.uk
Website: www.ducknet.co.uk

A catalogue record for this book is available
from the British Library

ISBN 1-85399-568-1

Printed in Great Britain by
Booksprint

Contents

Acknowledgements

I wish to thank Neil Cornwell for inviting me to contribute this volume to the *Critical Studies in Russian Literature* and for his encouragement and patience while I was at work on it. I also wish to thank Birgit Beumers, Richard Davies, Roger Keys, Aleksandr Ospovat, Andrei Rogatchevski, Tatiana Vladimirovna Tsivian and Evgenii Tsymbal, all of whom supplied me with materials used in this study.

I am, as ever, profoundly grateful for the energy, good humour and resourcefulness of the staff of the Library of the School of Slavonic and East European Studies, University College London.

Introduction

Nikolai Gogol wrote his most famous story, the Petersburg tale 'The Overcoat', in 1839-41 and it was first published in his *Collected Works* in 1842. This initial publication did not attract a large amount of attention, but within a very few years the story and its hero, the 'eternal titular counsellor' Akakii Akakievich, began their epic and continuing journey through the minds of readers and critics, provoking in them responses that are remarkable both for their intensity and for their variety.

Uniquely among Russian short stories, 'The Overcoat' has been repeatedly reworked by later writers, from Fedor Dostoevsky, whose *Poor Folk* was published in 1846, to the writers of post-Soviet Russia. It has also spawned films, theatrical productions, opera and ballet, and its influence has spread throughout the world.

Part One of this study looks both at the history of the story's critical reception in Russia and at its many remarkable reworkings, in fiction, film and other arts.

Part Two attempts a survey of critical interpretations. So many critics have contributed to the discourse the story has provoked, and taken up the points made by their predecessors, that full discussion of the evolution of the critical debate would require a study many times longer than this. When referring to the critical debate I have therefore attempted to quote either the first critic to make a particular point, or the one who has made it most effectively.

For this reason, too, the Bibliography contains brief annotations to all the articles or parts of books that are devoted specifically to 'The Overcoat'. Some critical studies, most notably Boris Eikhenbaum's 'How Gogol's overcoat is made', have provoked a resonance way beyond the study of this tale, and have been many times republished, both in Russian and in English. The bibliography contains references to the most important of these republications, and also indicates which edition is used in the text of this study.

To reduce the number of footnotes, references to works listed in the bibliography are incorporated in the text. When the bibliography includes more than one work by a particular author, or more than one edition of a particular text, the date of the edition being referred to will also be given.

The transliteration system used in the text is that of the Library of Congress, with the exception that diacritics are not used and the common

English form of surnames such as Dostoevsky and Belinsky is preferred. The name Gogol is given in the text without its final soft sign.

The standard Library of Congress system is used in the bracketed page references and in the bibliography. Thus, for example, I use Chizhevsky and Nikolskaia in the text but Chizhevskii and Nikol'skaia in the bracketed page references and the bibliography.

Translations from Russian originals are mine unless otherwise stated.

References in the text to the collected works of Gogol in Russian, Nikolai Gogol, *Polnoe sobranie sochinenii* (Complete Works), ed. N.L. Meshcheriakov and others (14 volumes), Moscow and Leningrad: Izdatel'stvo Akademii nauk SSSR, 1937-52, are given by the abbreviation PSS, the volume number and the page number, e.g. PSS, 10: 93. References to volume three of the Complete Works, the volume which contains 'The Overcoat', are given by volume and page number only, e.g. 3: 141.

References in the text to the collected works of other authors are given by the author's name, the abbreviation PSS, or SS, or S (standing for Complete Works, or Collected Works, or Works), the volume number and page number, e.g. Belinskii PSS, 6: 349.

Part One:

Receptions
and reworkings

Receptions and reworkings

In July and August 1839, in Marienbad, Nikolai Gogol began work on a story called 'The Tale of the Clerk who Stole Overcoats' ('Povest' o chinovnike kradushchem shineli'). The tale is told in comic vein, beginning, indeed, with a pun on the name of the department in which he works. The nameless hero, 41 years old but an 'eternal titular councillor', is mocked both by his colleagues and by the narrator, who describes him as a 'very good animal' and his tail-coat as 'the colour of a cowpat'. His single problem is that his worn-out coat will not withstand the Petersburg cold, and so he goes to the tailor Petrovich to get it mended. Alas, the tailor pronounces that 'Nothing can be done' with it, words which 'so confused' the hero that...but here the tale breaks off, before the desperate measures suggested in its title can be implemented.

Gogol continued to work on the story in Vienna, in August and September 1839 and again in St Petersburg at the end of the year, the work consisting both of corrections and additions to the existing text and of pushing the narrative further. Further details about the clerk are added, including the story of his birth and christening, and he acquires the name Akakii Akakievich Tishkevich, a surname which is described by the narrator as strange, but which may imply his meekness. These reworkings also temper the anecdotal and humorous tone of the original draft with passages which suggest a more sympathetic attitude to the hero, including the introduction of the 'humane passage' which would later play such a crucial role in interpretations of the story. In late December 1839 Gogol moved to Moscow and concentrated on the other major work he was writing at the time, the novel *Dead Souls*. His fourth and final period of work on his story would be in Rome in the spring of 1841. In drafts dating from this period the hero's surname becomes Bashmakevich or Bashmakov, before settling into its final form of Bashmachkin and, for the first time, the story bears the simplified (and significant) title 'The Overcoat' ('Shinel''). This is also the period in which the fantastic epilogue is written. The first announcement in the Russian press that the work is forthcoming also dates from the middle of 1841.

In the summer of 1842 in St Petersburg Gogol sent a copy of the story to the printers for inclusion in the third volume of his forthcoming *Collected Works* (*Sochineniia Nikolaia Gogolia*, St Petersburg, 1842). Certain references

3

in the tale to members of the government service then attracted the attention of the censor, and some phrases had to be softened for the first edition. Though copies of this volume were ready at the end of 1842 their release for sale was not permitted until late January 1843.

This was the only edition of the tale to appear in Gogol's lifetime, and it attracted what now seems to be remarkably little attention, lost as it was in a volume of his collected works, and overshadowed by the first publication that year of Part One of *Dead Souls*.[1] Unlike so many of his other works it is not referred to at all by Gogol in later years in his essays in self-justification and explanation or in his voluminous correspondence. Yet it would over time become perhaps the most famous tale in all of Russian literature, the most interpreted, the most fought over. Critics of every hue would argue over both the 'meaning' and the means of the tale, attempting to appropriate it for their various ideological and artistic schemas.[2] But uniquely the reception of this story would also take the form of a dazzling succession of literary and other reworkings, offering ample evidence of its continuing potency for succeeding generations, both in Russia and in other cultures. In a letter to his mother of April 1827, the eighteen-year-old Gogol had written:

> Man is strange with regard to his inner desire. He catches
> sight of something in the distance and the yearning for it will
> not leave him for an instant. It troubles his peace and forces
> him to use all his efforts to attain the essential. Sometimes
> something which seems to be the smallest trifle, but which
> for me is precious, torments me with yearning and with
> anguish at my inability to possess it.
>
>   (PSS, 10: 93, quoted by Stilman: 138-9)

This insight was later developed into the yearning/frustration plots of such early Petersburg tales as 'Nevsky Prospect' and 'Diary of a Madman', but in 'The Overcoat' Gogol gave the fullest and most effective expression to a basic structural model of lack – desire – gain after major strivings and privations – short-lived joy – loss – suffering – madness – death and vengeance that would be applied again and again by later authors in a succession of tales written as homage, stylisation or in polemical opposition.

The initial reception: Belinsky and the 'Natural School'

The contemporary critic whose name is most closely associated with the work of Gogol is, of course, Vissarion Belinsky. His first major article on the writer 'On the Russian story and the stories of Mr Gogol' (1835) elaborated a theory of literary realism associated with Gogol's work. In the words of Paul Debreczeny:

> In addition to singling him out as a leading poet, Belinsky
> gave a sharp definition of the nature of his works. Whether
> the critic's conception was true or not, and whether Gogol
> himself liked it or not, in any case, the young author now
> emerged in the consciousness of the public as a poet of
> reality, from whom a portrayal of, and comments on, society
> could be expected. (Debreczeny: 13)

After the appearance of Belinsky's article, 'it became virtually impossible to regard Gogol from a purely literary point of view' (ibid., 21). In this context one would expect him to seize upon 'The Overcoat' as fodder for his theories, and he did indeed long harbour a plan to write at length about the story; but in fact he never did so, and his actual references to it are sparse and superficial. He first alluded to it, in 1842, as 'one of the most profound of Gogol's creations' (Belinskii PSS, 6: 349), and the following year, in a review of the *Collected Works*, he again described it as a 'new work, distinguished by the profundity of its idea and feeling, the maturity of its artistic chiselling' (ibid., 661-2). In 1845 he listed 'The Overcoat' among works by Gogol that 'could have been written not only by a person with enormous talent and a brilliant way of looking at things, but also by a person, who, moreover, knows Petersburg not only by hearsay' (ibid., 8: 555). In 1847 he found that 'the presence of the tragic element is strongly felt in the ostensibly comic tale "The Overcoat", in the figure and the fate of the comic and pitiable Akakii Akakievich' (ibid., 10: 179), an idea that he expanded in his most extended comment on the tale in another piece from the same year:

> If in 'Taras Bulba' Gogol knew how to reveal the comic in
> the tragic, then in 'Old World Landowners' and 'The Over-
> coat' he managed to find the tragic...in the positive vulgarity
> of life. This is where, it seems to us, we should seek the
> essential particularity of Gogol's talent. This is not just the
> gift of displaying vividly the vulgarity of life, but even more
> the gift of displaying life's phenomena in all the fullness of
> their reality and their truth. (ibid., 10: 244)

Belinsky did not return to 'The Overcoat', but in the words of the last quoted sentence, with their stress on 'reality' (*real'nost'*) and truth (*istinnost'*), together with other ideas about the nature of Gogol's gift, he nevertheless was instrumental in establishing what would be a particularly influential reading of the story's essence.

1844 saw the appearance of 'The Theatrical Carriage' ('Teatral'naia kareta'), the first story by a young writer (born in 1822), Dmitrii Grigorovich. It tells of the life of a 'poor man', the theatrical prompter Ivan

Ivanovich,[3] the butt of the mockery of all those around him, but also the object of the sympathy of a young actress, a sympathy expressed through a dramatic verbal intervention. With its mix of the comic and the sentimental, this is one of the very first stories to be written directly under the influence of Gogol's tale, as Grigorovich himself admitted in his literary memoirs: 'We were all equally captivated by Gogol, almost everything that was being written in narrative form was a reflection of Gogol's tales, and predominantly of the tale "The Overcoat"' (cited by Dolotova: 191). The point was taken up by the Formalist critic Viktor Vinogradov:

> While he was constructing it, the author seemed to have Gogol's 'Overcoat' directly before his eyes, but he changed its compositional plan in such a way that the dramatic summit of his novella became the touching episode.
> (Vinogradov 1976b: 159)

Belinsky, too, had spoken repeatedly in the mid-1840s about Gogol's influence on the new generation of writers, contending in 1843 that:

> ...all new writers of novels and stories, the talented and the talentless, have somehow involuntarily succumbed to the influence of Gogol...Gogol killed two false directions in Russian literature: a strained idealism that stands on crutches and waves its cardboard sword...and a satirical didacticism.... Now...everyone is striving to portray real, not imaginary people; but since real people live on the earth and in society, and not in the air, not in the clouds, where only ghosts live, then, naturally, writers of our time along with people also depict society.   (Belinskii PSS, 8: 80, 81, 82)

He added, in 1845, 'Decidedly, Gogol is all Russian literature! If anyone wishes to speak of Russian literature, he will inevitably say at least something about Gogol; and if another wishes to speak of himself, he will again speak of Gogol' (ibid., 9: 356), before going on to signal the influence of Akakii Akakievich on the heroes of another emerging writer, Iakov Butkov. In another piece of that year he spoke of Gogol as having 'given a new direction to Russian literature', and referred to his 'school' as:

> 'ashamed of the *sensitive* [*chuvstvitel'nogo*] – that's true, because the *sensitive* or the *sentimental* [*santimental'noe*] is now the same as the vulgar.... But the idea that the school founded by Gogol should be ashamed of the emotional [*pateticheskogo*], that is decidedly a lie. Where is there more of the emotional than in the works of Gogol: 'Taras Bulba',

'Old World Landowners', 'Nevsky Prospect' and 'The
Overcoat'?   (ibid., 9: 375)

In 1846, in disapprobation of this tendency, the conservative critic Faddei
Bulgarin coined the term 'The Natural School' ('Natural'naia shkola'), but
the term was embraced with enthusiasm by Belinskii, who stated later that
year that Bulgarin was absolutely right to name the school founded by Gogol
'the *new natural school*, unlike the *old rhetorical* school, or the *unnatural*
school, that is to say the *artificial* school, in other words the *false school*.'
(ibid., 9: 650).[4] Viktor Vinogradov concluded his extensive 1929 study, *The
Evolution of Russian Naturalism. Gogol and Dostoevsky (Evoliutsiia russkogo naturalizma. Gogol' i Dostoevskii)*, with the contention that 'The return
to sentimental forms was not a "struggle with Gogol" for the consciousness
of his contemporaries, on the contrary, they saw it as the realisation of
Gogol's precepts, which they sought with particular insistence in the novella
"The Overcoat"' (Vinogradov 1976b: 187). Earlier in ths same work,
Vinogradov wrote of Gogol's followers in the following terms:

> The search for new literary forms led to the ideological 'load-
> ing' of the novella, to the switching into the plan of artistic
> creative works of philosophical, sociological and other 'extra-
> literary' material. Finding support in the personal initiative of
> the leader ('The Overcoat') and in the parallel 'philanthropic'
> strivings of French literature – the inclination towards 'civic',
> socio-philosophical sentimentalism aroused the renaissance
> of a cycle of sentimental plot schemes, devices of drawing,
> images, stylistic accessories, symbolism.... This wave swept
> over Dostoevsky, Grigorovich, Turgenev, Nekrasov...Tol-
> stoy and a number of other less important writers...
>   And in this growth of sentimental strivings, an exceptional
> role was played by Dostoevsky's novel *Poor Folk*.
>   (ibid,. 162)

The initial reception: Dostoevsky

Writing in public praise of Gogol in 1861, Dostoevsky recalls how 'out of
the loss of a clerk's overcoat he made for us a terrible tragedy.' ('A series
of articles about Russian literature' ['Riad statei o russkoi literature'],
Dostoevskii PSS, 18: 59). His first response to Gogol's tale, was of course,
the novel *Poor Folk (Bednye liudi)*, published in 1846, to which the words
quoted above are relevant, but which is a considerably more ambiguous
work than they would suggest, and has been called the most remarkable and
sophisticated of all the responses to Gogol's tale. It is also the only one of
the 'remakes' of the story for which we have Gogol's own assessment,

though this is based just on 'reading the first three pages and taking a look in the middle'. In a letter to A.M. Velgorskaia of 14 May 1846 he writes:

> You can see talent in the author of *Poor Folk* , the choice of subjects speaks in support of his spiritual qualities, but you can also see that he is still young. There is still a lot of loquaciousness and little concentration in himself: the whole thing would be much more lively and stronger if it were more compressed. Though I admit that I am saying this without reading it to the end, just having leafed through it.
>
> (PSS, 13: 66)

Like its model, *Poor Folk* tells the story of a poor St Petersburg copying clerk and his doomed love. In this case the object of Makar Devushkin's devotion is a young woman, Varvara Dobroselova, living, like him, in straightened circumstances. Throughout the tale, he makes constant sacrifices for the object of his love, but in the end he is tragically deprived of her and reduced to despair. This borrowing of the basic story outline of 'The Overcoat' is adumbrated by a plethora of plot details such as Makar's pride in his calligraphy, his mockery at the hands of his fellow clerks, including mockery of his name, and a number of visits to beseech help from 'important personages'. In this sense Makar is a double of Akakii Akakievich and the protagonist of a new version of the story. But as well as being the story's protagonist, he is also its reader, and stern critic, for in the course of the novel Varvara sends him both 'The Overcoat' and Pushkin's *The Tales of Belkin* to read. Makar infinitely prefers a story from the latter, 'The Station Master', which he takes to be a sympathetic tale. He both identifies absolutely with its hero, Samson Vyrin, and feels as if he had written the tale himself, adding, 'No, it's natural! You read it; it's natural, it's alive!' (Dostoevskii PSS, 1: 59). 'The Overcoat', on the other hand, outrages him, for he notices the parallels with his own experience and, with his literary theory based upon identification (a theory Gogol himself had mocked in the tale of the provincial police inspector in the first paragraph of 'The Overcoat', 3: 141), takes the whole thing to be a vicious attack on him.

His detailed response to the story in a letter to Varvara of 8 July is also an *apologia pro vita sua*, for he too has an unblemished record in the service, would like to be able to afford new clothing, but has been reduced by his penury to walking the streets on tiptoe to preserve his shoe leather. He is particularly incensed by what he perceives as the complete absence of sympathy from the writer, of whom he suggests:

> Well it would have been good if near the end he had turned over a new leaf, had softened things a bit, found room, for example, say even after the bit where they threw bits of paper

on his head, to say, well, that for all that he was a virtuous man, a good citizen, that he did not deserve such treatment by his comrades, that he was obedient to his superiors (this could have served as a sort of example), that he wished no one evil, that he believed in God and that when he died (if he really wants him to have to die) he was mourned. But best of all would be not to leave him to die, poor fellow, but to arrange that his overcoat was found, that that general, finding out about his virtues in more detail, would ask him back to his chancellery, would promote him and give him a good salary, so you see how it would be: evil would be punished and virtue would triumph, and his comrades at the office would be left with egg on their faces. At least that's how I would have done it.   (ibid., 63)

The story has profoundly discountenanced Makar, and he returns to it in a reference to 'lampoonists' who write about people walking around on tiptoe in his letter of 1 August, but his engagement with Gogol's text is not limited to these exercises in practical criticism. For Makar, as well as being Akakii's double and Gogol's reader, is also Gogol's rival. From the beginning of the tale his letters have been peppered with references to literature and he is greatly concerned about the style of his own writing. More directly, he wonders what it would be liked to be a published author himself, the author of *The Poems of Makar Devushkin* (ibid., 53). Within his letters he includes sentimental tales of 'poor folk', both in his recountings of the relentlessly tragic fortunes of his fellow tenants, the Gorshkov family, and in the tale of a poor beggar boy encountered on the street, of which he says:

I am forced to tell you, my dear, that I began to describe all this to you partly in order to pour my heart out, but more in order to show you an example of the good style of my creative writing. Because I am sure that you will admit, my dear, that recently I have started to get myself a style.

(ibid., 88)

This admission is followed later in the same letter by Makar's 'allegorical' and didactic sketch of an 'alternative' 'The Overcoat' which would follow the poetics of the Natural School. It would be the tale of a poor cobbler, desperate about a pair of boots he had inadvertently ruined, and of a rich man living in the same house, also dreaming of a new pair of boots, who might be persuaded by his wife to stop thinking of himself and to show concern for those around him.

However, the complexity of the dialogue in which *Poor Folk* engages with 'The Overcoat' is not exhausted by the multifariousness of Makar's connection with it. For Dostoevsky, too, is both reader and critic, re-writer and rival of his predecessor and the ambiguity of his take on the earlier tale is paramount. His hero Makar is naïve and myopic, sentimental and verbose, but all these qualities are a sign of his humanity. He could not, like his predecessor, be called a 'good animal'. His love object is a human being, not a thing. Like Akakii Akakievich he has a surname (Devushkin – Virginal) that can evoke ribaldry and a given name of Greek origin that suggests his unworldliness; but this name is not in itself absurd and is not a repetition of his patronymic, which already confers on him a crucial autonomy.

Dostoevsky also alters a key episode in Gogol's plot, for when at the height of his troubles Makar is summoned by 'His Excellency', the equivalent of Gogol's important personage, he is met, after initial sternness, with sympathy, understanding, a gift of money and a warm handshake (ibid., 93), in a plot move strikingly like Makar's rewrite of 'The Overcoat'. Above all Dostoevsky's construction of his work in epistolary form gives Makar the chance to *tell his own life* in first person narration. If Akakii *copies,* (*perepisyvaet*), then Makar *corresponds* with another human being (*perepisyvaetsia*); and Dostoevsky's own attitude to him is not finally apparent. His exasperating foibles are all too clear, but so is his innate kindness. As Dostoevsky wrote to his brother Mikhail on 1 February 1846:

> Our public has instinct, as any crowd does, but it doesn't have education. They don't understand how you can write in such a style. They are used to seeing the author's mug [*rozhu*] in everything: but I didn't show mine. And they're not quick enough to realise that it's Devushkin talking, not me, and that Devushkin cannot speak in any other way.
>
> (ibid., 28/1: 117)

Makar's spontaneous reactions to his reading of 'The Overcoat' may indeed be naïve, but the very fact that a reader who engages so directly with the text that he identifies himself with its protagonist is at the same time so offended by it fundamentally undermines Belinsky's pat formula of the tragic peeping through the comic mask. Makar is also alert enough to ask some troubling questions about the very *form* of the text, about the intention and the effect of its being written in the way that it is. 'Why write about someone that sometimes he is in such need that he doesn't drink tea?', he exclaims, and more crucially 'But why write this stuff?' (ibid., 1: 62, 63), questions which will be fully addressed for the first time only by Eikhenbaum. That they are also questions that trouble Dostoevsky is evident from the complex relationship his own text has with its precursor. As the émigré critic Alfred Bem reminds us, Makar ends his analysis of 'The Overcoat' with the words:

> You know it's an ill-intentioned little book, Varenka; it's just
> not plausible, because it couldn't happen that there would be a
> clerk like that. You know after such stuff a complaint should
> be made, Varenka, a formal complaint.   (ibid., 63)

And, Bem goes on to suggest, Dostoevsky has written this complaint on Makar's behalf: 'Isn't the whole story "Poor Folk" such a "complaint" against Gogol's "Overcoat"?' (Bem: 138).

In the letter to his brother quoted above Dostoevsky said: 'I work through Analysis, not Synthesis, that is I go into the depths, and, sorting things through atom by atom, I seek out the whole, whereas Gogol goes straight for the whole and is therefore not so deep as I am' (ibid., 28/1: 118). Critics were also quick to notice the polemical relationship of the two texts, and the ever more intricate discussion of this literary relationship has yielded particularly fruitful insights into 'The Overcoat' itself. The critic Apollon Grigorev, writing in 1851, said 'look at Akakii Akakievich from the sentimental point of view, imbue yourself with regard to him...with morbid sympathy...and you get Makar Alekseevich Devushkin...' and other Dosto-evskian heroes (Grigor'ev 1916: 36-37); and in 1864 the satirist Saltykov-Shchedrin called Devushkin a 'famous cadger...who somehow managed to cut himself at least a hundred sweaters full of holes out of Gogol's "Over-coat"' (Saltykov – Shchedrin PSS, 6: 497). In 1881 the critic Nikolai Strakhov called *Poor Folk* a 'bold and decisive *correction* of Gogol', and a condem-nation of his irony (cited by Bem: 134); while in 1902 the poet and critic Innokentii Annensky spoke of the 'whole abyss' that lay between Akakii Akakievich and Makar Devushkin (Annenskii 1979: 223). This idea was developed by the Symbolist writer and critic Viacheslav Ivanov, who wrote in 1911:

> As for Gogol, I see Dostoevsky and Gogol as polar oppo-
> sites: one of them has faces without souls and the other the
> faces of souls...Gogol could influence Dostoevsky only at
> the time of *Poor Folk*. Then 'The Overcoat' was a revelation
> for him...   (Ivanov 1971: 17)

Yet in the same sentence Ivanov would go on to describe Dostoevsky as a young story teller who was 'alien in spirit' to Gogol. The idea of the struggle between the two writers was also illuminatingly articulated by the Russian Formalist critics whose brilliant work of the 1920s would take the analysis of 'The Overcoat' on to a new level of sophistication. In particular Iurii Tynianov in a seminal study of 1921 drew upon the relationship of the two tales to make a subtle contribution to the theory of literary stylisation and parody. In Tynianov's view Gogol is a 'point of departure' for Dostoevsky, who tries out Gogol's devices to see which of them will suit him. The relationship between the two writers is therefore one of stylisation, 'not following the style, but playing with it', rather than 'imitation' or 'influence', and stylisation is close to parody. In the question of characterisation too, Dostoevsky 'clashes with Gogol' and it is particularly this aspect of the earlier story that so exasperates Makar Devushkin (Tynianov 1979: 199, 200, 207). Writing at the end of the decade the other leading Formalist critic Viktor Vinogradov stressed that the 'conversational-vocal verbal mosaic' (*razgovorno-rechevaia slovesnaia mozaika*) which Gogol had created with such exceptional artistry was of no use for the '"touching" spiritual effusions' favoured by Dostoevsky (Vinogradov 1976b: 165). Mikhail Bakhtin in his major early study of Dostoevsky writes as follows: 'As early as the first, "Gogolian" period of his writing, Dostoevsky depicts not the "poor clerk", but the *self-consciousness* of the poor clerk (Devushkin...)' and others (Bakhtin 1972: 80). Thus:

> Dostoevsky produced a sort of small scale Copernican revolution, by making what had been a firm and conclusive authorial definition an aspect of the hero's self-definition.... The dominant of the entire artistic vision and construction was shifted, and the whole world began to look new, even though Dostoevsky scarcely introduced any essentially new, non-Gogolian material.
>
> Not only the activity of the hero himself, but also the external world and daily life which surround him are drawn into the process of self-consciousness, transferred from the author's field of vision to the hero's field of vision.   (ibid., 82-3)

Returning to the subject in 1961, he epigramatically describes the birth of Dostoevsky from Gogol as 'the birth of the personality from the character', the first stage in his move from the 'type' of the poor clerk to the greater self-consciousness of his dreamers and 'underground men' (Bakhtin 1979: 324). Discussion of this remarkable literary relationship continues to this day, and a recent contributor has described Dostoevsky's story as 'the most brilliant "embodied" commentary on Gogol's "The Overcoat" in all Russian literature and criticism', and 'a colossal act of aesthetic necromancy' (Jackson 1993: 206, 207).[5] Thus the reception of *Poor Folk*, always bound up with discussion of its forerunner, not only elucidates the uneasy relationship of 'disciple texts' with their 'master text' and the pervasive ambiguity of their motivations, but also sheds light on what Gogol was trying to do and what he was not trying to do in 'The Overcoat'.

Though Dostoevsky's engagement with 'The Overcoat' would never be so intense again, connections have been found between it and a number of Dostoevsky's other works. In a recent study Olga Dilaktorskaia has shown the relationship between Bashmachkin and the important personage to be reflected in that between Goliadkin Jr. and Goliadkin Sr. in another 1846 work, *The Double* (*Dvoinik*) (Dilaktorskaia 1999: 191-3). Mikhail Epshtein has followed the evolution of Akakii's passion for calligraphy through the copying clerk hero Vasia Shumkov of the 1848 story 'A Faint Heart' ('Slaboe serdtse'), of whom it is said that 'you will not find such handwriting in the whole of Petersburg', to another Dostoevskian character with a passion for copying – which is indeed described as his only talent – Prince Myshkin, the hero of *The Idiot* (*Idiot*), of 1868. But as Epshtein points out, everything here, plot, character, and above all authorial attitude to the 'holy fool' protagonist is radically reworked, and *The Idiot* represents the end of the road of the Dostoevskian move away from Gogol (Epshtein 1988).

Other mid-century reactions

Ivan Turgenev was another of the mid-nineteenth-century writers whom Vinogradov (quoted above) suggested as having been influenced by 'The Overcoat', and Turgenev more than once acknowledged Gogol's influence on his early writing. Writing to Mikhail Pogodin in December 1851, he told him: 'If you see Gogol don't forget to bow to him in the name of one of the smallest of his pupils' (cited by Dolotova: 188). In a letter of 21 February 1852 to Pauline Viardot under the immediate impression of Gogol's death he wrote: 'For us he was more than a writer: he revealed to us our very selves' (cited by Pustovoit: 41). A number of his early works have been seen to bear the influence of 'The Overcoat'. Pustovoit compares the eponymous hero of the 1847 story 'Petushkov' in his lovelorn shyness, his tongue-tied speech and his general weakness to Akakii Akakievich, and the limited and bullying major who hectors him to the important personage (Pustovoit: 43-45). Simon Karlinsky finds the 1849 play *The Bachelor* (*Kholostiak*) – in which the kindly middle-aged government clerk Moshkin becomes attached to the orphaned young Maria Belova, who actually prefers him to her heartless young suitor – to be a polemic with Gogol's tale in the same way as is Dostoevsky's *Poor Folk*, based upon a desire to 'correct the Gogolian situation in "The Overcoat"' and an 'urge to bring things closer to what is probable and possible in real life...' (Karlinsky: 139-40).

One of Turgenev's most famous early tales, the 1852 'Mumu', is described in passing by the historian of Russian literature Prince Mirsky as 'a philanthropic story in the tradition of "The Greatcoat" and of "Poor Folk"' (Mirsky 1958: 198). On close examination this story turns out to be Turgenev's closest and most inventive reworking of the Gogolian original. It tells the tale of the peasant Gerasim, deaf and dumb from birth, brought from his village by his mistress, a querulous old widow, to work as yardman in her Moscow house. Like Akakii, Gerasim takes an inordinate pride in his work, and his dumbness makes it impossible for him to communicate closely with his fellow servants; but Gerasim is a huge man, repeatedly described as a *bogatyr* (the heroic figure of Russian folklore) and this prevents his fellows from mocking him. Also like Akakii, Gerasim finds his isolation in his own little room suddenly disrupted by the appearance of a love-object, in this case a fellow servant, Tatiana, who seems to reciprocate. In an echo of the plot of 'The Overcoat', the need to get a new article of clothing, in this case a new kaftan, which will make him seem more presentable, delays his visit to the 'important personage' in his life, the mistress, to ask for Tatiana's hand. The delay turns out to be fatal, for the capricious mistress decides to marry her off to another of her servants. This rival, Klimov, in another allusion to Gogol's text, has lived in St Petersburg and is a shoe-maker, a *bashmachnik* (an exact anagram of the name Bashmachkin) a term which is repeatedly used to identify him. So the poor, meek girl is married off to the drunken Klimov and Gerasim has gone through the tragic lack – aspiration – brief hopes of happiness – deprivation cycle of his Gogolian fellow. But the story does not end there. Instead the cycle is repeated, this time with a non-human love object, the eponymous dog Mumu, whom Gerasim saves from drowning on the very day on which he parts from Tatiana. Gerasim loves the dog unreservedly, and everything goes well until the mistress takes an interest in the dog, which, devoted to Gerasim, does not return her affections. Incensed, the mistress insists that Mumu be got rid of and she is taken away and sold. Gerasim is plunged into gloom, and searches half of Moscow. Then, miraculously, the dog finds its way home. Now Gerasim is more careful, keeping the dog out of sight during the day and taking it out only at night, but, alas, a bark alerts the insomniac mistress and she repeats her demand that the dog be disposed of. When Gerasim becomes aware of this he himself takes the dog back out to the river, ties it to heavy bricks and drowns it.

Thus the lack – acquisition – loss triad is repeated in 'Mumu' three times, but with interesting departures from the Gogolian model. Gerasim never goes to beseech his 'important personage' and his very lack of language makes it impossible to turn to those around him and ask for sympathy. Indeed he seems finally to acquiesce in his own desperate fate, a fate caused entirely by simple human malice. There is no Akakian rebellion here. And yet, he is avenged. After the drowning of Mumu he leaves Moscow for ever, and walks like a pilgrim with sack and stick back to his village, his *rodina*, where the wind and the stars seem to greet him. The mistress experiences anger at his departure and temporary remorse, and very soon she dies. The heirs dismiss the remaining servants. Gerasim may not be able to speak in his own defence, but the tone of the narrative is unwaveringly sympathetic, and Turgenev's recension of the Gogolian model reclaims the hero for humanity, its poignancy never dissipated by the dizzying shifts of tone that so discountenanced Makar Devushkin in his reading of 'The Overcoat'.

The influence of the story continued. In 1852 Panteleimon Kulish, who

would publish one of the first biographies of Gogol two years later, pro-
duced 'Iakov Iakovlevich', whose hero again tellingly bears the same name
as his father, and which Chizhevsky describes as 'surely inspired by Gogol's
"The Overcoat"' (Chizhevskii 1976: 387). In 1860 the poet Lev Mei wrote
'The Ten Copeck Coin' ('Grivennik'),[6] a Moscow-based story whose hero,
Spiridon Petrovich Bogoslovskii, has much in common with Akakii
Akakievich. He too is a copying clerk, who has to take care of every copeck,
who worries about finding the money to get new clothes and economises
on tea, and whose overcoat is bespattered by mud from a passing carriage.
He also takes inordinate pride in his handwriting. The poor clerk finds a
sparkling ten copeck coin in the street, and superstitiously considering that
this will bring him happiness he doggedly refuses to give it up to anyone,
even to those who are clearly poorer than he is. This selfish act leads
indirectly to the poor man's downfall, because, largely through the callous
intervention of his love rival, his refusal to part with the coin leads to the
suspicion that he has forged it. In another echo of 'The Overcoat' he has a
humiliating encounter with an important personage, in this case the father
of his love object. Dismissed from the house he quickly loses his job in the
service and very soon dies from drink. His funeral attracts but a single
mourner.

Spiridon's closeness to Akakii Akakievich is also indicated by his
initials, which as he himself stresses are SPB, a fact that associates him with
the so-called 'St Petersburg text', a continuing nineteenth-century narrative
of stories set in the capital of which Gogol's 'Petersburg Tales' are a crucial
component. Again his fate is similar: sudden and inordinate obsession leads
not to happiness but to total destitution and ultimate death. Mei adds a
multi-layered social context and psychological acuity to the ramifications
of the 'Overcoat' texts, but the narrator of 'The Ten-Copeck Coin' also
maintains an ironic lightness of tone, marked by a recurring Gogolian joke
about the need to say something about each of the several secondary
characters even when they do not merit it, a lightness adumbrated by the
story's subtitle 'An implausible event'. This is echoed in an amusing dream
sequence in which the coin itself counsels Spiridon to abandon his super-
stitious search for unearned happiness and return to his former hard work
and self-reliance (advice he conspicuously declines to take), and an ending
that insists that if only Spiridon had drunk his winnings in vodka he would
not have fallen into ruin. The greater distance in time from the publication
of Gogol's original makes it possible for Mei to move on from the polemical
moral engagement with Gogol of the young Dostoevsky and Turgenev. The
spry and distanced tone of the narration marks a new turn in the reception
of the tale, making 'The Ten-Copeck Coin' an elegant and witty pastiche
and suggesting a new, collusive, relationship with 'The Overcoat' that will
characterise many later homage texts.

The critical discourse around the tale also continued to develop. In his first response to it, in 1847, Apollon Grigorev suggested:

> In the image of Akakii Akakievich the poet sketched out the
> final shallowing of God's creation to such a degree that an
> object, and the most insignificant object, becomes for man
> the source of boundless joy and destructive grief, to such a
> point that an overcoat becomes a tragic *fatum* in the life of a
> creature created in the image and form of the Eternal; your
> hair stands on end from the maliciously cold humour with
> which this shallowing is traced.   (Grigor'ev 1982: 113-14)

In a number of articles of the 1850s Grigorev repeatedly stresses Gogol's
brilliant sobriety and artistic restraint, which he contrasts with the excesses
of his sentimental 'followers':

> And what mysterious sensitivity points out to a brilliant nature
> the limits in his creation, what protects him from two evils:
> from slavish copying of life's phenomena and from stilted
> idealisation, what makes it stop in time?.... One false move,
> it seems, and Akakii Akakievich would strike us not with a
> tragic but with a sentimentally lachrymose impression.
>   (Grigor'ev 1990: 77)

If Grigorev was alert to stylistic questions, others were more comically
alarmed by the story's social implications. In *My Past and Thoughts* (*Byloe
i dumy*) Herzen reports Count Sergei Stroganov's reaction to the story:

> 'What a terrible tale Gogol's "Overcoat" is', Stroganov once
> told Korsh, 'that ghost on the bridge will drag the overcoat
> from the shoulders of simply every one of us. Put yourself
> in my position and look at the story.'
>   'That's very difficult for me', Korsh replied, 'I'm not used
> to looking at things from the point of view of a man who
> owns thirty thousand souls.'   (Gertsen 1967: Book 2, 145)

At the other end of the ideological scale was the radical critic Nikolai
Chernyshevsky. In his mid-1850s 'Essays on the Gogol period in Russian
Literature' he had considered that 'the Gogol tendency...remains the only
strong and fruitful one in our literature' (cited by Pustovoit: 42), but in his
most extensive consideration of 'The Overcoat', in the 1861 essay 'Is this
not the beginning of a change?' ('Ne nachalo li peremeny?'), written in the
year of the liberation of the serfs, his position had changed. Chernyshevsky
finds Gogol to be unequivocally sympathetic towards his hero:

> Does Gogol mention any faults of Akakii Akakievich? No,
> Akakii Akakievich is unconditionally right and good; all his
> misfortune is ascribed to the lack of feeling, the vulgarity,
> the coarseness of the people upon whom his fate depends...
> Akakii Akakievich suffers and perishes from human cruel-
> heartedness. And Gogol would have considered himself a
> scoundrel if he had told us about him in another tone.
>
> (Chernyshevskii: 215)

But, invoking the fundamental nineteenth-century Russian question 'Who is to blame?', Chernyshevsky goes on to insist upon Akakii's own respon-sibility for his fate, calling him 'a complete ignoramus and a total idiot, capable of nothing', a reading which he says is clear from the story, but which Gogol does not elaborate upon because it would be pointless to do so – since all that writers could then do was to offer sympathy to their downtrodden heroes, which made them feel good. This led to the stories of writers like Grigorovich and Turgenev, 'completely imbued with the smell of Akakii Akakievich's "overcoat"'. Now, Chernyshevsky affirms, a new socially active generation of writers has come along, and 'sympathetic' but mendacious portraits of the common people will no longer do; it is time for harsh truths (ibid., 216-17). While Chernyshevsky's reading of Gogol's authorial attitude would not now find widespread support, the activist conclusions he drew from it were hugely influential for socially committed writers and critics, both in the late nineteenth century and into the Soviet period.[7]

The late nineteenth century

Such was Gogol's influence that by 1879 the novelist Ivan Goncharov could affirm: '...for the time being in Russian literature there is no getting away from Pushkin and Gogol. The Pushkin – Gogol school is still continuing, and all of us writers are only working through the material they bequeathed us' (Goncharov: 76). As if to reiterate this contention, Anton Chekhov included 'Akakii Akakievich got himself a new overcoat (1842)' as one of the 'important events' of Friday 2 April in his parodic 'Calendar of the *Alarm Clock* newspaper for 1882. March-April' ('Kalendar' "Budil'nika" na 1882 god. Mart-aprel'') (Chekhov PSS, 1: 156), and then, a year later, in 1883, produced a comic miniature pastiche of the ending of 'The Overcoat' in his story 'Death of a Functionary' ('Smert' chinovnika'), in which the comically named clerk Cherviakov (Mr Worm) inadvertently sneezes on the head of a general. The man makes nothing of it, but Cherviakov perversely considers this to show a lack of respect for him and keeps returning to the general's house and demanding to reiterate his apology until he is thrown out in exasperation. Upon which, 'walking mechanically home, without taking off his uniform, he lay down on the sofa and...died' (ibid., 2: 166).[8] Then in 1885 the Vicomte Melchior de Vogüé, a French historian of Russian literature, wrote in an article on Dostoevsky in *Revue des deux mondes*, 1885, No. 1:

> Il est vrai, Gogol avait fourni le thème dans sa nouvelle intitulée 'Le manteau'. 'Nous sommes tous sortis du "Manteau" de Gogol' disent avec justice les auteurs russes; mais Dostoïevsky substituait à l'ironie de son maître une émotion suggestive.   (cited by Reiser 1968: 185)

In 1886 in the chapter on Gogol in his *Le Roman russe*, de Vogüé returned to the phrase, stressing that the more he read Russian writers the more he was convinced of its rightness, and ascribing it to 'a writer who had been very involved in the history of Russian literature for the last four decades' (Bocharov and Mann: 183-4). Though he removed the phrase from the 1886 Russian translation of the Dostoevsky article it was reinstated in his 1887 book *Contemporary Russian Writers. Tolstoy. Turgenev. Dostoevsky* (*Sovremennye russkie pisateli. Tolstoi – Turgenev – Dostoevskii*). With time the phrase 'we have all come out from under Gogol's "Overcoat"' ('vse my vyshli iz gogolevskoi shineli') became perhaps the most cited in all Russian literary criticism, and it was almost invariably ascribed to Dostoevsky. It became nearly de rigueur to quote it in articles on the subject or to use it as an epigraph in stories written in Gogol's shadow. In 1968-72 Russian critics engaged in a lively debate about the history of the phrase and the case was made for ascribing it to Turgenev. The telling point was further made that, psychologically, Dostoevsky would seem very unlikely to have advertised a debt to a precursor with whom his relationship was extremely ambiguous.[9] Thus the phrase should properly be seen as anonymous, but its very vitality is itself significant. For if writers, readers and critics remain convinced of Gogol's centrality to Russian literature, then 'The Overcoat', along with the play *The Government Inspector* and the novel *Dead Souls*, is crucial to the Gogolian heritage. And in a sense the influence of the story exceeds even that of the other two great works, since as well as being constantly interpreted and re-interpreted, and used as a cultural paradigm, it continues to be re-worked and its 'little man' doubled by Russian and non-Russian artists to this day.

In the early 1890s the publication of a new seven-volume *Works* (*Sochineniia*) edited by N. Tikhonravov and V. Shenrok, Moscow, 1889-96, which for the first time included key drafts of his works, and of Shenrok's *Materials for a Biography of Gogol* (*Materialy dlia biografii Gogolia*), four volumes, Moscow, 1892-97, brought vital new material into the critical arena. A new view of Gogol was advanced in three essays first published in this decade by the writer and philosopher Vasilii Rozanov. In remarks on

Gogol at the beginning of an extended study of the *Legend of the Grand Inquisitor* section of Dostoevsky's novel *The Brothers Karamazov* (first published in 1891) Rozanov overturned the critical commonplace advanced by de Vogüé, and suggested that in fact all Russian literature was engaged in a struggle with Gogol's baleful influence, an influence that depended on the total lack of attention to the soul in his works. Gogol was a brilliant painter of external forms, who sold us his sick dreams as reality.

> Gogol looked at life with a dead gaze and in it he saw only dead souls. He absolutely did not reflect reality in his works, he just drew a series of caricatures of it with amazing mastery.... Caricature takes a single character trait, and the entire figure reflects it alone – both in the facial grimace and in the unnatural convulsions of the body. It is false, and it is remembered forever. That is what Gogol is like.
>
> (Rozanov 1970: 18-19)

Further invoking the 'monstrous phantasmagoria' displayed in Gogol's work, Rozanov suggests that the search for 'the human' in recent Russian literature – and particularly in such writers as Turgenev and Goncharov, Dostoevsky and Tolstoy – was an explicit rejection of Gogol. The suggestion that Gogol drew 'caricatures' of 'monstrous phantoms' was a frontal attack on those who, following Belinsky and Chernyshevsky, found Gogol motivated by 'sympathy' for 'tragic' (Belinsky) or undeserving (Chernyshevsky) figures. Rozanov continued the assault in another piece of 1891, 'A Few Words about Gogol' ('Neskol'ko slov o Gogole', reprinted as 'Pushkin and Gogol'), in which he asserts that the features of Gogol's characters, once apportioned, never change. The characters have no thoughts of their own and stand motionless in the poses into which the author has pressed them, and for this reason it is 'naïve' to see him either portraying reality, or founding the Natural School. Gogol lived in his own world and in it he hewed out a 'huge wax picture with wonderful mastery.'

> In this picture there are absolutely no living creatures: they are tiny wax figures, but they all make their grimaces so artfully that for a long time we suspected that they might be moving. But they are motionless.   (ibid., 261)

And if they seem to move it is because the author moves their legs for them, for they themselves are lifeless, 'made from some wax mass of words, and the mystery of this artistic making was known only to Gogol' (ibid., 262).

In his third piece, 'How the Akakii Akakievich type came about' ('Kak proizoshel tip Akakiia Akakievicha'), of 1894, with its title that directly echoes a startling phrase in the original, ('Takim obrazom i proizoshel Akakii Akakievich', 3: 142), Rozanov turned directly to 'The Overcoat'. His close reading of the drafts published by Tikhonravov led him to suggest that Gogol's method was to select a certain 'thematic' feature for his character and then to add only other characteristics that were similar. Therefore everything about Akakii Akakievich is ugly (*bezobraznoe*). Such a combination of features is unreal: 'but of course this is not the natural, diffused light we know in nature, but one derived artificially in a laboratory' (ibid., 273). Gogol is a writer who shuns reality, and all his characters from the 'radiant' Annunziata in 'Rome' to the 'emasculated' Akakii Akakievich are 'equally lifeless, without natural light on them, without movement, without the capacity for prolonged thought or developing feeling' (ibid., 276-7). The famous 'humane passage' was undoubtedly added later by Gogol as an 'outburst of profound grief in the creator at the sight of what he has created; he is the one who "trembles" when he completes the work of "savage coarseness", and "covers his face with his hand", and repeats the words that are ringing in his ears: "I am your brother"' (ibid., 280-1).

Rozanov's reading of 'The Overcoat' has recently been described as 'a sophisticated reformulation of some of [Makar] Devushkin's responses' and his 'effort to disconnect Gogol's art from any roots in Russian life' has been found to display 'a tendentious one-sidedness quite as damaging as Belinsky's troublesome insistence on seeing in Gogol's art a "full representation of reality"' (Jackson: 201, 205). Certainly all these three texts exude a kind of fascinated horror at Gogol's world view, but in so doing they draw our attention to the way Gogol's writing works – his literary style, his language, his devices of characterisation – and make it impossible to sustain an uncomplicatedly 'realistic' reading of his work and his world. His reading of the motivation of the 'humane passage' is not persuasive, but insights about the marionette-like quality of Gogol's characters and the fantastic quality of their world would be fruitfully developed by later commentators.[10]

The early twentieth century

The century opened with invocation of Bashmachkin from what might seem an unlikely quarter. Pouring out his wrath against the contemporary bureaucracy in a 1901 article entitled 'An internal review' ('Vnutrennee obozrenie'), Vladimir Ilich Lenin wrote:

> Having perfectly imbibed that spirit of bowing and scraping [*nizkopoklonstva*] and the paper attitude to their business which reigns in the entire hierarchy of Russian officialdom, they react with suspicion to anyone who is unlike Gogol's Akakii Akakievich or, employing a more contemporary comparison, the Man in a Case.
> (Cited by Nechkina: 570. The second reference is to Chekhov's eponymous hero.)

Alas, poor Akakii Akakievich, reduced to a byword for servility in political polemic. It does not even suit Lenin's purposes to mention his heroic final rebellion![11]

At the end of the decade, in 1909, the centenary of Gogol's birth was celebrated by the 'Gogol Days' in Moscow. Such occasions are usually characterised by the conservative reiteration of conventional positions. The Vicomte de Vogüé returned to his favourite ideas of Gogol as the great initiator and of 'all the powerful descendants [who] came out from Gogol's "Overcoat",' continuing:

> Akakii Akakievich's pitiful Overcoat is the cloak of a bibli-
> cal prophet, left for his disciples, whom it has helped to
> ascend into the heavens. This petty functionary, anatomised
> like a medical preparation, the object of mockery and morbid
> pity, will more than once serve as a model for Dostoevsky.
> (*Gogolevskie dni v Moskve*: 142-3)

A similarly conventional tone was adopted in a letter of greeting sent by a 'group of English writers' headed by Henry James, John Galsworthy and Arthur Conan Doyle:

> Gogol was...a pioneer, and the qualities most characteristic
> of Russian literature may first be traced in his writings....
> Above all we find in Russian literature a peculiar sympathy
> with all who suffer – with the unhappy and the failures, the
> oppressed, the outcasts and the victims of life in all classes, –
> people whose souls are not dead but, as it were paralysed or
> distorted by the world. And this peculiar sympathy, perme-
> ating all that is most distinctive in Russian art, is not a matter
> of patronage or even of pity. It is rather that close human
> kinship that holds a family bound together in good and evil
> fortune alike by the common tie of blood, that sense of the
> true brotherhood between all types of mankind.   (ibid., 249)

So the English writers continue to react to Gogol's work just like Akakii's fellow clerk, moved to hear his words as 'I am your brother'; but this was not the only position advanced at the *Days*. For the Symbolist poet Valerii Briusov, 'Gogol's creations are bold and terrible caricatures which, just by succumbing to a great artist's hypnotic powers, we took for decades as a reflection in the mirror of Russian reality' (ibid., 158).

Gogol's influence on the entire Russian Symbolist movement was im- mense. Blok and Bely, Briusov and Ivanov all wrote articles about him. Merezhkovsky wrote a pioneering study of the role of the devil in Gogol's works in 1906, and in 1911 a book about the relationship of his work, his

life and his religious views, in which he suggests that through Akakii
Akakievich's dead face at the end of the story 'there glimmers something
true, immortal, above the rational, something which exists in every human
personality and which cries out of it to people and to God' (Merezhkovskii
1972: 169). In the special centenary issue of the Symbolist journal *The
Scales* (*Vesy*), 1909, Bely insisted:

> ...people go on reading Gogol and they do not see that there
> is no word in the dictionary to name Gogol; we have no
> means to measure all the possibilities that he has exhausted:
> we do not yet know what Gogol is; and although we do not
> see the authentic Gogol, his creations, even though they are
> narrowed by our wretched powers of perception, are nearer
> to us than all the Russian writers of the nineteenth century.
>
> (Belyi 1994: 362)

In his later book on Gogol's literary style, Bely traced a number of stylistic
influences of 'The Overcoat' on his own novel *Petersburg*; he described the
functionary hero Apollon Apollonovich Ableukhov (again the name and
patronymic are tellingly the same and the 'odd' surname requires explanation in the text) as combining Akakii Akakievich's humiliations and the
important personage's haughtiness. (Belyi 1982: 303-7)

Two other major prose writers of the Symbolist movement, Sologub and
Remizov, wrote works that would seem to be explicit reworkings of Gogol's
tale. The very title of Sologub's 1905 story 'The Little Man' ('Malen'kii
chelovek') overtly addresses it to the Gogolian-Dostoevskian tradition, but
in this case the metaphorical is made physical, for the existential problem
of the hero, a clerk named Iakov Alekseevich Saranin, is that while he is
very small, he is married to a very large wife. He walks in perplexity through
the night streets of St Petersburg, where in true Gogolian fashion light
playing from the street lamps makes things seem to change in size. He goes
to see an Armenian (whose stressed 'eastern' qualities recall those ascribed
to the tailor Petrovich in 'The Overcoat'), and gets hold of a potion which
when administered to his wife will make her grow smaller. Alas, she swaps
the glasses round and he drinks the potion himself. His life becomes an alternation of trips to the office and visits to tailors to get ever smaller clothes.
Both the basic plot framework – lack – desire – temporary acquisition of
something that will resolve your problem, swiftly followed by its loss – and
the plot details recall 'The Overcoat', and this is now made explicit:

> At the office, in the department, at first they looked askance and
> laughed. Especially the young people. The traditions of the
> colleagues of Akakii Akakievich Bashmachkin are still alive.
>
> (Sologub: 187)

From this point on the references to the original come thick and fast. Saranin, whose very surname is probably a sly Gogolian allusion,[12] is summoned by his director, who asks him 'How were you so bold as to...?' (*Kak osmelilis' vy...?* [ibid., 188], compare *Kak vy smeete*, the words with which the important personage begins conversations with his inferiors [3: 165]), and the Gogolian clothes motif becomes overt when his wife arranges for him to become a living mannequin in the window of a fashionable clothes shop, modelling exquisite but ever smaller clothes. But Saranin, too, is eventually avenged upon his tormentors, for he still continues to diminish in size, and, in the final words of the story (reversing Gogol's words about Akakii's birth), 'Saranin ended' (*Saranin konchilsia*) (ibid., 193). So the story turns out to be another homage variant of Gogol's original, though in the view of V. Keldysh, 'Sologub goes considerably further in cranking up the absurd' (Keldysh: 97), thus suggesting a fruitful direction for later twentieth-century reworkings of the tale.

Remizov was a writer who frequently admitted to his love of Gogol and to some extent projected his literary persona on to that of Gogol – his Gogolian dreams were published in *The Fire of Things* (*Ogon' veshchei*, 1954) – and he, too, wrote several novels and stories with poor clerk heroes. The link with 'The Overcoat' is particularly interesting in *The Tale of the Tinkling Cymbal and Sounding Brass* (*Povest' o Ivane Semenoviche Stratilatove. Neuemnyi buben*), published in 1910. Like Bashmachkin, Stratilatov is a middle-aged copying clerk with a particular love for strange words, and is mocked by his fellow clerks; but in the course of the story his character changes (Stratilatov himself despises Gogol [Remizov 1922: 32]), and his relationship with other nineteenth-century literary forbears comes into play. In the words of A.A. Danilevsky:

> The fact that the sequence of the introduction into the narrative of references to the clarifying 'text-myths' opens precisely with Gogol's 'The Overcoat' is hardly by chance. Its pragmatics is in the realisation of the famous formula 'We all came out from under...'. Appearing at the start as a simulacrum of Bashmachkin, a petty clerk, a 'little man' worn down by reality, Stratilatov then within the bounds of a short narrative undergoes an evolution, one that had been accomplished long before by the heroes of Dostoevsky: from the still typically 'Gogolian' Devushkin through the hero of *The Double*, and, passing the 'underground man', to the image of the 'voluptuary, money-grubber and holy fool' Fedor Karamazov.
>
> (Danilevskii: 144)

Thus Remizov uses his tale for a meditation on the evolution both of a social type and of a literary and cultural tradition.[13]

A reiteration of the conventional reading of the character of Bashmachkin was provided, however, at an era's end. In a book that first appeared in 1914 and was reissued in the post-Revolutionary period, the Marxist critic V.F. Pereverzev found Bashmachkin a 'meek toiler' (*krotkii truzhenik*):

> Maybe this toil does lack objective meaning; it has enormous subjective meaning because it is the manifestation of the struggle for life, because in it one senses an argument over the life and death of man. In the meekness and spiritual mildness of Bashmachkin you can sense the submission to his fate and the unmurmuring endurance of a poor man cast down by life, and not satiated post-prandial good humour, you can sense spiritual tiredness and not spiritual indolence and obesity. That is why the image of Bashmachkin very quickly forces you to forget your smile, to fall into gloom and to burst into tears.   (Pereverzev: 135)

Alas, this was not the reaction of spectators at a 1916 theatrical staging of the tale in N.F. Baliev's Cabaret *The Bat* (*Letuchaia mysh'*) in Moscow. 'The Overcoat' was not among the works of Gogol that had been adapted for the stage during his lifetime or in the later nineteenth century. An adaptation in three scenes had been passed by the censorship in 1908, but the Baliev company's was the first production.[14] As the 'solitary call for help of the unfortunate Bashmachkin sank in the black abyss of the stone desert of the town', the wartime revellers continued to 'drink and eat, to the clinking of glasses and knives' (Tikhvinskaia: 370), callously echoing the indifference of Akakii's textual addressees.

From the Revolution to 1930:
the critical debate and the artistic response

The immediate post-Revolutionary period was a time of extraordinary vitality and invention in both the study of Gogol and the symbolic appropriation and remaking of his texts. In 'The Teapot' ('Chainichek'), a 1915 tale seen by Mirsky as belonging to the tradition of 'The Overcoat' (Mirsky 1989: 163), Remizov's poor and humiliated clerk hero Vorobushkin (Mr Little Sparrow) is so horrified by his own rebelliousness in demanding from his patron to be given the eponymous teapot that it gives him bad dreams and pangs of conscience. The teapot seems to grow to fill the whole town where he is attempting to have a restful holiday and causes him to flee back to Petersburg, where he belongs. The advent of Revolution brings change however. Even before the revolutionary year was over, Remizov published in the issue of the leading Socialist Revolutionary newspaper *The People's Cause* (*Delo naroda*) for 15 December 1917 his miniature 'Akakii

Bashmachkin'. The story's beginning reiterates the clichés of the character's life: 'There lived a little man, Akakii Bashmachkin...', who busied himself with his Departmental copying and was afraid of everyone...

> But then hunger and cold came, cold and hunger, and then
> in addition oppression and pressure, and the chisel, and the
> little man Akakii became enraged [*ostervenel*].
> And Akakii said to himself:
> 'My life is over, and my deeds are small, that's what we have
> been told since time immemorial, if I have to perish I have
> to perish, I don't want to work and that's all there is to it.'

So Akakii went home, to the horror of all his senior colleagues, who demanded that he come to his senses and return to work:

> But he replied – look how bold the man has become! –
> Gogol, are you listening..!
> 'It was you who said that my work was so unimportant and
> that I'm a nonentity [*a ia – mlia*], do it yourself, let's see if
> you can!'

And though they tied him up and threw him into prison, it made no difference and the work remained undone (Remizov 1990: 236-7). In his remarks on the story Lampl explicitly links it to Remizov's other politically satirical pieces of late 1917 and sets it 'under the Bolsheviks' (Lampl: 248), in what would seem to be a justifiable clarification of Remizov's enforced opacities. Thus within weeks of the introduction of the new regime Akakii Akakievich, whose meekness had, three years earlier, been his defining characteristic for Pereverzev, rebels and the story is reworked for explicitly political ends.[15]

The critical debate

Critics, too, were looking anew at Gogol. In 1919 the Futurist poet Aleksei Kruchenykh published his hand-written book *Melancholy in a Dressing Gown* (*Malakholiia v kapote*), which begins with the words 'Istoriia KAK anal'naia erotika nachalas' Akakiem Akakievichem Gogolia...' ('History as anal eroticism began with Gogol's Akakii Akakievich...' (Kruchenykh 1973: 259). The book's shock tactics have been well described by Vladimir Markov:

> ...in it he tried to demonstrate with quotations from all Rus-
> sian literature that poets and writers, whether they wanted to
> or not, produced *sdvigi* [shifts, J.G.] of sexual or scatological

meaning (the latter was not difficult to do, *kak* being the
Russian conjunction for "as" or "like"). Even the name of
Gogol's character, Akaky Akakievich, was, for Kruchenykh,
an excellent proof of this point.   (Markov: 342)

Thus Kruchenykh was the first Russian writer to draw direct attention to
what Sologub had merely hinted at, namely the possible faecal implications
of Gogol's hero's name, preceding by four years the interpretation of Ivan
Ermakov.

The main contribution to the reappraisal of the story was made by the
critics of the Russian Formalist school, and in particular by Boris Eikhenbaum. In a brief article of 1918, 'The illusion of *skaz*' ('Illiuziia skaza'),
Eikhenbaum sought to study the phenomenon of the first person narrator
who is strongly characterised by his manner of speech in a literary imitation
of oral tale-telling (*skaz*): 'The writer often thinks of himself as an oral tale
teller (*skazitel'*), and by various devices he attempts to give his written
speech the illusion of *skaz*' (Eikhenbaum 1924: 153). He included Gogol
among such writers, adding:

> Gogol is a *skaz* teller of a particular kind: with mimicry, with
> gestures, with grimaces. He does not just narrate, but per-
> forms and declaims...he himself created particular forms of
> *skaz* – with exclamations, and with little words of every kind.
>
> (ibid., 155)

Even this small contribution to the study of Gogol was of major importance,
drawing attention as it did to the role and 'personality' of the narrators of
his stories and distinguishing them implicitly from the author, as well as
characterising the kind of language and devices which Gogol's narrators
favoured. The following year Eikhenbaum was to develop and deepen his
insights in an article which has since become not only the most famous and
influential study of 'The Overcoat', transforming our understanding of the
story; not only the most succinct and persuasive example of Russian Formalist
theory in practice; but also perhaps the most suggestive and anthologised
contribution to the study of narrative voice, a true landmark in literary
studies. The article was called, with programmatic intent 'How The Overcoat Was Made' ('Kak sdelana shinel'').[16] According to his Formalist
colleague Viktor Shklovsky, it was suggested to Eikhenbaum by an intrigu-
ing chance remark of Osip Brik, 'Underneath an actor's mask is – grease-
paint' (Shklovskii 1977: 38). The study consists of three sections, a
definition of the *skaz* form; a study of 'The Overcoat'; and a consideration
of the famous 'humane passage' and the ending. Because of the article's
fundamental position in the reception of Gogol's story, we shall rehearse its
arguments in some detail here.[17]

In section one Eikhenbaum develops the insights sketched out in 'The illusion of *skaz*', beginning:

> The composition of a novella depends to a considerable extent on what role the *personal tone* of the author plays in its formation, i.e. is this tone the organising principle that creates more or less the illusion of *skaz*, or does it merely serve as the formal link between events and hence occupy an auxiliary position.   (Eikhenbaum 1969: 306)

In what he calls the 'primitive novella' or the adventure novel, as well as in comic novellas based on an anecdote, there is no need for *skaz*, since plot is all important.

> Composition becomes very different if the plot itself, as the weaving together of motifs with the help of their motivation, ceases to play the organising role, i.e. if the narrator in some way thrusts himself to the foreground, and, as it were, only makes use of the plot for the weaving together of separate stylistic devices. The centre of gravity is shifted from the plot (which is here abbreviated to a minimum) on to the devices of *skaz*; and the most important comic role is assigned to puns, which sometimes amount to nothing more than simple plays on words, and sometimes develop into small anecdotes. (ibid.)

Eikhenbaum goes on to distinguish between two types of comic *skaz*, the narrative and the reproductive, saying of the latter that it 'seems to conceal an actor, so that the *skaz* takes on the character of a game and the composition is defined not by a simple linking of jokes, but by a certain system of varying mimico-articulatory gestures' (ibid., 307). He then turns his attention to Gogol, and insists:

> Composition in Gogol is not determined by plot; his plots are always scanty, or rather, there is no plot at all, but only some comic premise (and sometimes even that is not at all comic *in itself*), serving, as it were, merely as an impetus or pretext for the elaboration of comic devices.   (ibid.)

He continues:

> ...the basis of a Gogolian text is *skaz* , and the text is made up of the actual elements of speech and verbalised emotions. Moreover, this *skaz* has a tendency not simply to narrate, not simply to talk, but to reproduce mimetically and through

articulation – words and sentences are chosen and put together not only according to the principle of logical speech,
but more according to the principle of expressive speech, in
which a special role belongs to articulation, mimicry, sound
gestures and so on. From this comes the phenomenon of
sound semantics in his language: the sound shell of a word,
its acoustic character becomes *meaningful* in Gogol's speech
independently of this logical or material meaning. Articulation and its acoustic effect are foregrounded as an expressive
device. That is why he likes names, surnames, given names
and so on – this opens up the scope for articulatory play of
this kind.   (ibid., 309)

He ends this general analysis by reiterating:

So plot in Gogol has only external meaning and is therefore
in itself static.... The real dynamism, and thus the composition
of his works, is in the construction of the *skaz*, in the play of
language. His protagonists are petrified poses. Over them,
in the form of a director and the real hero, reigns the merry,
ludic spirit of the artist himself.   (ibid., 311)

Section one concludes with Eikhenbaum turning his attention directly to
'The Overcoat', in which he finds that:

...the purely comic skaz, with all the devices of linguistic
play characteristic of Gogol, is linked with emotional declamation, which forms a sort of second layer. This second layer
was taken by our critics as the basis of the tale.   (ibid.)

Section two of the article looks at the specifics of these comic devices as
deployed in 'The Overcoat'. Eikhenbaum notes the important role played
by puns, based on 'similarities of sound, or etymological plays on words,
or on hidden absurdity' (ibid., 312). This is followed by a lengthy discussion
of the sound features and paronomastic qualities of the names Bashmachkin
and Akakii Akakievich, and of the words chosen to describe the hero.
Eikhenbaum insists that these 'words are selected and placed in a certain
order not on the principle of designation of certain features, but on the
principle of sound semantics' (ibid., 315). For Eikhenbaum 'There is no
neutral level of language in Gogol, no logical bringing together of simple
psychological or material concepts into ordinary sentences' (ibid., 316).
Rather, he alternates mimetic and articulated sound with intense intonation
– a long piece of emotional declamation can be resolved in bathos; for this
reason words themselves become '*strange*, enigmatic, unusual sounding,

they strike the ear – as if they had been broken up into their component parts
or invented by Gogol for the first time' (ibid.). He goes on to note that:

> 'The Overcoat' also contains another kind of declamation
> which makes an unexpected intrusion into the general pun-
> ning style: the sentimental-melodramatic style; this is the
> famous 'humane' passage, which has been so fortunate
> among Russian critics that from being a secondary artistic
> device it has become the 'idea' of the entire story: 'Leave me
> alone, why are you insulting me?'   (ibid.)

Eikhenbaum's profound attention to Gogol's devices and intentions leads
to a radical overturning of the conventional nineteenth-century interpretations of the meaning of this passage. He notes that it is not present in the
first draft of the story but instead of taking this as a reason to stress its moral
centrality, as had such critics as Rozanov, he interprets its addition as
stylistically motivated, adding a new tone of 'emotional declamation' (ibid.,
317) to the existing anecdotal style. He then offers an analysis of the speech
of characters in the story, of its distance from everyday speech, finding it
always to be stylised. Although the speech of Akakii differs from that of
Petrovich, they are both equally conventional (*uslovna*), 'the language
which marionettes might speak' (ibid.). As for the language in which the
tale is narrated, the *skaz*, this is equally contrived (*vyiskana*):

> In 'The Overcoat' this *skaz* is stylised as a special brand of
> offhand, naïve chatter. 'Unnecessary' details pop up seem-
> ingly without his willing it [*neproizvol'no*].... Or it takes on
> features of familiarity and verbosity.... He is also ready to
> digress from the main anecdote and put in intermediary
> ones.   (ibid., 317-18)

At the end of this section of his analysis, Eikhenbaum introduces the key
concept of the *grotesque* to define the complexity of the resulting style:

> What resulted was the grotesque, in which the mimicking of
> laughter is replaced by the mimicking of grief – and both of
> them take the form of play, with a conventional succession
> of gestures and intonations.   (ibid., 319)

In the final section of his analysis, Eikhenbaum tries to establish how the
different devices are linked. It is of course the *skaz* that does this, and in
'The Overcoat' it is not a narrative *skaz* but one of declamation and mimicry,
performed not by a tale teller so much as by a comic actor (ibid.). Shifts of

tone are present from the start of the work. The practical tone of the introduction gives way to the personal, which takes the character of a 'grotesque
leer or grimace' (ibid., 320). This prepares us for the shift to the pun on the
surname and the anecdote about Akakii Akakievich's birth and christening.
The comic tone continues until it is suddenly broken off by a sentimental-
melodramatic digression with the characteristic devices of the sentimental
style. It is Eikhenbaum's conclusions about this 'humane passage' and
its implications for the entire tale that have been most influential and
contentious:

> This device raises 'The Overcoat' from a simple anecdote
> into the grotesque. The sentimental and intentionally primitive
> content of this passage (in this sense the grotesque coincides
> with the melodramatic) is conveyed by means of a tensely
> rising intonation, which has a solemn, emotionally height-
> ened character.... We are accustomed to understanding this
> passage literally: an artistic device which transforms a comic
> novella into a grotesque and prepares the 'fantastic' ending
> is interpreted as a 'sincere' intervention of the 'soul'...for
> scholarship such naïveté is no triumph, because it reveals
> scholarship's helplessness. Such an interpretation destroys
> the entire structure of 'The Overcoat' and its entire artistic
> intent. Proceeding from the basic proposition that no single
> sentence in a work of art *can*, in and of itself, be a pure
> 'reflection' of the author's personal feelings, but rather is
> always both construct and performance, we *cannot and have
> no right* to see in a passage like this anything other than a
> specific artistic device. The usual habit of identifying some
> particular opinion [*suzhdenie*] with the psychological con-
> tent of the author's soul is a false path for scholarship. In this
> sense the soul of the artist as a man *experiencing* this or that
> mood always remains and should remain outside the con-
> fines of his work. A work of art is always something that is
> made, fashioned, contrived; it is not only artful but also
> artificial, in the good sense of that word; and therefore there
> *neither is nor can there be* any place in it for the reflection
> of the empirical reality of the soul.   (ibid., 320-21)

The melodramatic episode is there to contrast with the comic *skaz*, a fact
that is underlined by the return, as soon as it is completed, to playful punning
chatter. This pattern of interweaving opposed styles defines the entire composition of the story as a grotesque:

> The grotesque style...gives scope for a *play with reality*,
> breaking up its elements and displacing them freely, so that
> normal psychological and logical correlations and associa-
> tions no longer apply in a world that has been constructed
> *anew*.   (ibid., 322)

Gogol can thus link the unlinkable: 'in a word he can play with all the norms
and laws of real spiritual life' (ibid., 323). The death of Akakii Akakievich
is narrated in the same grotesque fashion, with alternating comic and tragic
details and sudden changes of tone. For Eikhenbaum the ending of 'The
Overcoat' is no more fantastic or 'romantic' than the entire tale. Rather it is
' a new "deception", a device of reversed grotesque' (ibid., 325). And the
anecdotal ending leads us away from the sad story and the melodramatic
episodes back to the comic *skaz* of the beginning of the story, so that
everything is resolved in laughter.

Eikhenbaum's extraordinary achievement was to refocus study of 'The
Overcoat' from the 'moral' of the story to its linguistic and narrative devices,
and particularly to the figure of the narrator himself. Even the Russian title
of his article, 'Kak sdelana "Shinel'"', would itself seem to contain a
punning allusion to the frequency with which the word 'kak' (how) is used
by Gogol in passages associated with Akakii Akakievich – another indica-
tion that the dominant feature (*dominanta*, a key Formalist concept) of the
tale lies in its language. The Overcoat and its hero are made of *words*, and
words are *how* (kak) they are made. In so doing he revealed the story to be
constructed with a hitherto unsuspected wit, sophistication and complexity.
For this reason his reading of the story would be as influential as Dostoevsky's had been seventy years previously and would, like *Poor Folk*,
provoke a subgenre of criticism of the story engaged in dialogue with his
contentions. This dialogue was particularly intense among other Russian
critics throughout the 1920s, but after the demise of the Formalist school
the dialogue was taken up by émigré and Western critics, notably Dmitrii
Chizhevsky, and it continues to this day.

Critics agree that Eikhenbaum's contentions – particularly about language,
the narrator, the grotesque – must remain a central part of any understanding
of the story and its workings, but some of the most perceptive of them go
on to stress that his concentration on stylistic questions made it impossible
for him to cover other aspects of the work adequately – particularly, in a
sophisticated restating of nineteenth-century critical positions, the question
of reception. If readers, even the most sophisticated, also *read for the plot*,
then attention to the plot and the ideas it rehearses and to their relationship
with the formal devices must also play a part in a synthesising reading of
the tale. For Eikhenbaum 'The Overcoat' is 'about' its devices; for Driessen,
Eikhenbaum 'robs the story of all its content' (Driessen: 200), and for de Lotto,

in her fascinating recent study of hagiographic sources, his reduction of Gogol's hero's name to a 'sound gesture' and ignoring of its profound semantic content is a 'brilliant mistake' (*genial'naia oshibka*, de Lotto: 62).

At the time, however, this idea was taken up with alacrity by other critics. For Tynianov, whose 1921 study (discussed above) was mainly concerned with the 'parodic' relationship to 'The Overcoat' of Dostoevsky's *Poor Folk*, the name Akakii Akakievich is a 'verbal mask' which has 'already lost its link with semantics, has consolidated itself in sound and has become a sound mask, a phonetic mask'. This mask is 'equally material and spectral', making it easy and natural to replace Akakii with a ghost (Tynianov 1979: 203). A critic loosely associated with the Formalists, Aleksandr Slonimsky, also turned to 'The Overcoat' in his 1923 study of the comic in Gogol. Following on from Eikhenbaum he found that there was nothing comic about the plot of the story, but that comic effects were created by the alternation of comic and serious episodes, all manipulated by the sharp contrasts in the narrator's diction (Slonimskii: 331-3). For Slonimsky too, 'the comic effect depends on the displacement of semantic categories' (he too invokes the idea of the 'verbal mask'), as when Petrovich is said, 'despite...having a completely pock-marked face', to be good at mending overcoats (ibid., 355-6).

The following year the story was addressed from a very different critical position by Ivan Ermakov, a practising psychoanalyst and follower of Freud, under whose auspices the master's works had begun to be translated into Russian. Ermakov begins by conceding Eikhenbaum's achievements, but reinterprets Gogol's *skaz* as organically linked to the content of his stories, which he describes as 'nothing other than an authorial confession, the repentance of a suffering, self-flagellating soul' (Ermakov 1999: 242). *Skaz* is an utterly appropriate strategy for a writer simultaneously motivated both to confess and to conceal. Gogol uses his works to lay himself bare, to reveal what he considers to be his own sinfulness. For all this, and despite additional contentions that Gogol had a 'functionary complex' (*kompleks chinovnika*) that his correspondence was repeatedly concerned with bodily functions, that 'it was obviously himself, his sins, his shortcomings which Gogol embodied in "The Overcoat"' (ibid., 245), Ermakov's analysis of 'The Overcoat' is dismayingly conventional, and generally too unfocused. Akakii Akakievich is a typical 'exister'. His fate is against him. He is humiliated from the very start. In the light of Freud's contention that the overcoat is a male symbol, Ermakov goes on to suggest that erotic desire is always punished in the story, just as sexual attraction is always punished in Gogol's work (ibid., 255-6). He has referred earlier in his study to the consonance of Akakii's name with 'the children's pejorative "kaka"' (ibid., 245), and in its final section, like Eikhenbaum before him, he looks at the 'sound structure' of the story, finding all the other names to have insulting and unmasculine implications. Thus Ermakov queasily combines elements of a psychoanalytical study of the author, a character study of the hero and some attention to formal questions. The

Formalists themselves were unimpressed. In his 1925 study of Gogol and the Natural School, Vinogradov humorously confessed: 'I am not going to speak about Professor Ivan Ermakov's *Studies in the Analysis of the Work of Gogol* since I lack a sense of humour' (Vinogradov 1976a: 200). A full-blooded psychoanalytical study of the work would only be produced by the American critic Daniel Rancour-Laferriere six decades later.

Vinogradov was the most prolific Formalist student of Gogol, writing three books about him during the 1920s.[18] His main contributions to the study of 'The Overcoat' lie in establishing its relationship to other 'poor clerk' tales and to the evolution of the Natural School; an analysis of its relationship to Dostoevsky's *Poor Folk* (discussed earlier); and a 'correction' of Eikhenbaum's reading of *skaz* in 'How Gogol's Overcoat is Made'. In *Gogol and the Natural School* (*Gogol' i natural'naia shkola*, 1925) Vinogradov contends that by concentrating on intonation as a 'syntactically organising factor' and 'paying no attention to semantics' Eikhenbaum has produced a reading of the artistic construction of the story that is 'one-sidedly distorted' (Vinogradov 1976a: 197). Later he finds that:

> ...the contrast between the sentimental-emotional notes and the dominant tone of 'comic mockery' seemed so sharp that the uniting of these two forms of speech in a single image of the narrator could only be forced and mechanical. Gogol is not satisfied with it.   (ibid., 222)

Vinogradov returns to the question of the *skaz* form of 'The Overcoat' in his important 1926 article 'The Problem of *skaz* in stylistics' ('Problema skaza v stilistike'), where his scepticism about Eikhenbaum's analysis is more extensively articulated. Eikhenbaum is attempting a stylistic definition of the 'reproductive' comic *skaz* where, naturally, jokes and puns are prevalent:

> Consequently the verbal material of 'The Overcoat' is examined by Eikhenbaum not on a semantic plane, but only from the point of view of its 'mimico-pronunciatory force' and its sound effects. What is studied is not the structure of the *skaz* in its own sense, but only its 'phonetics'. An intonational sketch of 'The Overcoat' is drawn. And Eikhenbaum's work has the unquestionable value of a sharp description of the mimico-declamatory aspect in one of the forms of comic *skaz*. But the whole concept of *skaz* in all its scope is not thereby clarified.   (Vinogradov 1980: 43)

At the end of the decade, in his book *The Evolution of Russian Naturalism. Gogol and Dostoevsky* (1929), Vinogradov was explicitly concerned to establish the contemporary reaction to 'The Overcoat' as a move towards using sentimentalism in the new poetics of naturalism (Vinogradov 1976a: 151). Through his new synthesis of the comic and the sentimental, Gogol revived and reinvigorated the flagging 1830s theme of the poor clerk. 'The Overcoat' itself was 'a destruction of comic cliché in the depiction of the adventures of the titular councillor,' something Gogol emphasised by complicating the grotesque surface by the introduction of the 'touching episode' which softened the initial mockery and made significant changes to the work's structure (ibid., 158-9). This literary-historical contextualising is also, of course, a 'correction' to Eikhenbaum's reading and Vinogradov goes on to contend that:

> Eikhenbaum did not appreciate the historical sharpness of the artistic intent of the reworked 'Overcoat', and his article 'How the Overcoat is made', while containing interesting comments on certain of Gogol's stylistic devices, does not reveal the artistic structure of 'The Overcoat' itself.   (ibid., 159)

By now Vinogradov has cast away all caution in his assessment of the limitations of Eikhenbaum's method.

The other leading Formalist writer on prose, Viktor Shklovsky, was disappointingly reticent on the subject of 'The Overcoat', though he, too, makes a stirringly blunt contribution to the definition of *skaz* in a 'Letter to Eikhenbaum' in his *The Third Factory* (*Tret'ia fabrika*), of 1926, which begins:

> I am going to write to you about *skaz*. You define *skaz* as an orientation [*ustanovka*] in a narrative towards the spoken word.
> But even if that is true, can you really examine *skaz* outside the realm of plot [*siuzhet*]?.... So *skaz* is (at least much of the time) a plot device and cannot be examined outside the realm of plot...*Skaz* reshapes a plot, converting the groundwork of the narrative into one aspect of the plot: *Skaz* is not the issue.
> (Shklovskii 1977: 56-7, modified translation)

Shklovsky would not return to the subject of 'The Overcoat' until three pieces written decades later in his exasperatingly discursive late style, where he says that Eikhenbaum was wrong, 'and all we Formalists were wrong', to refer to the name of Akakii Akakievich as a 'sound gesture' (Shklovskii: 1959: 406), and makes some not very interesting points about the readerly sympathy that he evokes.

A considerably more productive engagement with Eikhenbaum's ideas was provided in the analyses of the tale offered by Mikhail Bakhtin and his close literary associates. Bakhtin's contribution in his *Problems of Dosto-evsky's Poetics*, first published in 1929, to the continuing discussion of the relationship between 'The Overcoat' and *Poor Folk* has been discussed above. The book also challenged Eikhenbaum's reading of *skaz*:

> The problem of *skaz* was initially raised for us by Eikhen-baum. He perceives *skaz* exclusively as *an orientation towards an oral form of narration*, an orientation towards oral speech and its corresponding linguistic features.... He completely fails to take into account that in the majority of cases *skaz* is above all orientation towards *someone else's* speech, and after and in consequence of that towards oral speech.
>
> (Bakhtin 1972: 327)

Bakhtin considers this emendation to be crucial to an understanding of the phenomenon, since it influences our understanding of the narrator figure, and of his social status, which is usually inferior, and which, of course, influences the attitudes and values that he will display in the course of his narration. The usefulness of this 'addition' to our understanding of the function of the narrator in 'The Overcoat' is obvious, and Bakhtin further stresses the need to distinguish 'the parodic and the simple *skaz*' (ibid., 332) when elaborating authorial intention.[19]

The nature and function of Gogol's language and his *skaz* method was also addressed in studies published at the end of the decade by Bakhtin's close colleagues Voloshinov and Medvedev.[20] Voloshinov's 1929 study *Marxism and the Philosophy of Language* (*Marksizm i filosofiia iazyka*) suggests that in Gogol's writings 'characters' speech sometimes loses almost all its referential meaning and becomes decor instead, on a par with clothing, appearance, furnishings, etc.' (Voloshinov 1973: 121). Later, in a discussion of what he terms 'particularised direct discourse' (*ovesh-chestvlennaia priamaia rech'*), he adds, in a passage of direct relevance to the characters in 'The Overcoat':

> The authorial context here is so constructed that the traits the author used to define a character cast heavy shadows on his directly reported speech. The value judgements and attitudes in which the character's portrayal is steeped carry over into the words he utters. The referential weight of the reported utterances declines in this modification but, in exchange, their characterological significance, their picturesqueness, or their time-and-place typicality, grows more intense.... Such is the way direct discourse is usually handled by Gogol...
>
> (ibid., 134)

Medvedev's stance was more overtly polemical. In his 1928 book *The Formal Method in Literary Scholarship* (*Formal'nyi metod v literaturovedenii*), revealingly subtitled *A Critical Introduction to Sociological Poetics*, Medvedev quotes Eikhenbaum's theory, and goes on to discuss the relationship of the *skaz* to the whole artistic world of the tale:

> ...story is not dispensable (in non motivated art) or mere motivation for the development of plot (brakings, digressions etc.). The story develops together with the plot: the event being narrated and the event of narration itself merge in the single event of the artistic work....
>
> In the same way, the plane of *skaz* contains the full depth of the narrative. Eikhenbaum is wrong in asserting that 'humaneness towards one's inferior fellow man' and Akakii Akakievich's 'insignificance' are only motivation for the device of grotesque change from punning intonation to that of sentimental melodrama.
>
> The same principle organises the way the author sees and conceptualises the life of someone like Akakii Akakievich and the intonation of the *skaz* about him. The fictional event in the life of Akakii Akakievich and the event of the actual *skaz* about it merge in the historical event of Gogol's story. In this way, *The Overcoat* entered the historical life of Russia and became an active factor in it.   (Medvedev 1978: 127)

In a later passage discussing Eikhenbaum's characterisation of the 'humane passage' as grotesque device, Medvedev objects, in the name of ethical criticism and a commonsensical theory of reception, to the removal of the work from 'the whole ideological horizon':

> We know that everyone interprets and understands the 'humane passage' in *The Overcoat* as a socio-ethical, 'confessional' objectification. If it is considered the interference of the soul and the reflection of the personal feelings of the author, the same grounds compel us also to place the aesthetic objectification as Eikhenbaum understands it, i.e. the grotesque device, in this category...
>
> The matter under consideration does not involve the interference of 'the soul' or the reflection of spiritual facts, but the entrance of direct socio-ethical evaluations into the artistic work.... To exclude the ethical aspect from the artistic construction of *The Overcoat* is to misunderstand this construction.   (ibid., 148-9)

Medvedev broadens the attack on Eikhenbaum's, and by extension all Formalist analysis, from an accusation of misunderstanding the workings of *skaz* to a far-reaching dissatisfaction with a critical method that has no space for explicit engagement with ethical questions. Certainly, in the intellectual climate that the Soviet Union was now experiencing, such a position was no longer tenable. But these 'corrections' notwithstanding, Eikhenbaum's article took the critical analysis of 'The Overcoat', and of narrative prose in general, on to a new level of acuity, and initiated a decade of extraordinarily stimulating and productive critical debate.

The artistic response

If the Revolution provided an impetus to the understanding of Gogol, then, conversely, Gogol was instinctively turned to for help in understanding the Revolution. Revolutionary Russia was immediately interpreted in Gogolian terms by the philosopher Nikolai Berdiaev, who saw in Gogol a contemporary artist who anticipated Bely and Picasso. For Berdiaev:

> In the revolution that same old eternal-Gogolian (*vechno-go-golevskaia*] Russia, the inhuman, half-bestial Russia of muzzles and snouts has been uncovered. In the unendurable revolutionary vulgarity there is the eternally Gogolian. The hopes that the revolution would reveal a human image in Russia, that the human personality would rise to its full height after the autocracy fell have turned out to be in vain.... There is no longer any autocracy but Russian darkness and Russian evil remain. Darkness and evil are buried more deeply, not in the social shell of the people, but in its spiritual kernel.... Scenes from Gogol are being played out at every step in revolutionary Russia.... At the base lie the old Russian lies and deceit which Gogol saw long ago....
>
> The Russian revolution is a tragicomedy. It is the end of the Gogolian epoch. And maybe the most sombre and hopeless element in the Russian revolution is the Gogolian element in it...Russia absolutely must free itself from the power of Gogol's ghosts.   (Berdiaev: 125-7)

Shklovsky, too, when he describes the privations of winter in Civil War Petrograd and asserts that 'The Arctic Circle became a reality and passed somewhere near Nevsky Prospect' (Shklovskii 1986: 25) is using an image out of 'The Overcoat' in which Akakii Akakievich crosses a vast St Petersburg square at night and sees a sentry box 'at the edge of the world' (*na kraiu sveta*, 3: 161). The fantastic and estranged new world could best be assimilated in fantastic Gogolian terms. Many of the leading prose writers of the post-revolutionary decade, most notably Zamiatin, Zoshchenko and Bulgakov, stressed their closeness to Gogol and reworked his texts or incorporated his characters. The group of young Petrograd writers emerging under Zamiatin's tutelage, the Serapion Brothers, were also ready to admit their Gogolian heritage, none more strikingly than Veniamin Kaverin, who was later moved to conclude:

> Who does not know Dostoevsky's famous formula: 'We all
> came out from under Gogol's "Overcoat"?'. Now, in the
> middle of the twentieth century we ought to add: 'And out
> of Gogol's "Nose".'   (Kaverin: 6)

Evgenii Zamiatin described Gogol in his 1924 autobiography as the 'friend of his childhood', his books the solace of a lonely child, and the influence of this reading is apparent throughout Zamiatin's career in a continuing and inventive reworking of the 'obsession text' of Gogol's 'Petersburg Tales'.[21] Of particular interest in this context are three stories both written and set in revolutionary Petrograd. In the brief sketch 'The Dragon' ('Drakon') of 1918, an arresting updating of an episode from Gogol's story set in icy, fiery, foggy Petersburg, a 'dragon' man in oversized peaked cap and overcoat (*shinel'*), who comes in and out of view in the swirling fog, boasts of how he captured and shot a 'bastard intellectual', presumably at the same time relieving him of his coat (Zamiatin, S, 3: 68-9). Two stories of 1920, 'The Cave' ('Peshchera') and 'Mamai' model themselves closely on the structure of the whole story. In 'The Cave', the vicious Petersburg weather that is a 'strong enemy' of clerks like Akakii Akakievich has worsened to such a degree that mammoths roam the glaciers of the city. The meek hero Martin Martinych, desperate to warm his flat for his bed-ridden wife's name-day, becomes obsessed with getting firewood, an object of desire that is literally a matter of life and death. His plea to a potential benefactor, his neighbour Obertyshev, is turned down with the suggestion that 'books burn very well' (Zamiatin, S, 1: 455). So Martin is forced to turn to theft and steals some of his neighbour's logs; the neighbour complains to the House Representative, Selikhov, who comes to call. Selikhov tells an anecdote that again replays the episode in 'The Overcoat' noted in 'The Dragon', this time from the opposite angle, telling them:

> I was on my way home and on the Field of Mars [in the centre
> of the city, J.G.] I saw a man coming towards me just wearing
> a waistcoat, I swear! 'What's up?', I say. 'Oh, nothing', he
> says, 'They've just stripped me of my clothes so I'm running
> home to Vasilevskii Island.' What fun!   (ibid., 458)

In elemental revolutionary Petersburg there is no 'man on point duty' for the robbed man to appeal to, and he goes out of his way to minimise the encounter. Nor can there be any vengeance for Martin. For though Selikhov loathes the callous Obertyshev and encourages Martin to 'go and stuff his logs down his throat' (ibid., 459), the sense of imminent death is all pervasive and instead Martin gives his wife a phial of poison he has been saving and himself walks out into the icy dark where the mammoth roams.

If 'The Cave' offers a reworking of 'The Overcoat' of almost unbearable poignancy, then 'Mamai' provides a comic variant. In this story the city is, in a marine image like the one used in 'The Overcoat', a vast ocean, and its houses are stone liners. The story begins with another variation on the theft of clothes motif as the house manager, Elisei Eliseich, who plays a role akin to that of the 'important personage', is asked: 'Aren't you afraid of going around in a fur coat (*v shube-to*), that they'll take it off you?' (ibid., 445). The hero of the story, Petr Petrovich Mamai, is a meek, middle-aged, balding clerk, frightened of women, and twice referred to as a 'little man' (*malen'kii chelovechek*, ibid., 449). He is an avid collector of old books and admires their elegant lettering; and like his predecessor he has a female love object, in this case a book dating from the time of Catherine the Great, *A Description of the Beauties of Saint Petersburg (Opisatel'noe izobrazhenie prekrasnostei Sankt-Piterburkha)*. Alas, he is deprived of the object of his desire, for mice have eaten the money he has secretly been saving for it and stored under the floorboards; but perhaps beneath the comedy there is also serious intent. For the choice as love-object of this book about historical St Petersburg pays explicit homage to the Petersburg obsession text in the tradition of which Zamiatin is writing and his hero's very name, Petr Petrovich, like that of Akakii Akakievich's tailor, associates him with the city and its founder. At the same time it draws attention to an eighteenth-century Petersburg culture that is now lost forever. As the story tells us, its protagonists wander:

> in a strange, unfamiliar town – *Petrograd*.... So like, in one
> way – and so unlike – the *Petersburg* from which they had
> sailed off almost a year previously and to which they were
> unlikely ever to return.... No, not Petersburg!   (ibid., 450)

Thus in these stories, Zamiatin uses a dialogue with 'The Overcoat' to offer a lament for people deprived not simply of an overcoat or a book but of their whole way of life, and for a city that had just lost its status as the country's capital and was about to suffer an even more ignominious change of name, severing its official connection with its founder for seventy years.

For the rest of his career Zamiatin would continue to use the template of Gogol's Petersburg tales. Christopher Collins has offered an illuminating analysis of the close similarities of characterisation and plot between 'The Overcoat' and his 1928 story 'The Sloop' ('Ela') (Collins: 83-86). But in emigration Zamiatin would return to the theme with parodic intent in the 1934 story 'The Watch' ('Chasy'). It is set, like its predecessors, in post-revolutionary Petersburg, a place where 'merry bandits send passers-by home wearing only their collar and tie' (Zamiatin, S, 2: 145). A chatty, amused narrator tells us the story of red-haired (*ryzhii*) Semen Zaitser, an 'ex-trainee tailor' from Pinsk, but now a functionary who signs orders for the frozen city's supplies of firewood and is therefore mockingly styled a 'great man' (*velikii chelovek*). He has just traded a load of wood for a fine gold watch, which he wears to impress his secretary Verochka, with whom he is secretly in love. While he is walking Verochka home late at night, a man in 'a military overcoat without epaulettes' approaches and asks for a match. Zaitser know that this is merely a ploy to steal his watch. Indeed, seeing a gold watch on the man, he heroically grabs it back from him. The next day for Verochka and all his office colleagues he is a hero – until, that is, he looks in his desk drawer and finds there...his own gold watch, which he had not in fact been wearing the previous night, a fact he foolishly confesses to Verochka. As the story ends he is mocked by Verochka and all his colleagues, ridiculed as a 'little foolish man' (*malen'kii smeshnoi chelovechek*) in the office wall newspaper, and, in the tale's final words, 'departs forever from his office, from Verochka's heart and from the story' (ibid., 153). The tailor who became a clerk and tried to be an 'important personage', and then to emulate the exploits of the spectral Akakii Akakievich, has ceased to exist at all.

Zamiatin died in Paris in 1937, but even in death he remained true to his Gogolian heritage, for, according to Remizov's obituary, he died 'of angina pectoris, the death of Akakii Akakievich Bashmachkin, the hero of Gogol's "The Overcoat"' (Remizov 1989: 117).

In a diary entry for 10 August 1923 Mikhail Zoshchenko's wife records of her husband: 'As he often likes to do, he drew a parallel between himself and Gogol, in whom he's very interested and with whom he finds much in common' (cited by Scatton: 27-8), a perception that would also soon become a critical commonplace. In a number of his 1920s stories Zosh-chenko transfers episodes from 'The Overcoat' into the Soviet present. In 'Love' ('Liubov'), of 1924, Vasia Chesnokov (Mr Garlic) is seeing his girl-friend Mashenka home through the snowy Petersburg streets when they are set upon by a robber who demands his fur coat and boots. Incensed, Chesnokov suggests he takes Mashenka's instead. The robber demurs, and Chesnokov is left with neither coat nor girl. In 'Swinery' ('Svinstvo'), 1923, the anguished search for a suitable name for the baby Bashmachkin is replayed in revolutionary circumstances. Two stories take the whole 'Overcoat' plot, but give their heroes animal love objects. In 'Misfortune' ('Beda'), 1923, Glotov, a peasant from the village of Gnilye Prudki (Putrid Pondlets), scrimps and saves for two years, cutting down on food and cutting out cigarettes and moonshine, to buy a longed-for horse. Eventually he goes to market and after heroic bargaining he gets it. Realising that the acquisition of the animal is an 'event' in his life he decides that he must 'wet its head' in celebration (*vsprysnut'*, compare 'we must wet the new overcoat', *nuzhno vsprysnut' novuiu shinel'*, 3: 157). After a day and a half's heroic drinking he has lost the animal, 'But, brother, you wet its head' (*Zato, bratok, vsprysnul.* Zoshchenko SS, 1: 167). In 'The Nanny Goat' ('Koza') published the same year, the object of desire is the eponymous animal. The hero of the story is Petr Zabezhkin, a Petersburg clerk who has worked at the same desk for twelve years, and who before the Revolution held the rank of Collegiate Registrar, the lowest rank of all. Lonely and in constant fear of losing his job, he dreams of an encounter that will transform his life. His dreams of comfort become centred on the goat – getting it will surely bring prosperity; and so he embarks upon a ruthless and cunning emotional assault upon the large lady, Domna Pavlovna, whom he takes to be its owner. Alas, once they have agreed to marry he incautiously mentions the goat – only to find that it is not hers. His dastardly plans are revealed. In Domna Pavlovna's words: 'Oh, you scoundrel, you canine idol, was it the goat you were aiming for?' (Zoshchenko SS, 2: 26). She throws him out, he loses his job and his life is ruined.

It will be obvious from the details of these stories that the poignant and tragic elements of Gogol's story have been replaced by broad laughter, both at new Soviet conditions and at eternal human foibles. Zoshchenko's heroes bring disaster upon themselves, without the intervention of fate. Cathy Popkin has examined a whole series of Zoshchenko's 1920s stories involving the removal of coats and other garments:

> But if Gogol's 'Overcoat' presents certain obstacles to an unreservedly empathic reading, Zoshchenko's coat capers nearly preclude it, foregrounding instead the insistence on articulating the trivial, refuting, while appearing to accept, the injunction to adopt the 'important themes' both of the present and of Russian literature's great nineteenth-century literary forebears.   (Popkin: 72)

The influence of Gogol on the writings of Mikhail Bulgakov has also been widely attested, both by the writer himself and in the critical literature, though for Bulgakov the key Gogol texts are *Dead Souls* and *The Government Inspector*.[22] Nevertheless, traces of 'The Overcoat' can also be seen throughout his career. In his first long story, 'Diaboliad' ('D'iavoliada'), of 1924, a satire on Soviet bureaucracy, a quiet clerk named Korotkov (Mr Meek) makes a mistake copying a document, is dismissed by his terrifying superior, loses a sense of his own identity and falls prey to demonic forces, goes mad and eventually kills himself. As Marietta Chudakova writes, we have here a hero 'formed "with the participation"' of Akakii Akakievich and the heroes of Gogol's other Petersburg tales (Chudakova 1980: 182).

In a story written the next year, 'The Heart of a Dog' ('Sobach'e serdtse'), the dog turned man decides to designate himself Poligraf Poligrafovich 'and the name itself is chosen in circumstances which recall the christening of Akakiy Akakiyevich (another pairing) in "The Overcoat"' (Milne: 116). Indeed the 'strange' name has been chosen by 'looking through the calendar' (Bulgakov SS 2: 172). He later appears in a second-hand leather jacket and trousers, acquired because he has 'got myself a post' in an institution of which these are the sinister badges (ibid., 198). There are also several echoes of 'The Overcoat' in the work Bulgakov was writing over the last decade of his life, the novel *The Master and Margarita* (*Master i Margarita*), a story of a great love aspired to, gained, lost, and then regained with demonic intervention leading to a fantastic resolution. The motif of the loss of clothes runs through the novel, and is specifically used in the scene at the Variety Theatre in chapters 12 and 14 of the novel as a punishment for unacceptable aspirations. Above all the links are apparent in the device of the chatty, unreliable narrator and in the epilogue, in which, after the events of the story are seemingly over, rumours spread through Moscow about demonic forces and ghostly apparitions – including the story of 2,000 people stripped of their clothes in a Moscow theatre. All of these events are gleefully reported by the narrator, who then 'explains' them, only to open up new enigmas.

Echoes of the story can also be found in other leading writers of the period. Sofia Poliakova sees elements of Akakii Akakievich in both the features and the behaviour of Parnok, the hero of Mandelshtam's 1928 novella 'The Egyptian Stamp' ('Egipetskaia marka') and finds the plot to be repeated in the theft first of his morning coat by the tailor, Mervis, and then of his shirt. She concludes: 'One has to assume that Mandelshtam was counting on the recognition effect, which, as in the uncovering of any reminiscence, gives mental joy to the reader' (Poliakova: 288). The Gogolian heritage is positively embraced by Kavalerov, the hero of Olesha's 1927 novel *Envy* (*Zavist'*), who is both a great fantasist and a great reader. When he first meets Ivan Babichev, in the words of Andrew Barratt:

> ...Kavalerov (in an obvious plagiarism of Gogol's *The Overcoat* [*Shinel'*]) introduced himself to Ivan as a 'little man', abused by a figure of authority: 'Kavalerov told Ivan of how he had been evicted by an important personage (*znachitel'noe litso*) from his [i.e. the important personage's, A.B.] house...Ivan told him the same thing, he too had been evicted by an important personage.
> (Barratt 1981: 30, quoting from Part 2, chapter 4 of the novel)

Akakii Akakievich was also co-opted by the actor Vladimir Iakhontov for his *Petersburg*, a 'literary montage' of episodes from 'The Overcoat', Pushkin's *The Bronze Horseman* and Dostoevsky's 'White Nights', performed at the Sovremennik theatre in Moscow in 1928. Iakhontov had started these one-man shows the previous year in an attempt to 'look anew at the classical heritage in the light of revolutionary reality', but the very nature of the genre meant that little light was cast on the figure of Bashmachkin himself (Danilov: 457-58).

Political intentions of a very different kind lay behind the use of the story in G. Alekseev's 1927 story 'The Fur Coat' ('Shuba'). Set in the mid-1920s in a provincial Soviet town, it tells of Drigulin, a poor miller who is helped onto his feet by his old friend Dondysh, now the Chairman of the local Executive Committee of the Party. Flushed with success, he orders himself a lavish fur coat of kangaroo fur [!], a hubristic act that will have tragic consequences. For his boasting about the coat arouses the envy of Dondysh, who tries to persuade him to sell it on to him. When Drigulin refuses, the Chairman assaults him with a regime of heavy taxes until he is forced to give it up to the tax inspector and Dondysh can buy it at auction. Seeing his coat on Dondysh's back, Drigulin falls into paralysis. As Tatiana Nikolskaia has pointed out, the story is intended as a protest against the political drive for egalitarianism (*uravnilovka*), and the use of the seemingly innocent pastiche form serves as a veil for masking politically subversive thoughts (Nikol'skaia: 283-4).

One of the most ambitious and exciting of the engagements with Gogol's story during the 1920s was the film made for Leningradkino in 1926 by the young directors Grigorii Kozintsev and Leonid Trauberg from a script by Iurii Tynianov, and entitled *The Overcoat. A Film Play in the Manner of Gogol* (*Shinel'. Kino-p'esa v manere Gogolia*). All the leading Formalist critics, and especially Eikhenbaum, Shklovsky and Tynianov, became directly involved in the workings of the new Soviet cinema, as critics and theorists, but also practically, as the writers of screenplays. More than once during the decade, Tynianov, who had in *Dostoevsky and Gogol* (*On the Theory of Parody*; discussed earlier) seen all artistic evolution as rebellion and reinterpretation, expressed his exasperation with the vogue for films which attempted merely to 'illustrate' the classic works of nineteenth-century literature. In the preface to his screenplay of *The Overcoat* he writes:

> The film story *The Overcoat* is not a film illustration of Gogol's famous story. Illustrating literature for the cinema is an arduous and inauspicious task, since the cinema has its own methods and devices, which are not the same as those of literature. The cinema can only try to reincarnate and reinterpret literary heroes and literary style in its own way. That is why we have before us not a Gogol tale, but a film

> tale *in the manner* of Gogol, where the story is made more
> complicated, and the hero is dramatised in a plane which is
> not given by Gogol, but which is as it were suggested by
> Gogol's manner.   (Tynianov 1973: 78)

For this reason, the screenplay was not drawn solely from 'The Overcoat.'
The first half of the film, in which Bashmachkin is still a young man, is
based mainly on another Petersburg tale, 'Nevsky Prospect', and, as if to
emphasise this point, the film's first intertitle consists of that story's famous
opening line, 'There is nothing better than the Nevsky Prospect, at least in
Petersburg.' All in all, according to the calculations of Iurii Tsivian, it used
'at least ten' other Gogol sources, both published stories and unpublished
fragments (Tsiv'ian 1986: 15), as well as character names and plot details
from the work of Dostoevsky. The Bashmachkin of the film is a character
who did not exist, strictly speaking, in Gogol's work, but his experience,
like that of Korotkov in Bulgakov's 'Diaboliad', is that of a composite St
Petersburg hero. Likewise the artistic space of the film is not limited to that
of any particular story but is rather the 'mythological' Petersburg developed
in the nineteenth century through the writings of Pushkin, Gogol, Dostoevsky and others. Akakii Akakievich's nocturnal wanderings, dwarfed by
imperial statuary, echo the encounter of Pushkin's Evgeny with the statue
of the Bronze Horseman The grand but empty imperial centre of the city,
with its granite, its huge buildings and imposing interiors, its soldiers and
government officials, contrasts with the marginal Petersburg of brick, small
houses and bustling street crowds.

If Tynianov brought to the film the result of his subtle musings, both
about nineteenth-century Petersburg culture and about the relationships
between the two art forms, then the contribution of the two young directors
was no less seminal. In 1921 in Petrograd they had 'patented' Eccentrism
in theatre and, together with Sergei Iutkevich, had founded the *Factory of
the Eccentric Actor* (*Feks*), an experimental group with its roots, according
to their 1922 manifesto, in circus, jazz and music hall, and had proclaimed
as their slogan 'We prefer Charlie's backside to Eleanora Duse's hands.'
They brought this raucous modernity to their work in cinema from 1924,
and its influence, and their admiration for Chaplin, are also evident in the
eccentric acting styles of the completed film. At one point they even thought
of Chaplin in the part of Akakii Akakievich, since they felt 'some sort of
almost imperceptible likeness: a little man in the enormity of a strange, alien
world' (Kozintsev SS 4: 109).[23] Indeed, Kozintsev insisted that it was the
experience of the snowbound 'cruel' St Petersburg winter of 1920-1, and
the sense that the Revolution had snapped the threads between two eras, that
evoked an overwhelming sense of unreality and disorientation and led them,
inevitably, to the weirdness and nightmare in Gogol's writings (Kozintsev
1978: 26-7).

A crucial role is also played by the cinematography of Andrei Moskvin, full of light and shadows and grotesque, distorting angles, and the film's overall design, playing with the sizes of people, objects and buildings, and its use of Cubist shapes and Constructivist design for interiors and stairwells. The sense of estrangement is enhanced by the fact that the film is, of course, shot in black and white, (as Vaiskopf 1978: 48 points out, the palette of the original story is dominated by blacks, whites, and greys), and is silent, addressing the viewer only through the often intentionally confusing inter-titles, and through various examples of calligraphy, including the final title, in which Akakii Akakievich 'writes his own death'.

As Tynianov noted in a 1929 memoir of his work with the Feks, the critical reaction to this clearly polemical work was savage:

> One critic called me an insolent illiterate, and, if I am not mistaken, proposed cleaning up the Feks with an iron broom.... Another's reasoning was as follows: the classics are national property; the scriptwriter and the directors have distorted a classic – the Public Prosecutor's Office should try them for plundering national property.   (Tynianov 1979: 347)

With time, however, the compelling intellectual and visual boldness of this embodiment of a distorted world, plunged in frost and snow, and prey to dream and devilish temptation, has come to be acknowledged as a brilliant and pioneering creative re-imagining of Gogol's story and his world. Later film versions have not managed to emulate it; but during the final years of his life, from 1969 to 1973, Grigorii Kozintsev made extensive notes for a new film, to be based on all of Gogol's Petersburg tales, and to be called *Gogoliad* (*Gogoliada*) (Kozintsev SS 5: 174-306). Recalling how in 1926 he had set the 'nonentity' Akakii Akakievich against the grand scale of the imperial capital, he planned now to show him on a more human scale, not just as a petty copy-clerk, but 'capable of dreaming'. As well as the fantastic, his character would contain elements of Neo-Realism, and his plea for pity should ring out with 'Shakespearean force' (ibid., 181, 183, 182, 198). Though the project never came to fruition, the notes Kozintsev made for it, which were begun while he was working on his film of *King Lear*, contain an extraordinary range of subtle connections with the sensibility of other artists, and provide fascinating evidence of the way a great film director's perception of the text changed over a lifetime.

The 1930s and 1940s; émigré readings

The post-Revolutionary years were an extraordinarily fruitful time both for the analysis of Gogol's story and for the appropriation of it for a variety of artistic and ideological purposes. Two major books on Gogol appeared in

1934. Andrei Bely's *Gogol's Mastery* (*Masterstvo Gogolia*) provided a hugely ambitious analysis of Gogol's style. In the context of 'The Overcoat' it is particularly interesting on Gogol's 'squadron' of odd names, whose 'intention is to instil terror through their triviality', among which he lists the names rejected for Akakii Akakievich (Belyi 1982: 216), and on Gogol's 'repetition of little words [which] plaits together the musculature of the story like glands' (ibid., 246). Aleksandr Voronsky's *Gogol* provides a traditional social interpretation of Akakii Akakievich as victim of inhumanity and, more suggestively, calls him an 'automaton' adding: 'Akakii Akakievich is not capable of offending anyone, he is quiet and meek, but he is also terrifying: it is not man who exists for him, but paper' (Voronskii: 472). Voronsky also makes the case for the role of the 'Gogol manner' for Soviet writers: 'It's time for Gogol's rights to be re-established. Socialist Realism has no reason to deny Gogol this' (ibid., 517). But in fact these books were the last flowerings of a free discourse about Gogol's work in the Soviet Union for several years. Belyi died in 1934. Voronsky's book was withdrawn and almost the entire print run destroyed after his arrest. For 1934 was also, not coincidentally, the year of the First Congress of the Union of Writers of the USSR, at which the concept of Socialist Realism was officially promulgated. Under these circumstances Gogol and his heroes would become petrified for several years in socially 'progressive' poses (see Karlinsky: 285-9). The one major achievement of Soviet Gogol scholarship of the next two decades would be the publication of the Academic Edition of his works, 1937-52, which, with its full apparatus of drafts and variants, remains the fullest edition of 'The Overcoat'.

Two other silenced writers turned to 'The Overcoat' in the terrible circumstances of these years. In 1943-4, in 'A Petersburg Tale', the eighth poem of his sequence 'The Lay of the Exploits of Gogol' ('Slovo o podvigakh Gogolia'), the poet Aleksei Kruchenykh writes:

> Lord my God,
> Do not let me drink
> Burning the remains of my thoughts in the stove
> ....,
> The hellish vengeance of Akakii Akakievich...
>   (Kruchenykh 1999: 302)

The most poignant of all the 'conversations' with Gogol is that of Daniil Kharms. On 11 April 1937, as the pressures on him mounted, he wrote in his diary: 'If you have nothing to note down, then at least follow Gogol's example and write that today you can't write anything' (Kharms 1991: 496-7); later that year, on 14 November, he put Gogol at the top of a list of his favourite writers (Nikitaev: 49). And three months before the diary entry, on 6 January 1937, he wrote 'Blue Notebook No. 10' ('Golubaia tetrad'

No. 10', also known as 'The Red-Haired Man'), his bleakest miniature tale:

> There lived a red-haired man, who had neither eyes nor ears.
> Nor did he have any hair, so it was a convention to call him
> red-haired.
> He could not speak, since he had no mouth. He also had no
> nose.
> He did not have even hands or legs. And he had no belly,
> and he had no back, and he had no backbone, and he had no
> innards. There was nothing. So it is not clear [literally not
> understood], who is being talked about.
>   We had better not talk about him any more.
>
>   (Kharms SS 2: 330)

Robin Aizlewood has pointed out the Gogolian features of this text, including the loss of body parts, which recalls 'The Nose', and the failure of the
narrator to narrate (Aizlewood: 101-03). The story also recalls 'The Overcoat', another tale characterised by narratorial incompetence, and some of
the bodily features of the protagonist recall Akakii Akakievich. He, too, was,
in one of the first things we learn about him, 'a little red-haired' (*neskol'ko
ryzhevat*, 3: 141). He, too was losing his hair (ibid.). He, too, 'could not speak'.
Like Sologub, in the story discussed earlier, Kharms presents the 'erasure' of the little man literally, but he also 'erases' the text, reducing it to
an absolute, imploding minimum. As Aizlewood also suggests, if, in a story
written in 1937, the hero has 'disappeared', become a 'non-person', someone
it is 'better' not to talk about, then the chilling political implications of this
narrative are obvious. Thus Gogol's tale is reworked as a parable of the
extinguishing both of people and of literature, a symbolic end of the road.
    In this context it is unsurprising that some of the most innovative inter-
pretations of Gogol were now being written and published in emigration. In
'Pan Micholski's Waistcoat' ('Zhilet Pana Mikhol'skogo'), a short story of
1932 by Ivan Bunin, set in Kiev in the 1840s, the hero decides it is time to
marry. He chooses a pretty bride with a dowry, and makes all other necessary
preparations, including ordering 'some pairs of trousers, some frock-coats,
some tail-coats and some waistcoats in the very latest fashion' (Bunin SS
7: 288). He is then unexpectedly invited to a reception for a writer he considers to be 'terribly commonplace' by the name of...Nikolai Gogol. Much
of Kievan society has turned out for the occasion, but the foppishly dressed
writer of 'The Overcoat' only has eyes for...Micholski's jacket, which its
wearer describes as 'very fine, only it did not look like the skin of a frog, like
the one worn by our guest from the capital, but like the skin of a chameleon'
(ibid., 290). The next day Micholski's tailor arrives and begs him to give up
the final jacket he is making him (which is using the last velvet in Kiev) to
the writer. But in a superb comic thwarting both of Gogol's obsession and

the reader's expectations, Micholski refuses point blank to give up the garment, exclaiming 'He may be Gogol, but he hasn't got a jacket like this and he's not going to get one!', adding that he values it considerably higher than 'any of his *Dead Souls* !' (ibid., 290).

There were also a number of important critical studies. Konstantin Mochulsky's book on *Gogol's Spiritual Path* (*Dukhovnyi put' Gogolia*), appeared in Paris in 1934. In Alfred Bem's piece about 'The Overcoat' published two years later, 'Gogol's world is a marionette theatre, a brilliant masquerade, which evokes laughter or tears, but not sympathy for his heroes' (Bem: 132). The following year Dmitrii Chizhevsky, who was associated with the Prague Linguistic Circle, published another pioneering critical study, 'The Composition of Gogol's Overcoat.' Chizhevsky drew upon and extended Eikhenbaum's analysis of formal questions, but combined this with an attention to the story's moral and philosophical concerns. The stylistic feature that he dwells upon most illuminatingly is the abnormally frequent use of the word 'even' (*dazhe*) in the story. Chizhevskii has calculated (and later critics have not chosen to challenge him) that the word is used 73 times, and that it appears in clusters at key points in the narrative. It is used to remind the reader of the presence of the *skaz* narrator, and to create comic effects, since it works antithetically and illogically, for dilution rather than intensification. It is associated with all of the protagonists, and reveals the inner hollowness of their worlds. Moving on to a consideration of Gogol's motivation in writing the tale, Chizhevsky bluntly rejects the Belinskian line:

> Putting it quite simply, it was said that Gogol wanted to protest in his story against the position of the minor official. If one examines Gogol's story closely, one must in all events say that this protest, if at all intended, is strangely absent. Does Akaky Akakievich offer convincing proof that the 'little man' is also our 'brother'?...
>
> We are convinced that Gogol has no intention of exploring the social aspect of his theme in the story, and that, on the contrary, he had something entirely different in mind, namely the development of a theme intrinsic to his philosophy of life, the problem of man's 'own place'. (Chizhevskii 1976: 387)

He goes on to suggest that 'the theme of the story is the kindling of a human soul.' But, alas, for Akakii Akakievich this kindling is aroused by a passion for something 'worthless', a 'useless object' (ibid., 389). 'The world – and the devil – capture man not only with greatness...but also with trivialities, with commonplace things...with the love for an overcoat' (ibid., 392). For Chizhevsky the overcoat is a devilish temptation arranged by the demonic Petrovich (ibid., 393).

Chizhevsky concludes his analysis with a double attack: on the socio-political criticism that has 'built a high wall of political, social and other prejudices around Gogol'; and on the recent Formalist contribution, which 'with its sharp polemical tendency has more or less wholly ignored the ideo-logical context of Gogol's work' (ibid., 397). In his view formal and ideological aspects are linked – the constant undermining use of the word 'even' is connected with the moral attention to the idea of destruction by the trivial. He concludes:

> Gogol's plot can in no way be termed anecdotal, humoristic
> or sentimental. Gogol's basic idea here is *serious* and *gloomy*,
> the fate of his hero is *terrible* and not ridiculous.   (ibid.)[24]

For all the perspicacity of Chizhevsky's stylistic discoveries, and for all his scorn for critics who 'see Gogol primarily as a critic of "Russian conditions"' (ibid.) his article is clearly driven by the need to read meaning in(to) the story. No such impulsion is felt by Vladimir Nabokov, who devoted a chapter to the story in his 1944 book *Nikolai Gogol*, which reads in part like an eloquent 'hands off' sign for the literarily unsophisticated. For Nabokov:

> Neither the person who wants a good laugh, nor the person
> who craves for books 'that make one think' will understand
> what *The Overcoat* is really about. Give me the creative reader;
> this is a tale for him.   (Nabokov 1961: 140)

Nabokov lays great stress on the absurdity of Gogol's world and on the 'conjuror's patter' of his language. He shows (without reference to Chizh-evsky) how insertion of the word 'even' can 'make the harmless sentence explode' (ibid., 142). He insists that 'the *real* plot (as always with Gogol) lies in the style' (ibid., 144). He gives a bravura description of the piece's construction:

> So, to sum up: the story goes this way: mumble, mumble,
> lyrical wave, mumble, lyrical wave, mumble, lyrical wave,
> mumble, fantastic climax, mumble, mumble, and back into
> the chaos from which they all had derived. At this superhigh
> level of art, literature is of course not concerned with pitying
> the underdog or cursing the upperdog. (ibid., 149)

He concludes: 'if you are interested in "ideas" and "facts" and "messages", keep away from Gogol' (ibid.).

This was, as Cyril Bryner has shown, light years from the way the story had traditionally been recommended to English-speaking readers, 'under the false pretence of realism, mangled by inadequate translations' (Bryner: 509). The 'new' reading was also given support in 1949 in Wellek and Warren's seminal *Theory of literature*:

> In their day, Gogol's 'The Cloak' and *Dead Souls* were apparently misread, even by intelligent critics. Yet the view that they were propaganda, a misreading explicable in terms of isolated passages and elements in them, is scarcely to be reconciled with the elaborateness of their literary organisation, their complicated devices of irony, parody, word play, mimicry, and burlesque.
>
>   (Wellek and Warren: 239; also cited by Bryner: 506)

This was a book recommended to generations of students of literature, but its influence was eclipsed among students of Russian literature by Dmitrii Mirsky's canonical *A History of Russian Literature*, edited by Francis Whitfield from books published by Mirsky during his period of English emigration in the 1920s, and also first published in a single volume in 1949. Though Mirsky dutifully ascribes the interpretation that the story is imbued with 'poignancy of pity for the poor and insignificant man' to the contemporary readers of Gogol's tale (Mirsky 1958: 159), his study does not, and could not be expected to, refer to the more sophisticated interpretations that were appearing in Soviet Russia at the time he was writing it.

The 1950s and later: the international dimension

The *grand projet* of the Soviet *Complete Works* was finally completed in 1952, the year of the centenary of Gogol's death. This date also coincided with the last months of Stalinism and the stamp of Soviet orthodoxy is apparent in the flood of centenary publications, e.g. in the selection made for *Gogol in the Memoirs of His Contemporaries* (*Gogol' v vospominani- iakh sovremennikov*, Moscow, 1952). The decade also provided remarkable evidence of the universal appeal of the story. In 1951 in Paris Marcel Marceau staged the story as a romantic mime drama, a production explicitly sourced in the words 'heard' by Akakii Akakievich's young colleague 'I am your brother.' The production did not include the important personage or the fantastic ending, concluding with the tragic theft of the overcoat, described by Marceau as a crucifixion. The production was revived for the 150th anniversary of Gogol's birth in 1959 (see Boiadzhev). In a later Parisian stage production the hero was a Gaullist *fonctionnaire* (Shklovskii 1970: 22).

In 1952 the Japanese film director Akira Kurosawa released *Living* (*Ikiru*), the story of the last months and the death of Kanji Watanabe, a minor civil servant. The previous year Kurosawa had made a version of

Dostoevsky's *The Idiot* and he would later make films from works by Gorky and Arsenev; he has spoken of his fascination with Russian literature. In his *The Space of Tragedy* (*Prostranstvo tragedii*), first published 1973, Grigorii Kozintsev, who had directed the Soviet film version of 'The Overcoat', wrote that 'In *Living*, which is made from a Japanese work, it is not difficult to find a link between the mummy-like functionary and Gogol's Bash-machkin' (Kozintsev SS 4: 18). The film scholar Hyangsoon Yi has recently shown just how closely the plot and characterisation of *Living* follow those of 'The Overcoat'. Both heroes lead pitifully uneventful lives which are dramatically transformed before their premature deaths. Both make auda-cious challenges to authority and are accorded far more attention in death than in life. Watanabe's acquisition of a new hat has a meaning comparable to Bashmachkin's quest for a new coat. Though Yi adduces no evidence of Kurosawa's knowledge of the Gogol text, he does prove the extent of their shared concerns and devices, and the rightness of Kozintsev's insight.

Another 1952 film, *The Cloak* (*Il Cappotto*), made by the Italian film director Alberto Lattuada, is explicitly based on Gogol's story, which it transposes to contemporary Italy. According to the Soviet critic V. Turitsyn, Lattuada foregrounds elements of both comedy and social protest. After he gets his new cloak, the clerk, Carmine del Carmine, is invited to the mayor's New Year ball for the first time. There he makes a speech in defence of the poor and is thrown out. He has his coat stolen, catches a fever and dies. In the film's coda, as del Carmine's shade searches for his coat, the mayor is moved to repentance.

Three years later, in 1955, the story was reworked by the British play-wright Wolf Mankowitz in his *The Bespoke Overcoat*, set among the Jewish garment trade of London's East End. It was filmed the following year by the director Jack Clayton. It tells the story of the clerk, Fender, played by Alfie Bass, who had worked for the Ranting Warehouse Clothing Company for 43 years, before being forced to retire, at the very point when he had just made the first payment on a 'bespoke' overcoat from the master tailor Morry (Moishe), played by David Kossoff. Though Morry lets him have the new coat, Fender gets ill, lies in bed railing at his ill treatment by the 'governor' (who had only recently become the boss of the family company, and whom Fender remembered as a snivelling boy), and dies. After his death he returns to Morry, and insists that he must have a sheepskin coat from Ranting, so the ghost and the tailor go back to the warehouse and get the coat. Then Fender disappears and Morry prays for the repose of his soul. The film is studio-shot in black and white, with atmospheric, shadow-filled interiors. It is informed with details of Jewish life, and imbued with sympathy for the little man and his dreams, in this case of life in sunny Clacton. It won a prize at the Venice Film Festival, a British Academy of Film and Television Award, and the 1956 Oscar for Best Short Subject.

The decade ended with a new Soviet film version of *The Overcoat*, directed by the actor Aleksei Batalov. Batalov had sprung to prominence in the Thaw years, starring in a number of films imbued with a new sympathetic attention to the concerns of the individual. *The Overcoat*, his directorial debut, despite numbering Boris Eikhenbaum among its consultants, was also shot through with Thaw humanism. The film opens with the face of a pretty baby, gurgling as his doting mother chooses him a name. This blandly charming scene sets the tone for the whole film – though Akakii Akakievich is duly mocked by his colleagues and robbed of his prize possession, he is buttressed throughout by the sympathetic concern of his landlady, the bluff tailor Petrovich and, especially, Petrovich's down-to-earth wife. Rolan Bykov, the actor playing Akakii, deploys a whole gamut of ingratiating comic turns. Batalov has added a number of new characters – a money-lender, a coffin-maker, a crazy old man with a large manuscript to be typed – but they serve only to slacken the film's atmosphere. He also adds several ill-judged touching details: when Akakii chooses cat fur for his collar, a nearby cat miaows winningly at him; when he leaves for work in his new overcoat, the landlady's silly dog fails to recognise him and barks aggressively – and all of this is orchestrated by antiseptic and intrusive background music.

Comparisons with the Kozintsev-Trauberg film are instructive. There, too, were characters and episodes not in the original tale, but they all contributed to the evocation of the madness and danger that suffuse Gogol's Petersburg. This *Overcoat* makes nothing at all of St Petersburg – neither the grand imperial centre, nor the dark, demonic forces lurking just below the shiny surface. The theft takes place not in a wide space on the edge of the world, but in a covered arcade. And the fantastic ending also goes for nothing. Alas the lesson of this *Overcoat* is that to filter the story through a sieve of bloodless sentimentality is to make it, and its hero, null and exasperating.

In 1977 the German composer Gerhard Rosenfeld wrote a three act opera of the story, from Gerhard Hartmann's libretto. It was premiered at the German National Opera House in Weimar on 4 July 1978 (Sadie, 4: 43).

The late Soviet period

During the Brezhnev years Russian critics turned again to 'The Overcoat' with new critical approaches, and as innovative studies of the work began to appear once more, a lively new debate grew up around Gogol's meanings and devices. New appropriations of the story also showed how effective a vehicle it could be for resistance to Soviet orthodoxy. Boris Vakhtin's *The Sheepskin Coat* (*Dublenka*) was first published in *Metropol'*, a collection which a number of writers attempted to publish without prior submission to the censorship in 1979. It advertises its literary heredity by using the words 'We all came out from under Gogol's Overcoat' as its epigraph. The critic Julian Connolly has shown in potent detail how much the characterisation, the plot and the narrative style of the story owe to its predecessor. The hero, Filarmon Ivanovich Onushkin, is an ageing minor bureaucrat, ignored by his colleagues. His odd name and the odd way of its choosing are explained by the narrator: his revolutionary but ill educated father had come across the word *Filarmoniia* and, taking it for the name of the wife of the People's Commissar for Enlightenment, had named his son in her honour. (His surname, as Connolly has noted, also contains an allusion to 'The Overcoat', since *onuchki* are foot-wrappings and the word is used by Petrovich, who suggests Akakii Akakievich make some from his old coat, 3: 151). Onushkin, like his predecessor, spurns entertainment in the evenings, preferring to stay at home copying – in his case taking notes on works of Marxist-Leninist aesthetics. The plot links again are obvious. In Connolly's words:

> The everyday routine of an ordinary government bureaucrat becomes disrupted when he aspires to a more daring life-style, for which the symbol is a new sheepskin coat. Having obtained the coat, he runs afoul of his superiors, loses his coat, and is removed from his job.   (Connolly: 74)

At this point, he turns to a well placed patron, Taganrog, who fails him. All of Onushkin's tribulations are told in a careless, half-mocking style by the narrator, never more so than in the epilogue, which, while suggesting various versions of what might have happened to him after his disgrace, casts doubt on each of them, only to end with the words 'Who needs him?' (*komu on nuzhen?*, Vakhtin: 203).

Yet the story does also add elements not present in the original, in particular a young wife, who has run away and left him. The attentive reader will here spot two further sly allusions to the surname of Gogol's hero, since within three lines of being introduced the wife is identified as a *bashkirka* (a Bashkir) with a face like a *basmach* (a Central Asian anti-Soviet guerrilla, ibid., 167). It also adds an extensive subplot in which a Comrade Biceps explicitly plays the role of a contemporary Khlestakov.

Above all the whole motivation for Vakhtin's story seems more localised. Onushkin desires his sheepskin coat both for erotic reasons, to draw him closer to the glamorous avant-garde poet Elizaveta Petrovna (who provokes his first 'non-Party dream'), and because it is the height of Soviet fashion – but to get it he is sucked into a web of Party corruption around Comrade Biceps. Vakhtin's anti-Party satire has many targets: the secret shops for Party members; Party literary theory and Party artistic censorship; above all the underground parallel supply system where everything can be got for a price. However, as Connolly notes, the story lacks 'the apparent open-endedness and multi-dimensionality of Gogol's artistic vision', rather using its model for a tale focused on his own satiric impulses (Connolly: 84).

Like Vakhtin's hero, the protagonist (a man tersely named Narator) of

Zinovii Zinik's *Russian Service* (*Russkaia sluzhba*), published in Paris in 1983, is a meek and middle-aged Soviet functionary. His Akakian heredity is most vividly expressed in his role checking departmental documents for the orthographical mistakes he alone can recognise, an activity supported by evenings spent reading orthographical dictionaries. He, too, is mocked by his colleagues, and tormented by the obscene antics of the women workers of a sewing factory, with whom he shares a hostel. But when he asks these harridans his sacramental Akakian question, 'When will you leave me in peace?' ('Kogda vy menia v pokoe ostavite..?', Zinik: 93) no one is moved to pity; instead they make a complaint about him and he is deprived of his bonus.

Like all his clerkly predecessors, he is awakened by an object, in this case an umbrella given to him on his fortieth birthday, which, through a chain of circumstance, leads to a high temperature and three days in bed, and to a 'resurrection' consisting of listening to foreign broadcasts, carelessness at work (he lets through an orthographical mistake), and to eventual defection to England. However, his afterlife in the free world brings only a repetition of his Soviet tribulations. Working for a Russian Language Radio Station broadcasting from London, he tries to turn his redundant orthographical skills into instruction about stress in spoken Russian, but his feckless colleagues are not interested. He repeats the tribulations, real and imagined, of Akakii Akakievich. His clothes are stolen; he loses his beloved umbrella; his lack of English makes him express himself in odd, disconnected particles; he is tormented by the London cold and rain; he is spurned by his fellow workers and threatened with dismissal by the head of the service; he becomes the object of the erotic attentions of his landlady, but once she realises that the sum total of his Soviet persecution was mockery for his orthographic punctiliousness, her ardour cools. At the end of the novel, another umbrella is the cause of his death. He leaves his life for a second time, and is replaced at work, unmourned and unavenged.

Perhaps the most poignant of the losses which *Russian Service* narrates is that of the Russian language itself (another central Gogolian concern), maimed by Soviet linguistic reforms and Soviet boorishness, or forgotten through emigration and the passage of time. By the end the novel has become one of the saddest and most thoughtful reworkings of the master tale.

The émigré writer Vladimir Voinovich used 'The Overcoat' as a model for a jollier work, his satire on the venality of Soviet writers, *The Fur Hat* (*Shapka*), first published in London in 1988. It tells the story of Efim Semenovich Rakhlin, a prolific writer of dull adventure stories, and an unsuccessful member of the Union of Soviet Writers. Rakhlin's tranquil life is thrown into confusion when he learns that the Writers' Union is giving out fur hats to members and that the kind of fur you get is a measure of your importance. He does not need a new hat, indeed he has a perfectly serviceable one; but when he finds out that the one he is being offered is made of domestic cat (the kind of fur eventually used for the collar of Akakii Akakievich's coat), his sense of self-worth is offended. Thus begins his obsessive crusade for justice, which involves visits to two important personages, both Union functionaries but one of them also a KGB General. Both meet him with indifference and mockery. This causes him to go mad, to bite the finger of the second important personage, the chief editor of a literary magazine and also a member of the Communist Party Central Committee, and to have a stroke. Eventually Rakhlin dies, but not before, through the agency of a third important personage, his wife's Marshal lover, he has had his revenge on Lukin, the Party Functionary General. In accordance with the Gogolian model, a little man and writer-copyist (all Rakhlin's novels are comically the same), content with his lot, is awakened to aspiration by the desire for an article of clothing; he loses (in this case never gets) the object of his desire; he turns to important personages who fail to help him; he becomes obsessed, rebellious and mad; he avenges himself on the important personage; and he dies (the last two points are in reverse order from the model.) The template is used for a sharp but very local satire on contemporary Soviet literature, and on the manner in which it is fatally compromised by a precise system of ranks and by its dependence on Party patronage. Voinovich had himself suffered greatly at the hands of Soviet 'writer' bureaucrats, culminating in his forced emigration in 1980, but the revenge enacted by *The Fur Hat* was swift and sweet. The publication of the novel coincided with the heady opening up of the Soviet arts of the mid-Gorbachev years. The following year the story was published in the Soviet Union; and in 1990 it was produced on the Moscow stage and a Soviet film was made from it, directed by Konstantin Voinov.

Recent versions

In the first century and a half since its publication, 'The Overcoat' had become a stage production, a number of films, a mime and an opera. Grigorii Kozintsev, in his notes for the unmade film *Gogoliad*, had planned a dance for Akakii Akakievich and the overcoat, in the spirit of *West Side Story* or a 'Chaplin idyll' (Kozintsev SS 5: 180, 181). Now, in 1990, the story did become a ballet, created by the Danish choreographer Flemming Flindt for Rudolf Nureev. This was one of the last roles Nureev danced, and the poignant suitability of the role of the 'shambling and pathetic clerk' (Mackrell) was widely noted by critics (Mackrell; Watson: 437).

The last decade has also seen two extremely inventive productions on the Moscow stage. The *School of Russian Imposture* company, also styled the First Russian Conceptual Theatre, was founded in 1988. In 1993, directed by Zhak (Vadim Zhakevich), work began on their production of *Overcoat No. 2737 and a half (Shinel' No. 2737 s polovinoiu)* – the number is derived from adding together all the numbers mentioned in Gogol's text. Onto a set consisting of a large spiral of white sand, which later turns into snow or sea, wander two men, both of whom announce that they are there 'instead of Akakii Akakievich'. The text of the production consists of a collage of extracts from Gogol's story, and is interspersed with eclectic sound effects ranging from American rock to a French chanson, from a Russian romance to a Soviet demonstration. In this visually and aurally startling production Akakii Akakievich, like some character out of Beckett, never appears; instead, the characters, and the repetitions of key passages of the text, worry away at his essence.

The opposite approach is taken in *Bashmachkin*, in which Akakii Akakievich is the only character. This poignant monodrama was created in collaboration in 1994 by Aleksandr Feklistov, Aleksei Burykin, Oleg Menshikov and Igor Zolotovitsky, with a brilliant cupboard-like set designed by Sergei Iakunin, but was staged without the help of a director. The production was sponsored by the Bogis Theatrical Agency, which was founded in 1992 to support productions that the big state theatres were unlikely to attempt. It boasts a bravura performance by Aleksandr Feklistov as the ungainly, childlike Bashmachkin. He sits at a makeshift desk mouthing the words in a document, or paces his cluttered room, rehearsing his devastating encounters with Petrovich and the important personage, speaking lines which in the story belong to these characters or to the narrator. Later he dances with a series of enormous overcoats, before being plunged into his final despair.[25]

The continuing fruitfulness of the literary dialogue with Gogol in works published during the first post-Soviet years by writers from Andrei Bitov to Aleksandr Solzhenitsyn is apparent from an article published by the critic Andrei Nemzer in 1994. The following year, the émigré writer Vasilii Aksenov published 'Three Overcoats and a Nose' ('Tri shineli i nos'), a charming and witty memoir of growing up anti-Soviet in the 1950s. As a young medical student in Kazan, aping the new *stiliagi* (teddy boys) he has seen on his rare trips to Moscow and 'Piter' (Leningrad), he gets a tailor to sew him a jacket with superwide shoulders and a large slit up the back, and, despite being ridiculed in the Komsomol wall newspaper, he wears it through the freezing winter, since he hates his own winter coat 'more than Iosif Vissarionovich Stalin' (Aksenov: 140). Then, wonder of wonders, he sees in the local *Komissionyi magazin* (a shop where second-hand goods were sold on commission and an almost mythical feature of Soviet life), a wonderful old camel-coloured American coat with a belt with a metal buckle and buttons 'like cracked nuts'. He falls in love with it, he knows that for the whole of its life destiny has been drawing it towards him. The coat helps get him thrown out of the Medical Institute, and he moves to Moscow, where it keeps him warm on nights spent in railway stations, and on to Piter, where his horrified aunt buys him something new and suitably 'Stakhanovite'. The beloved coat just 'disappears', having 'done its duty' by de-Sovietising him. But a Petersburg friend – we are now in 1956 – takes him to a pawnshop where he buys a new coat à la Yves Montand, which he wears that autumn as he dreams of leading a rebellion in support of the Hungarian Revolution. Alas, as he staggers drunkenly home one night to his lodgings on the edge of town, three men emerge from the darkness and 'in a literal sense, like Akakii Akakievich, they shook me out of my new coat.' Here the homage to Gogol's text is made overt, since he continues that for the rest of his way home:

> I could not say precisely where I was: in the middle of the
> page of the album in which I am now writing this story...or
> in the middle of the street.. a street still occupied by those
> same, absolutely unchanged Petersburg ghosts and devils,
> desirous of our most dear overcoats...   (ibid., 143)

So he goes to a *Komissionyi magazin* on Nevsky Prospect, where from under the counter he gets a light-grey coat made up in the latest Parisian style. He is wearing this coat when once more he calls for a move to the barricades, but though two 'Leningrad Lumpen' attempt a citizen's arrest, this time he, and his coat, survive. Aksenov's brilliant tale is both a revealing memoir of the de-Sovietisation of Soviet youth and an affectionate tribute to his literary master. Yet again Gogol's garment is revealed by an imaginative follower to be almost miraculously capacious.

Perhaps the longest, most ambitious and most intense engagement with Gogol's story has been that of the Russian animator Iurii Norshtein. Norshtein began work on his film of the story in 1981, and after lengthy interruptions caused by the withdrawal of official support and by chronic lack of funding, he is still at work on it today. He has filled his enforced periods of inactivity with serious thought both about Gogol's intentions in the story and about the practical problems of its realisation as an animated film, thoughts which have found expression in a number of fascinating published lectures and interviews. For Norshtein the story is 'a chapter of the bible. It is like the Life of Saint Akakii. This story seems to me to be a repository of human conscience' (Norshtein 1988: 18). He is not interested in making a simple 'screen version', insisting that 'the original text cannot dictate its laws' (Norshtein 1999a: 110); on the contrary, 'the authenticity of a film arises when you are tormented by the very same questions, and they torment you with the same force as they tormented the author of the story' (Norshtein 1999b, 10: 108). He can, however, learn practical lessons from Gogol, whose 'unique vision' and sudden changes of focus preceded the practical inventions of the cinema (Norshtein 1992: 98). Some sequences from the incomplete film have been widely shown and have stunned audiences, particularly with the power of their drawing and their 'Rembrandtian' play of light (thus drawing yet another major artist into Gogol's orbit). In a sequence of Akakii Akakievich sitting at home, completely absorbed in his copying, he looks, with his enormous head, like a defenceless child or a little animal, taking us back to the image of the 'good animal' of Gogol's first draft.

Ever since it was written, Gogol's 'Overcoat' has provoked an imaginative response in writers and artists, who have continued to revisit it with a wide variety of intentions and approaches, using a great range of protagonists and settings, in a large number of languages and cultures and in a great variety of media. Some essential quality in Gogol's original has triggered this ever-widening response. The critical debate around the story has also shown enormous vivacity and in recent decades has encompassed a lively and unprecedented dialogue between Russian and Western critics of the story, and some exciting new insights into its workings. The contributions of recent Russian and Western scholarship will be incorporated into Part Two of this study.

Notes to Part One

1. For a more detailed analysis of the composition of the story, see the notes, 'Kommentarii' by V.L. Komarovich, in Gogol', N. *Polnoe sobranie sochinenii*, ed. N.L. Meshcheriakov and others (14 vols), Izdatel'stvo Akademii nauk SSSR: Moscow and Leningrad, 1937-52, volume 3, 'Povesti', 1938, pp. 675-90. And see the early drafts, including the text of 'Povest' o chinovnike kradushchem shineli', and the variants., ibid., pp. 446-61 and pp. 521-49. See also Gogol', N. *Peterburgskie povesti*, with notes by O.G. Dilaktorskaia, 'Litera-turnye pamiatniki', Nauka: St Petersburg, 1995. [Text, pp. 88-109; 'Drugie redaktsii i varianty', pp. 194-203; 'Primechaniia', pp. 285-9.]

2. For surveys of the reception of the story and the 'battle for Gogol', see especially Debreczeny, on the reception by Gogol's contemporaries; Karlinsky, pp. 280-94; Maguire 1976; and Pakhlevska.

3. The device of giving their heroes the same given name as their fathers, just as Bashmachkin had been, was commonly used by writers who were reworking Gogol's story. It will be used in several of the stories discussed later in this survey, but I shall not draw the reader's attention to it on every occasion.

4. For a useful brief survey of the Natural School see the entry by John Schillinger in Victor Terras (ed.) *Handbook of Russian Literature*, (Yale University Press: New Haven and London, 1985), pp. 293-5. For a nuanced reading of Belinsky's evolving attitude to Gogol's work, see, e.g. Jackson.

5. For another suggestive recent study of the literary self-consciousness of Dostoevsky's text see R. Epstein Matveyev.

6. The word *grivennik* plays a role in the relationship between Akakii Akakievich and Petrovich in 'The Overcoat'. It is the sum Akakii thinks he will need to add to persuade Petrovich to mend his old coat (3: 149). Though he gives this to him (3: 152, 153), it fails to work its spell and Petrovich insists on making a new one.

7. For a detailed analysis of Chernyshevsky's readings of Gogol', see Berliner.

8. The same device is repeated in the late story 'Man in a Case' ('Chelovek v futliare'), in which the hero, Belikov, thrown down the stairs in exaspera-tion by Kovalenko, goes home, takes to his bed...and dies in a month.

9. For the full debate see Reiser 1968; Bocharov and Mann; Reiser 1971; Dolotova.

10. On Rozanov's reading of Gogol, see Jackson; Erofeev; and Pakhlevska, pp. 96-102.

11. Gogol was quoted by Lenin more than any writer other than Saltykov-Shchedrin. A quarter of his Gogolian allusions were to Manilov in *Dead Souls*. For an analysis of Lenin's Gogoliana, see Nechkina. For a list of them, see Chernevich.

12. The name Saranin suggests the vulgarism *srat'* (to defecate). This predates the faecal allusions noted in the name A*kak*ii A*kak*ievich by later readers and critics including Kruchenykh, Ermakov and Rancour-Laferriere.

13. On the relationship between Remizov's story and 'The Overcoat', see also Slobin, pp. 61, 64, 71.

14. On theatrical productions of Gogol's stories, including 'The Overcoat', see Danilov.

15. When the story was incorporated into Remizov's 1927 book *Vzvikhrennaia rus'* (*Russia in the Whirlwind*) it acquired the new title 'Sabotage'.

16. From the time of its first reprint in 1924 it was retitled 'How Gogol's Overcoat was Made'.

17. Quotations of the article are based on the 1974 translation by Robert Maguire, but with some significant changes. I therefore give page references in the quotations to the 1969 Russian edition.

18. For an overview of the Formalist contribution to the study of Gogol, and in particular the work of Vinogradov, see Maguire 1985.

19. Bakhtin returned to 'The Overcoat' in studies that were written and published much later in his career, developing his analysis of the role of the story's narrator and also stressing the link of the narrative to the 'popular sphere', a point he makes only in passing in his 1929 study. These points will be addressed in Part Two of this study.

20. I do not address here the vexed question of Bakhtin's contribution to the authorship of these texts, referring to them conventionally by the authors under whose names they were published.

21. For a detailed discussion of Zamiatin's Gogolian obsession texts, see Graffy 1990.

22. For the relationship between Bulgakov and Gogol, see especially Chudakova 1979; Chudakova 1985; Milne.

23. It is fascinating to note in this context that the role of Akakii Akakievich was played by Chaplin's rival, Buster Keaton, in a production entitled *The Awakening*, shown on American television on 14 July 1954. See Weddle, p. 20.

24. Chizhevsky's article has also provoked a detailed response by later critics. See especially the studies by Clyman, Driessen, Knudsen, Seemann and Wissemann.

25. For an interesting review of this production, see Sokolianskii.

Part Two:

Readings
and interpretations

The story of the gradual composition of 'The Overcoat' over the years 1839-41 was outlined at the beginning of Part One of this study.[1] Very soon after publication of the tale in 1842, critics began to search for sources and derivations for its plot, both in Gogol's life and through comparison with the writings of his contemporaries.

1. Sources, parallels, contexts

Direct triggers

The most commonly suggested source for the story, one that is indeed ritually invoked by critics, is an episode recounted by Gogol's friend Pavel Annenkov, and first published by him in 1857. Annenkov tells of Gogol being present at the telling of a 'chancellery anecdote' about a 'poor clerk' who loved shooting birds and who, by effort and economising, managed to save 200 roubles and buy himself a Lepage rifle. The first time he set off in his little boat along the Gulf of Finland in search of prey, he placed the gun at the prow, and, as he later realised, fell into deep thought, coming to only when he suddenly realised that the gun was missing. It had clearly snagged on some thick reeds and fallen into the water, but all his attempts to find it were in vain. The clerk went home and was confined to bed with a fever. He did not get up again until his colleagues, who had learnt of his misfortune and made a collection, presented him with a new gun. Even afterwards, every memory of the event brought a deathly pallor to his face. In Annenkov's narrative, everyone who had heard the anecdote laughed...'except Gogol, who listened to it pensively and bowed his head. The anecdote was the first thought of his marvellous story 'The Overcoat', and it dropped into his soul that very evening'. (Annenkov: 77.)

The links between this anecdote and 'The Overcoat' are too obvious to be spelled out; but so are the differences, and they were well pointed out by Rozanov in the 1890s. The clerk described by Annenkov is seen to have a perfectly ordinary and acceptable masculine enthusiasm and is not mocked for it by his colleagues. With their help he returns to his pastime – the tale has neither an unhappy ending nor a fantastic epilogue. In addition, as Rozanov points out, the story was told at a circle which used to meet in 1834, five years before Gogol began to write 'The Overcoat' (Rozanov 1970: 266-9). Gogol's *radical reworking* of this source – if such it was – should make us wary of announcing 'the first thought' behind the story, which has as complex and ambiguous a relationship with a number of posited sources and triggers, as the later 'reworkings' discussed in Part 1 of this study have with Gogol's own story.[2]

Another source from Gogol's life that is regularly mentioned by critics is found in a letter to his mother of 2 April 1830:

Proof of my thrift is the fact that I am still walking around
in the same clothes I had made when I arrived in Petersburg,
and from this you can conclude that the tail-coat I go around
in every day has become rather decrepit, and not a little worn
out, since I have not been in a position to get myself not only
a new tail-coat, but even a warm coat, which is essential for
the winter. Fortunately I have got a little used to the frost, and
I survived the whole winter in my summer overcoat [*shineli*].
(PSS, 10: 169-70)

Critics have also drawn attention to other widely circulating anecdotes such
as the recent robbery of a number of 'persons of consequence' at night in
the Petersburg streets, related by Pushkin in a diary entry for 17 December
1833, a period of his great closeness to Gogol (Stilman: 143-4; Dilaktorskaia
1986: 171; see Pushkin PSS 1937-59, 8: 33); and a tale of a respectable citizen,
robbed of his overcoat at night near the Tauride Gardens and unable to get
help from the policeman on duty (Dilaktorskaia 1995: 286).

Contemporary literature

In addition to the several anecdotes related above, critics have stressed that
'The Overcoat' should be seen in the context of the already well established
tradition in both Russian and Western European literature of writing about
urban life (Nilsson 1975: 12). A particularly important sub-genre of this
writing was stories about the lives of poor clerks. These tales, which were
widespread in the 1830s, could be comic and satirical or sentimental and
moralistic, and though Gogol was not alone in combining elements of both
styles, his complex synthesis reinvigorated the genre.[3]

Vladimir Odoevsky's story 'The Brigadier' ('Brigadir') is among the
stories that have drawn particular critical attention. It was written in 1833,
at a time when the two writers were close friends, and begins as the unnamed
narrator records the death of an acquaintance who had lived an unnoticed
life and died mourned by no one. Suddenly the dead man appears to the
narrator and tells the true story of his life. Nilsson (1982: 69-70) draws
attention to the parallels and suggests a possible influence, but it should be
stressed that the life experience, the ostensible worldly success of Odoevsky's hero puts him worlds away from Gogol's poor clerk. Another writer
with whom Gogol was personally acquainted was Nikolai Pavlov, and the
links between 'The Overcoat' and 'The Demon' ('Demon'), the latter's
1839 tale of the poor Petersburg clerk Andrei Ivanovich, were remarked
upon in 1851 by Apollon Grigorev, who insisted that Gogol's was a far
better story, since Pavlov had 'tried too hard to be deep' (Grigorev 1916:
21. See also Karlinsky: 138-9). The close plot parallels were examined in a

comprehensive article by Elizabeth Shepard which also pointed to the 'equally obvious differences' in tone and in the ending. She concludes that Gogol's story 'can be read as a direct reply to "The Demon"', as a refutation of Pavlov's view of human, or at least Russian, nature', and that Gogol may well have had a 'polemical lining in his garment' (Shepard: 297, 298, 301). There are even closer parallels of setting, character, plot patterns and narrative structure between 'The Overcoat' and Andrei Kropotov's 'The Story of the Dark Grey Caftan' ('Istoriia o smurom kaftane'), as has been revealed in an absorbing recent article by Alessandra Tosi. The story was published in 1809 and was thus one of the first tales on the theme of the poor clerk. Both heroes are minor civil servants obsessed with an article of clothing, though where Akakii Akakievich is meek, Kropotov's Panfil (also a rare name of Greek origin) is brazen. Kropotov's tale does not have a fantastic ending. Tosi suggests that, though there is no definite proof, it is likely that Gogol knew this work, given Kropotov's role in the Russian literary process – he was cited by Bulgarin in 1849 as a precursor of the Natural School.

Pushkin

One writer whose influence upon his own writings Gogol was quite ready to admit to, perhaps even to exaggerate, was Aleksandr Pushkin. On 7 October 1835 he wrote to Pushkin asking 'Please, give me a plot, any one, funny or unfunny, but a purely Russian anecdote' (PSS, 10: 375); and in his 1847 'Authorial Confession' ('Avtorskaia ispoved'') he wrote that Pushkin

> gave me a plot of his own, from which he himself had wanted to make a kind of long poem, and which in his words, he would not have given to anyone else. This was the plot of *Dead Souls*. (The plot of *The Government Inspector* was also his.)
> (PSS, 8: 440)

In this context it is not surprising that echoes, particularly in the area of theme and the delineation of character, have been found between 'The Overcoat' and several of Pushkin's major works. V.E. Vetlovskaia has looked closely at the parallels between the story and Pushkin's play *Boris Godunov* (written 1824-5, published 1831), a work that Gogol is known to have admired, and about which he wrote, in 1831, a piece of prose, half literary criticism, half story, which is one of his first works to be set in Petersburg. In a 1988 article Vetlovskaia establishes links between the loss of the Tsarist purple and the clerk's overcoat, noting the concern of both texts with the ladder of hierarchy and Gogol's comparison of Akakii Akakievich's fate with that of 'tsars and the rulers of the world' (3: 169). She also compares the pretender Akakii Akakievich, in his ragged *kapot*, to the false Dmitrii, Grishka Otrepev ('Grishka Rags'). In a later article she further develops the momentous implications of the loss of an article of clothing, noting that in the play's most important scene Boris cries 'Will a shadow [*ten'*] really tear the porphyry from me?' (Vetlovskaia 1998: 13).

The ageing protagonists of 'The Overcoat' and Pushkin's Belkin tale 'The Station Master' are both deprived of what they love more than anything else in the world (Samson Vyrin loses his daughter, who elopes to Petersburg), but when Dostoevsky's Makar Devushkin was given the two stories to read he infinitely preferred the latter, [mis]reading it as motivated by pity for the little man. As Sergei Bocharov has noted, Devushkin's perceptions are guided by his radically different reaction to the *telling* of the two tales, and Bocharov has offered an illuminating comparison of the different narrative methods of the two authors, contrasting the Gogolian *skaz* with the 'concentric circles' of Pushkin's narration, and stressing once again the dominant role of the *skaz* in the work. It is his callously indifferent *language* that gives Gogol's narrator his power over Akakii Akakievich (Bocharov: 235).

Especially suggestive links can be established between 'The Overcoat' and Pushkin's two 'Petersburg tales' 'The Queen of Spades' ('Pikovaia dama'), first published in 1833, and *The Bronze Horseman* (*Mednyi vsadnik*), first published in full in 1837. Akakii Akakievich, like German, the hero of 'The Queen of Spades', is presented as an outsider figure, lost in the fantastic city, tempted to find the key to inclusion and acceptance by his fellows. He 'sacrifices the essential in the hope of acquiring the superfluous', gets it at a price, but loses it, and goes mad. At the name-day party he is shown, like German, sitting watching on the margins of a card game but treated with indifference by the other guests (3: 160). The important personage is also presented as a marginal figure desirous of social acceptance, and his anxious tics of triple verbal repetition, his motto of 'severity, severity, severity' (3: 164) and the triple questionings of his supplicants (3: 165) recall the 'three true cards' of 'calculation, moderation and assiduity', with which the neurotic German attempts to contain his wild passions.

'The Overcoat' contains a direct allusion to *The Bronze Horseman* in the scene where Akakii Akakievich's colleagues repeat the 'eternal anecdote' about the commandant who is told that the tail of the Falconet statute (the 'Bronze Horseman') has been cut off (3: 146), an anecdote that recalls the central episode in Pushkin's poem in which the statue is verbally attacked by Pushkin's hero. Both Pushkin's Evgenii and Gogol's Akakii Akakievich are 'little men' driven to rebellion by the loss of their 'life's companion' (*podruga zhizni*, 3: 154). In both cases the hero blames his woes upon the actions of a powerful authority figure and his rebellion takes the form of a sudden eruption from muteness into language. In *The Bronze Horseman* Evgenii looks up and curses the statue of Peter the Great with the words 'Just you wait!' (*Uzho tebe!*), and is promptly driven mad by his own brazenness. Akakii Akakievich also has to look up to the figure of power, climbing the staircase on which the important personage puts his subordinates in their place and later being thrown down it. He, too, is driven to foul curses in his delirium (*skvernokhul'nichal*, 3: 168, curses which directly follow the words 'your excellency'; in the first edition of the epilogue the social rebellion is even more explicit, as Akakii Akakievich cries out 'I don't care whether you are a general...I shall get the overcoat from you' 3: 456). In both works the foul Petersburg weather threatens the safety and the 'home' of the protagonist. If in *The Bronze Horseman* Parasha's home is destroyed by the flood and the Neva, bursting its banks, is compared to a band of robbers, so in 'The Overcoat', once Akakii Akakievich ventures out of the safety of his home, he is attacked by wind and rain, frost and snow; and the square where he is robbed is likened to the sea (3: 161). Both works (as does 'The Queen of Spades') contain scenes of fantastic visions in which the attack on figures of authority is reiterated; but there are crucial differences in the area of authorial attitude to the hero. Pushkin writes himself into the cityscape of *The Bronze Horseman* and famously addresses his hero as 'my poor, poor Evgenii' ('bednyi, bednyi moi Evgenii'). Gogol, by contrast, has rendered himself invisible behind the mask of his loquacious narrator, and although the latter also calls his hero 'our Akakii Akakievich' (3: 165) as he supplicates the important personage, and 'poor Akakii Akakievich' as he dies (3: 168), this is by no means typical of his treatment of him.[4]

Dickens

Of the Western European writers mentioned in comparative critical analysis of the 'poor clerk' tales, by far the most interesting connections have been established with Dickens. The general outline of the relationship between the two writers is delineated in Igor Katarsky's 1966 book on Dickens's reception in Russia. Katarsky records the philologist Fedor Buslaev's memoir of having seen Gogol reading Dickens in the Caffè Greco, Rome, in the winter of 1840-1 (Katarskii: 28-31) and reports that the first comparison between the two writers, by Shevyrev, dates from 1841. In general their shared mastery of the comic and in particular comic names, their interest in the fate of the little man in the big city, their enthusiasm for the grotesque and the caricatural have all been noted in the critical literature and Gogol is said to have been the writer who taught the Russians to appreciate Dickens (Katarskii: 67-78).[5]

If Katarsky mapped out the territory of the two writers' relationship, then a brilliant and absorbing article published two years later by Kenneth Harper, has, by the simple expedient of wondering which work of Dickens Gogol might have been reading in his Roman cafe, established fascinating points of connection between 'The Overcoat' and Dickens's *Sketches By Boz*. The *Sketches*, first published in book form in English, 1836-7, were translated into German, and partially translated into Russian in 1839-41. One piece published in St Petersburg in 1839 was entitled 'English Manners'

('Angliiskie nravy') and was an amalgam of two pieces from the 'Characters' section of the *Sketches*, 'Thoughts about People' and 'Shabby-Genteel People.'

'Thoughts about People' begins as follows:

> It is strange with how little notice, good, bad, or indifferent,
> a man may live and die in London. He awakens no sympathy
> in the breast of any single person; his existence is a matter
> of interest to no one save himself; he cannot be said to be
> forgotten when he dies, for no one remembered him when
> he was alive.   (Dickens: 215)

It continues to describe a poorly dressed clerk, Mr Smith, who has 'no variety of days', merely sitting at his office desk all day working. After work he walks home 'to his little back room at Islington' where he chats to his landlady's little boy. On occasion he has to visit the office of his conde-scending employer in Russell Square. After these encounters he 'backs and slides out of the room, in a state of nervous agitation...'. Dickens concludes: 'Poor, harmless creatures such men are; contented but not happy; broken-spirited and humbled, they may feel no pain, but they never know pleasure' (ibid., 217).

'Shabby-Genteel People' tells of a man encountered in the Reading Room of the British Museum and of the terrible shabbiness of his clothes. After a while the man disappears, and the narrator wonders if he has killed himself, but a week later he returns.

> He had undergone some strange metamorphosis, and walked
> up the centre of the room with an air which showed he was
> fully conscious of the improvement of his appearance.
>   (ibid., 264)

On close inspection it is established that his clothes have been 'revived':

> It is a deceitful liquid that black and blue reviver.... It betrays its
> victims into a temporary assumption of importance; possibly
> into the purchase of...some trifling article of dress   (ibid.)

Alas, after a week of 'incessant small rain and mist' the reviver disappears and the wretched man never tries again to improve himself.

Harper quotes judiciously and at length from both the English original and the Russian translation, enabling him to draw up a convincing list of connections between the two works, and in particular to suggest that the introduction into 'The Overcoat' of the notorious 'humane passage', not present in the original drafts, may in part be due to Dickens's influence. Thus another major writer is drawn into Gogol's orbit.[6]

Hagiography and Early Russian Literature

The initial impetus for the number of recent studies looking at 'The Overcoat' in the context of hagiographical writing was provided by F.C. Driessen in the chapter of his 1965 book devoted to the story. Driessen records that he has found eight saints by the name of Akakii in Bukharev's *Lives of All the Saints*, including the sixth-century St Akakii commemorated on 29 November, who 'lived for nine years in the service of a certain evil *starets* [elder, J.G.] and suffered all insults without complaint', and then, after his death, appeared to the elder and induced him to repent. Driessen concludes that 'the similarities with the main figure in "The Overcoat" are so great that, in my opinion, there is no question of chance' (Driesssen: 194), but he does not go on to develop his insight.

The legend of St Acacius [Akakii] of Sinai was recorded by the seventh-century monk and abbot of the monastery on Mount Sinai, St John Climacus in his book *The Ladder to Paradise* (in Russian the *Lestvitsa raiskaia*), a work well known to Gogol.[7] This version of the saint's life is given in German in a fuller study of the legend published by K.D. Seemann in 1967. Then in 1972 John Schillinger translated a version from a *Lives of the Saints* published in Moscow in 1875 and made detailed comparisons between the *Life* and Gogol's story. Writing in 1847, Apollon Grigorev had drawn attention to the implications of having the fate of 'God's creature' decided by something as trivial as an article of clothing (see Part One, p. 16), and Schillinger makes the same point, leading him to conclude that it must have been Gogol's intention to produce 'a travesty of the saints' calendar account of St Acacius of Sinai, and to some extent of hagiography itself' (Schillinger: 36). But he makes no attempt to consider Gogol's spiritual writings, and a number of later critics will challenge the use of the term travesty. It is, however, a term also favoured by Alex Emerson-Topornin, who in a footnote to his 1976 study of demonic motifs in the story suggests that the episode of Akakii's christen- ing may be a '*travestic syndesis*' of three biblical episodes, the conception of Isaac, the conception and christening of St John the Baptist and the Annunciation (Emerson-Topornin: 54, note 12); and by Krivonos, who also notes that Akakii is born on the eve of the feast of the Annunciation and calls his birth, from a father who is spoken of in the past tense, a 'travesty of the theme of immaculate conception' (Krivonos 1996a: 51). In the same vein, Chizhevsky had seen the whole story as 'to some extent an inversion of the parable of "the widow's mite"' (Chizhevskii 1976: 393).

In a piece published in 1982, E.A. Surkov makes a comparison between the story and another hagiographical text, the *Life of Feodosii Pecherskii*, and finds 'The Overcoat' to have an orientation to the genre of the Saint's *Life* as a whole, for example by its motif of poor and torn clothing; but he also stresses the links of the story to contemporary German Romanticism, leading him to find 'The Overcoat' of 'mixed genre'. This broadening of the hagiographic context continues in other studies published in the 1980s and 1990s. Erkki Peuranen, writing in 1984, as well as discussing St Acacius of Sinai, examines the life of another St Acacius, who was among the forty martyrs killed at Lake Sevan in Armenia in the year 320, and whose feast day is on 9 March. Peuranen notes in particular that these saints were tormented by cold, also a key motivating factor for Gogol's Akakii.[8] Olga Dilaktorskaia, in her 1986 book on the Petersburg tales, while establishing detailed parallels with the life of St Acacius of Sinai, also contends that the story contains echoes of the *Lives* of several other saints and that Gogol's use of these sources involves contrast and subversion as well as echo and borrowing. She notes that comic elements are not unknown in the hagiographical tradition and concludes that by simultaneously following the hagiographical canon and transforming and parodying it Gogol can construct Bashmachkin's particular character (Dilaktorskaia 1985: 166). For Mikhail Epshtein, comparing Bashmachkin and Dostoevsky's Prince Myshkin, both characters obviously bear traits of the hero of a *Life*. But whereas Akakii Akakievich betrays the saintly in the name of the satanic, making of 'The Overcoat' an 'upturned Saint's Life', Dostoevsky's Myshkin becomes ever more saintly, thus 'turning it over again': '*The Idiot* is a nineteenth-century *Saint's Life*, an index of the possibility of a saintly life in that vulgar environment where Gogol demonstrates its senselessness and destruction' (Epshtein: 74-5).

Julia Alissandratos also goes beyond comparisons with the life of St Acacius, pointing out that the version of this life in the Sinai Patericon 'does not realise any of the themes of the encomiastic narrative pattern found in Russian saints' lives' (Alissandratos: 25). She shows, however, that the story engages with several set elements of the encomiastic narrative, both in the first part, dealing with ancestors, birth and naming, and in the epilogue, concerning posthumous deeds. She suggests that Gogol distorts and profanes the initial sequences of the hagiographical text through a 'dense, continuous parodic play' involving humour, ridicule and scatology, which 'provokes forbidden laughter'; and that in the ending of the tale 'parody gives way to tragic contrasts based on "zero" realization, or denial' (ibid., 34). This leads her to conclude that Gogol's story 'presents the predicament of any modern person trying to live by the medieval standards advanced by traditional Russian culture through the church's teachings' and that Gogol thus offers a 'subversive critique of the hagiographical tradition and the cultural values it represents' (ibid., 39).

In an article of 1993, V. Linetsky suggest that the form upon which the story is based is in fact the *exemplum*, a 'short narrative used to illustrate a moral', used primarily in mediaeval sermons and also traceable back to the writings of the early Church Fathers (Cuddon: 315-16); Linetsky contends that this formal allegiance explains all the rhetorical devices of repetition and digression used in the story and the de-individualisation of its hero (Linetskii: 42). But the most ambitious and rewarding of all the studies of the hagiographical context is provided by Cinzia de Lotto in another study of the same year. De Lotto stresses how important a role spiritual writing, including the *Lives of the Saints* and the Writings of the Church Fathers, had come to occupy in Gogol's life by the beginning of the 1840s. He had a particular interest in *The Ladder to Paradise* and his 1840s letters are full of references to monastic ascesis. The critical period in the change of Gogol's world view, from the autumn of 1839 to May 1840, coincided with the writing of 'The Overcoat' and may have influenced changes in tone introduced in later drafts (de Lotto: 60). The relationship of Gogol's story to sacred writings is complex. Akakii Akakievich is presented with many monkish qualities – asceticism, obedience, meekness, lack of passion, and his 'monkish' path closely parallels that described in *The Ladder*. But he abandons the monkish path when he is tempted into disobedience by the new overcoat, which is associated with money and calculation, and which causes him to succumb to the 'devil of lechery,' to inappropriate laughter and other vices. De Lotto also shows the very close parallels between Akakii Akakievich's early 'monkish' behaviour and his subsequent fall into sin and the models and warnings contained in the *Rule* of monkish life composed by the fifteenth-century monk Nil Sorskii, which has also been seen to have influenced *Dead Souls*. De Lotto concludes from the detailed comparisons she has provided that 'The Overcoat' bears a 'conscious' influence both of *The Ladder to Paradise* and of Nil Sorskii's *Rule*, an influence that is consistent with Gogol's contemporaneous programme of spiritual self-education and with his literary penchant for taking his subjects from pre-existing sources (de Lotto: 83).

In the most recent of her three articles on the story, V.E. Vetlovskaia quotes the legend of St Akakii in full from *The Ladder to Paradise* (Vetlovskaia 1999: 18-19) and points both to parallels between the two texts and to contrasts, leading her to conclude that Gogol's Akakii, who lacks firmness of spirit as well as strength of holiness, 'is not the hero of a *Saint's Life*' (ibid., 29). Nevertheless, she insists that the points of comparison with the source are to be taken seriously and challenges the use of the words 'travesty' and 'parody' by earlier commentators (ibid., 23-4). She notes that the saint whose feast day is celebrated on the day of Akakii's birth, 22 March, is Saint Vasilii, martyred by Julian the Apostate by being skinned alive, and compares this with Akakii's loss of his coat and his later vengeful removal of the coats of his tormentors (ibid., 25-7). Following O.V. Evdokimov, she further compares the behaviour of Akakii to a famous nineteenth-century Holy Fool (*iurodivyi*) Ivan Grigorevich Bosoi, formerly a poor clerk.

Thus in the thirty-five years since Driessen's passing allusion to a saintly source for Bashmachkin's name a number of scholars have provided compelling evidence for Gogol's immersion in spiritual writings and in his use not just of the *Life* of St Acacius but of a number of other works as subtexts for his story.[9] His particular interest in *The Ladder to Paradise* of St John Climacus gave rise to the widespread use of the image of the heavenly ladder in his writings, as early as the 1829 story 'A May Night, or The Drowned Girl' ('Maiskaia noch', ili utoplennitsa'; Voropaev and Vinogradov: 174).[10] In this context it is noteworthy that the image of a *lestnitsa* (ladder or stairway) is also frequently used by Gogol in the Petersburg tales, but that in accordance with his presentation of St Petersburg as a place of danger and dark forces, these stairways are always profaned. There are several such stairways in 'The Overcoat', each with negative connotations consistent with a reading of Akakii Akakievich's life as that of a monk seduced away from holiness. The stairway that Akakii Akakievich climbs to visit Petrovich at the beginning of his adventures is described as 'completely steeped in water and slops' and with a foul smell that 'eats the eyes' (3: 148). Though the second stairway he ascends, the one that leads to the apartment of the colleague who is giving a name-day party, is brightly lit (3: 159), the illumination is provided by a lamp (*fonar'*), which is always the source of a deceitful, demonic light in Gogol's Petersburg tales. Indeed, after his indulgence in drink at the party, he finds his beloved coat on the floor, descends the same stairway (3: 160) and embarks upon the journey through the nocturnal city during which he will be robbed of his prized possession. An attempt to get it back leads to his climbing a third staircase, this time the one on which the important personage arranges for his inferiors to meet him when he arrives at work so as to assert his authority (3: 164). After his disastrous encounter with the important personage Akakii Akakievich almost falls to the floor and 'could not remember how he got down the stairs and went out into the street' (3: 167). At the end of the story the important personage also attends a relaxing party and then 'went down the stairs, got in his sleigh and said to his coachman: "To Karolina Ivanovna's"' (3: 172), only, like Akakii before him, to be robbed of his overcoat. Thus, in direct contrast to the heavenly ladder of the church fathers, which has as its source the image of Jacob's ladder in Genesis, chapter 28, the *lestnitsy* of 'The Overcoat' are either ascended to temptation and trial or descended into disaster.

Archetype and folk belief

For the cultural historian Eleazar Meletinsky:

> Gogol's work is extremely rich in archetypal motifs, including fantastic-mythological ones, and various folkloric elements, which can be traced back to them; it is characteristic of his work to use archaic genre structures such as the fairy-tale (magical or based in everyday life [bytovaia]), the true story [bylichka], the legend and the heroic epos   (Meletinskii: 72)

The concept of the fairy-tale is also invoked, with specific reference to 'The Overcoat', by James M. Holquist, who suggests:

> The combination of pathos and low humor, Petersburg realia and the supernatural, which characterizes the story makes it almost impossible to define in terms of genre – unless one sees it as a new kind of fairy tale.   (Holquist: 362)

Holquist further suggests that it is Gogol's achievement to have maintained the attributes of such tales, 'an infinite deceptiveness, the ever-present possibility of metamorphosis, rapid alternations of the comic and the sinister, the all-pervading presence of hostile forces, and many more', but to have stripped them of the literary trappings of the conventional literary fairy-tale, 'and to have shown them at work in a great modern city, convincing, but not real' (ibid.). Fairy-tale elements are also detected by V.Sh. Krivonos, who suggests that it is its 'fairy tale quality' (*skazochnost'*) that gives what happens in Gogol's Petersburg an infantile quality, and likens his heroes, including Akakii Akakievich, who treats his overcoat like a human being, to the infantile heroes of folklore (Krivonos 1996b: 125, 127). In another study published in the same year, Krivonos notes the presence in the Petersburg tales, including 'The Overcoat', of the folkloric motifs, also used by Gogol in his earlier stories, of the enchanted space and the search for treasure. All the heroes of Gogol's Petersburg tales search for and acquire something which is then devalued (Krivonos 1996a: 46-9). He further finds a 'fairy-tale colouring' to the description of Akakii Akakievich's birth and his 'instantaneous maturation' (ibid., 52).

   Both these fairy-tale motifs and the use of anecdotes rooted in urban folklore, noted earlier, link the sensibility of 'The Overcoat' to popular belief. The most pervasive application of this belief system in the story is through the use of popular ideas about the play of demonic forces. In April 1829, shortly after he moved to Petersburg, Gogol had written to his mother asking for information on the 'habits and customs of our Little Russians', including information about 'spirits or house spirits' and 'beliefs, terrible tales, traditions, various anecdotes and so on' (PSS, 10:141). The fates of the protagonists of Gogol's first collection of stories *Evenings on a Farm Near Dikanka*, published in 1831-2 and set in the Ukrainian countryside, were constantly affected by their encounters with devils. The first critic to engage in detail with Gogol's interpretation of the demonic was the Symbolist writer Dmitrii Merezhkovsky, in 1906, and the role of the devil in 'The Overcoat' was raised by Chizhevsky in 1937. Since then critics have found more and more evidence of the demonic presence in all his writings. Though devils are no longer directly participant in the 'Petersburg Tales', the imagery, characterisation and plot details of these later works can all be seen to have demonic implications.[11]

According to popular belief one of the deceptive wiles of the devil is to cause you to lose your way.[12] This motif is repeatedly connected with Akakii Akakievich's encounter with the overcoat: after Petrovich has pronounced his dreadful sentence that the overcoat must be replaced, Akakii Akakievich goes out into the street as if in a dream, and instead of going home wanders around, noticing nothing. The demonic implications of this loss of way are adumbrated by semantic play: 'On the way a chimney-sweep [*trubochist*] struck him with his whole dirty [*nechistym*] side and blackened [*vychernil*] his whole shoulder' (3: 152).[13] When he wears it for the first time 'he felt every moment of every minute [*vsiakoi mig minuty*] that he had the new overcoat on his shoulders' but 'he did not notice the way at all and suddenly ended up at the department' (3:157). Thus Gogol establishes moral identity between the acquisition of the overcoat and the 'loss of path'. He is similarly lost as he walks through the dark to the fateful party (3: 158) and again after he leaves it, where he is first diverted by 'some lady' and then robbed, lost in the middle of a vast square (3: 160-1). Krivonos notes that the theft itself is replete with demonic implications, including the fact that it takes place after midnight, 'the time when evil spirits are activated,' that it happens 'in the middle of a terrible desert', 'a favourite place for devils to attack ascetics,' and that the thieves themselves, like devils, seem to be disguised (Krivonos 1996b: 123, 127, note 12). The motif of the lost path is later also applied to the important personage, both by the suggestion that on being made a general he 'somehow got confused, lost his way' ('kak-to sputalsia, sbilsia s puti', 3: 165), and later, in physical terms, as he makes his way to see Karolina Ivanovna in the epilogue (3: 172).

Devils are also able to disguise themselves by changing their size, and this play with the instability of physical features is manifested in a curious phrase associated with the tailor Petrovich (whose many demonic qualities will be discussed in Section 2). Arriving at Akakii Akakievich's home, 'he took the overcoat out of the handkerchief [*nosovogo platka*] in which he had brought it; the handkerchief had just come from the laundress's; he then folded it up and put it in his pocket for use' (3: 156).[14]

Devils can also notoriously inflict illnesses and violent death. The extraordinary suddenness with which, after his encounter with the important personage, Akakii Akakievich 'succumbs to a quinsy' (which causes him to lose his voice, 'completely swell up and take to his bed', catch a 'powerful fever' and die very quickly [3: 167-8]) can also be interpreted as a demonic punishment. The immediate cause of his demise is, of course, the treacherous Petersburg weather, but according to popular belief that too is caused by demonic agency. Devils are linked with particular times of the day and year, and their activity is especially associated with the hours of darkness and with cold weather and the attendant wind, snow and frost (Novichkova: 397-435; Vinogradova: 166). It is remarkable how frequently the bad Petersburg weather is invoked in 'The Overcoat'. On the very first page of the story 'the Petersburg climate is to blame' for Bashmachkin's 'haemor-rhoidal' complexion. The overcoat plot is later introduced by the contention that 'There is in Petersburg a powerful enemy [*sil'nyi vrag*] of everyone who receives a salary of four hundred roubles a year' and that 'This enemy is none other than our northern frost.... Between eight and nine in the morning... it begins to give sharp and stinging blows to everyone's noses, without dis-crimination' (3: 147). This has led de Lotto to remind us this is also the time when the devil attacks monks on their way to morning prayer (de Lotto: 71); and Alissandratos stresses that the word 'enemy' (*vrag*) is 'frequently applied to the Devil himself, especially in the hagiographical tradition', making the frost the chief demonic force in the story, and Petrovich and the robbers of the epilogue ('a traditional hagiographic category of agents of the Devil') its diabolic accomplices (Alissandratos: 34-7). Aware of the inimical force of nature, Petrovich warns Akakii Akakievich that he cannot mend his old overcoat since a single breath of wind will cause it to fly into pieces (3: 150).

When he first wears his new coat Akakii Akakievich finds it 'warm...and good' (3: 157), but it cannot save him from nature's wiles. As he walks home through deserted streets from the assistant desk-head's party, 'only the snow sparkled through the streets' (3: 161), and the theft takes place in a square that is 'like a sea around him', its wetness signalling that it is a favourite domain of devils (Vinogradova: 171). When he comes round and gets to his feet he 'senses that it is cold in the field, and he has no overcoat' (3: 161). Then, after he is bawled at by the important personage, he 'walked through the snowstorm which was whistling through the streets' (3: 167) and is assailed by the wind, which in a remarkable phrase that makes its demonic powers obvious, 'blew on him from all four directions, in the Petersburg manner' (3: 167). This 'powerful beating' (*sil'no...raspekanie*) recalls the powerful (*sil'nyi*) enemy the frost, and causes him to get a powerful (*sil'naia*) fever and to take to his bed, where again 'thanks to the magnani-mous help of the Petersburg climate' (3: 167) his illness progresses unex-pectedly speedily and leads to his death. But this wind is no respecter of persons: when the important personage attempts to visit his mistress after a merry evening party 'a gusting wind, which would suddenly get up God knows from where and for no discernible reason, would so cut into his face, throwing scraps of snow at it...or suddenly throw [his collar] over his head with unnatural force' (3: 172).

Time

The forces of nature also appear to work 'unnaturally' in the story's treat-ment of time. Preparations to acquire the overcoat seem to take place in a climate of eternal winter. It is the fierce cold that leads Akakii Akakievich to realise his old overcoat must be replaced (3: 147). Once the decision has been made that he must have a new coat he begins a period of saving money to pay for it, and 'each month he called in to Petrovich at least once to discuss the overcoat' (3: 155). He then gets an unexpectedly large bonus which means that after 'about another two or three months of minor starvation' (3: 155) he and Petrovich go to order the cloth, which 'they had thought about six months previously and it was a rare month when they had not gone to the shops to compare prices' (3: 155). Petrovich then spends 'only two weeks' (3: 155) making it. Yet when he finally brings it round to Akakii Akakievich 'already quite firm frosts were beginning and, it seemed, threatening to get even stronger' (3: 156); nor do these frosts abate as Akakii Akakievich returns from the name-day party (3: 161), when he visits the important personage (3: 167), or even after his death, when the important personage is deprived of his overcoat.[15]

This impression of permanent winter is adumbrated by the idea that the town is 'on the edge of the world' (3: 161) and by other indications of life lived outside of time. On the first page of the story its hero is called an 'eternal' (*vechnyi*) titular consellor (3: 141) and the same word is used to describe his 'eternal idea about the future overcoat' (3: 154). It is unknown when (*kogda, v kakoe vremia*) his family got the name Bashmachkin (3: 142) or when (*kogda i v kakoe vremia*) he started work in the department (3: 143); indeed he has always been seen in 'one and the same [*odnom i tom zhe*] place, in the same [*tom zhe*] position, in the same [*toi zhe*] job, as the same [*tem zhe*] copying clerk', to the extent that people said he had been born 'completely ready, in his uniform and with a bald patch on his head' (3: 143). When an attempt to get him to take on greater responsibility fails, he is 'left to copy forever' (*navsegda*, 3: 145). His mother, too, seems to exist outside of time, being described as deceased (*pokoinitsa*, 3: 142) while she is clearly still alive, and spurning the calendar as a source for her son's name, preferring to 'copy' that of his dead father.

Thus both Akakii Akakievich and his family seem to exist statically in a ritual world where time is undifferentiated; and the 'plot' of the story is precisely a consideration of the effect of an 'event' upon this timelessness, of the devastating change that time and desire can wreak.[16] In Paul Waszink's words, when Akakii Akakievich decides to order a new overcoat, he leaves 'the atemporal stage of myth in order to enter that which is governed by the laws of linear (historical) time' (Waszink: 295). From then on, the gradations of linear time, from the months to the weeks to the days and the minutes, are keenly felt by Akakii Akakievich and meticulously monitored by the narrator. In celebration of his acquisition, Akakii Akakievich goes out in the evening for the first time in several years and looks at everything around him as at a novelty (*novost'*) (3: 158). Mikhail Vaiskopf has noted that the word 'time' (*vremia*) occurs no fewer than 31 times in the story (Vaiskopf 1978: 53); and it is notable that, though the narrator can continue to forget crucial information, he seems ever more alert to the temporal questions which he disdained to address at the beginning of the story, 'timing' Akakii Akakievich's death and not forgetting to tell us (in a final example of absurd chronological exactitude) that after the theft of the important personage's overcoat, it takes his coachman 'about six minutes, or slightly more' to drive him home (3: 173), before his story finally sinks back into the nocturnal Petersburg darkness from which it has emerged.

The Petersburg Text

In June 1827, while he was still a schoolboy in Nezhin, Gogol wrote to his friend Vysotsky of his hopes for the future:

> In my thoughts I already place myself in Petersburg, in that jolly little room looking out over the Neva, since I have always thought of finding myself such a place. I don't know if my ideas will come to fruition, and whether I really shall live in a such a paradisiacal place [*v etakom raiskom meste*].
> (PSS, 10:101)

This dream of the town as paradise was not securely based. In the words of the cultural historian Vladimir Toporov: 'In the *mythopoetic* and *providential* perspective the town arose when man was expelled from paradise and the bad times set in: man was left to his own devices and from then on he had to take care of himself' (Toporov 1987: 121). Life in the city was associated with 'unprotectedness, uncertainty, a fallen state, in a certain sense with being abandoned by God, and, finally, with labour and suffering' (ibid.).

A number of distinctive factors of its history and geography – its creation by an act of Peter the Great's will, at a huge human cost, on land that was unsuitable, on the margin of Russia, with a ferocious climate and strange, 'unnatural' light – predetermined St Petersburg as the most amenable of Russian cities to such 'mythological' interpretation. Throughout the nineteenth century and into the twentieth, Pushkin, Gogol, Dostoevsky, the Symbolists, Akhmatova and Mandelshtam, Pilniak and Zamiatin and others after them, incorporated and embellished these factors into what can be read as a single 'Petersburg' text (Toporov 1984), making of the city a place of dream and mirage, of fantasy, danger and excess. Gogol's Petersburg tales represent a crucial stage in the evolution of this text, both through their variations on the type of the bachelor Petersburg clerk, its typical denizen,[17] and through their stress on the pervasiveness of deceit in a city in which 'everything is not what it seems' ('Nevskii Prospekt', 3: 45).

The evocation of the city in 'The Overcoat' is entirely consistent with this mythological reading. Its climatic harshness and temporal uncertainties have already been discussed. Spatially too, it is an unknowable place. As Nilsson has noted, the main body of the text is bereft of topographical indicators – places are named only in the 'fantastic' epilogue (Nilsson 1975: 8-9), and indeed, when the narrator attempts to trace Akakii Akakievich's route to the assistant desk-head's party, 'everything there is in Petersburg, all the streets and houses merged and got mixed up so much in my head, that it is extremely difficult to get anything out of there in an orderly form' (3: 158).

For both Akakii Akakievich, who comes straight home after work and 'writes to his heart's content' (3: 146) and the important personage, who 'is, by the way, completely content with his domestic family tendernesses' (3: 172), the home (*dom*) represents a haven of calm and safety (Lotman 1968: 43-4), but, alas, both of them are tempted out into the world of danger and risk. This outside space is a place in which you wander and lose your way (see above), for it is a place of deserted streets (*pustynie ulitsy*, 3: 158, 161) and an 'endless square...which looked like a terrible desert' (*strashnoiu pustyneiu*, 3: 161), or like a sea (ibid.), with a sentry booth standing 'seemingly on the edge of the world' (ibid.). The marginal streets Akakii Akakievich walks through are badly lit (3: 158), their hovels low to the ground (3: 161). It is a world without colour, where the predominant black, white and grey (Vaiskopf 1978: 48) are mitigated only by the reddish quality (*ryzhevatost'*) of Akakii Akakievich's thinning hair (3: 141), the 'reddish-floury colour' (*ryzhevato-muchnogo tsveta*) of his uniform (3: 145), and the haemorrhoidal colour of his complexion (3:141). It is an alien, non-Russian space, inhabited by 'Russian foreigners' (3: 145). It is also a place of erotic temptation – both Akakii Akakievich and the important personage are tempted into chasing after 'ladies', but these seductions are deceptive and are thwarted.[18] It is, finally, a place of catastrophe, madness and death. In Toporov's words:

> One of the undoubted functions of the Petersburg text is as a funeral rite for those who have perished in Petropolis, which has become for them a true Necropolis.
>
> (Toporov 1984: 21)

In this respect, Akakii Akakievich's experience of marginality, exclusion, mockery, loss, indifference, sickness and death is pre-ordained not just in the view of his mother, who exclaims 'No, now I see...that, clearly, such is his fate' to be named as he is (3: 142); not just in the view of the narrator who has provided so much detail 'so that the reader can see that it happened completely by necessity' (3: 143); but also because he is a denizen of this fatal city and the doomed hero of one of its lethal texts.

2. The Protagonists

The narrator

It may seem perverse to begin a discussion of the story's protagonists with its narrator, but it is crucial to bear in mind that 'The Overcoat' is *his* story, that everything we learn about the character and experiences of Akakii Akakievich, the tailor Petrovich and the important personage, about the Petersburg climate and the Petersburg bureaucracy, is filtered through his consciousness and language, through his garrulous, meandering *skaz*.

For Boris Eikhenbaum, the first critic to have paid close attention to the role of the narrator, he is a comic actor, and his tale is a virtuoso performance of declamation and mimicry (Eikhenbaum 1969: 319). Following in the footsteps of Eikhenbaum and the many other critics who have succeeded him, it is possible to produce a detailed characterisation of this narrative performance.

First it is a narration that is aware that it is a narration, a story that refers to itself as a story. The narrator alludes disparagingly to the mocking tone adopted by other writers 'who have the laudable habit of attacking those who cannot bite' (3: 142), though the same charge can in fact easily be laid at his own door. He knows the rules of narration, introducing Petrovich and his wife with brief descriptions as convention demands (3: 148). He refers to the reader (*chitatel'*, 3: 143; *chitateliu*, 3: 154), and to himself as the 'narrator of this tale' (*rasskazyvaiushchii siiu povest'*, 3: 168); announces that 'our poor story [*istoriia*] is unexpectedly taking a fantastic ending' (3: 169); but stresses that this is 'the fantastic direction of a nevertheless completely authentic story' (*istorii*, 3: 170).

If the last two phrases suggest some measure of narratorial uncertainty, then this incompetence is echoed in the ostentatious and persistent motif of the narrator's failures of memory. He cannot remember: what town the police inspector worked in (3: 141, in only the fourth sentence of his story); when and how the name Bashmachkin came from *bashmak* (3: 142); or when Akakii Akakievich started work in the department or who appointed him (3: 143). He does not know who the general is on Petrovich's tobacco tin (3: 150); or on what day Petrovich brought Akakii Akakievich the overcoat (3: 156); or how his departmental colleagues found out about it (3: 157); or where the functionary who gives the party lives, 'because our memory has begun to betray us powerfully' (*sil'no*, 3: 158). He does not know why Akakii

79

Akakievich smirked when he looked at the picture of the lady: he makes suggestions, but then abandons them because 'after all you cannot climb into a man's soul and find out everything he thinks' (3: 159, perhaps a fairly concise conventional description of a writer's role). He does not even know, and here he is protesting too much, why the tipsy Akakii Akakievich follows the lady in the street after the party (3: 160). He does not know how Akakii Akakievich spent the night after the loss of his overcoat: 'this is left to judge to the person who can in some degree imagine another's situation' (3: 162). He does not know what post the important personage occupies (3: 164); or why the important personage finds Akakii Akakievich's manner familiar (3: 166); or whether the doctor's words are heard by Akakii Akakievich, and whether they have a shocking effect upon him, though he *does know* that Akakii Akakievich has lots of visions, which he describes in detail (3: 168). He does not know who Akakii Akakievich's heirs are, and he 'did not bother to find out' (3: 168). He refuses to make a judgement about why the important personage should visit Karolina Ivanovna, who is neither better nor younger than his wife (3: 172).

This is a profoundly contradictory state of affairs. There is a great deal that the narrator does not know, has forgotten, or has never troubled himself to discover, and we, the readers, know this *because he tells us so*. But his forgetfulness and ignorance are partial – there are also all sorts of things (some of them similar, some of them seemingly harder to establish) that he does know. Sometimes, of course, what he knows is itself unreliable and a further sign of his fecklessness – when he refers to the name Bashmachkin and suggests a derivation from the word *bashmak* (shoe), he notes that 'both his father, and his grandfather and even his brother-in-law walked around in boots' (3: 142). As several critics have pointed out, this remark is doubly careless: a man's brother-in-law (*shurin*) does not share his surname, and furthermore, Akakii Akakievich cannot have a *shurin* (a 'wife's brother' and not a 'sister's husband', Russian is very precise about these terms) since he is not married. Thus the narrator's incompetence and forgetfulness is continually made overt. These are things that it is clearly important that *we know that he does not know*; or does not consider important; or *considers it important to tell us that he does not know*; or perhaps Gogol considers it important that we learn these things about his narrator.

The narrator's incompetence is also manifested in a marked penchant for digression and irrelevance. He is a master of the irrelevant detail. At the christening we learn far more than we need to know about the names not chosen and the 'most excellent' godfather and the godmother 'a woman of rare virtues' (3: 142). Later, when Akakii Akakievich's fussy landlady suggests he goes to the police inspector, she does not fail to mention, and the narrator does not think to delete, that 'she even knows him, because Anna, the Finnish girl, who had previously worked for her as a cook, was now employed by the police inspector as a nursemaid, and that she often sees him himself, driving past their house, and that he also attends church every Sunday, and prays, and at the same time looks merrily at everyone, and that, consequently, everything points to his being a good man' (3: 162).

In fact the narrator's own narration is similarly hectic and disorientating. The first paragraph lasts over three pages, and takes us from 'a department', through Akakii Akakievich's birth and christening to his work in the department and his mockery by his colleagues, ending with the extended reaction of the young clerk to Akakii's plea for pity (3: 141-4). An *eight page* paragraph takes us from Akakii Akakievich's realisation that he will have to have a new overcoat to his entering into the square in which he will lose it (3: 153-61). It is *immediately followed* by another paragraph which leads from the loss to the encounter with the important personage (3: 161-6). The entire 'fantastic' epilogue also consists of a single paragraph (3: 169-74).[19] Just as Akakii Akakievich and the important personage get lost in the snow-bleached streets, so Gogol's reader gets lost in the maze of his narrator's endless paragraphs, finding it almost impossible to track down 'important' details; and when they come they are often bathetic, as in a sentence lasting an entire page which describes the various evening pastimes of everyone else in Petersburg only to end by telling us that 'Akakii Akakievich did not give himself up to any diversion' (3: 146). This bathos is canonised by the ending of the story itself: after the rhetorically expressed revelation that Akakii Akakievich's death is not the end of his tale (3: 169), the narrator takes us into a world of fantastic apparitions for which he offers no explanation, finally plunging into low gossip about a puny Kolomna policeman being knocked off his feet by an 'ordinary adult piglet' (3: 173) and a ghost with a huge moustache which 'completely disappeared in the nocturnal darkness', taking the story with it (3: 174).

The narration is also notoriously characterised by absurdity and illogical details. As discussed in Part One, Dmitrii Chizhevsky has shown just how illogical is the use of the narrator's verbal tic, the word *dazhe* (even). One example of the device may here suffice: when Akakii Akakievich goes to see Petrovich, there is so much smoke in the kitchen that 'one could not see even the very cockroaches' (3: 148). In a variation on the scheme of non sequitur, we have just been apprised of Petrovich himself that 'despite his squint [logical, J.G.] and the pockmarks all over his face [illogical, J.G.], he did rather a good job of mending functionaries' and all sorts of other trousers and tail-coats' (3: 148). In Bakhtin's words, 'both individual alogisms and more developed verbal absurdities are very widespread in Gogol' (Bakhtin 1975: 488), and the unquestioning enthusiasm for the absurd detail throughout 'The Overcoat' casts further doubt on the narrator's reliability. Thus he relays without demur that the policeman on duty did not try to help Akakii Akakievich because he thought the robbers 'were his acquaintances' (3: 162), and in the epilogue he blithely reports that another policeman, on the very point of having apprehended the functionary-dead-man, experienced an overwhelming desire to take a pinch of tobacco ('so as to freshen up for a time his nose, which had suffered from frostbite six times in his life'), thus leading the dead man to sneeze so powerfully that he bespattered the eyes of the policeman and his two companions, temporarily blinding them, and was able to effect a getaway (3: 170). Such details themselves 'bespatter' the text and have a similar effect on the reader, repeatedly enabling the narrator and his text to 'get away'.

Another significant feature of the narration, consonant with Eikhenbaum's idea of the text as performance and regularly remarked upon by critics, is his dizzying shifts of tone. It is not possible to establish a consistent narratorial attitude towards Akakii Akakievich. Ostensible sympathy is accompanied by demeaning detail. He is repeatedly rendered ridiculous: we learn of the 'watermelon and melon rinds' that fall on his hat as he walks down the street (3: 145) and of the decision to wash his underwear less frequently and walk over stones and flagstones on tiptoe in the name of economy (3: 154). And though the narrator has not bothered to find out about Akakii Akakievich's heirs, he has established, and bothers to apprise the reader of, the components of their inheritance, including 'three pairs of socks, two or three buttons that had come off his trousers...' (3: 168).

As if to underline this tonal instability, the list is directly followed by the second of the two 'humane passages', and the one in which the narrator himself expresses sympathy for Akakii Akakievich's sad fate. Yet it is striking that this sympathy is expressed through negatives and low comparison: 'a creature not defended by anyone, not dear to anyone, not interesting to anyone, who did not even attract the attention of an observer of nature, who would not miss the chance to put a common fly under a pin...' (3: 169; the negations are, of course, doubled in the Russian original, *nikem ne zashchishchennoe*, etc.). It is also striking that, after building itself up to a rhetorical high point, this passage suddenly stops in mid-paragraph and cedes to yet another change of tone and another example of the narrator's inability to resist the irrelevant detail, thus providing further evidence that repining over Akakii Akakievich's tragic fate is a tone to be tried on like any other. In the words of Gavriel Shapiro the narrator is trying out the *memento mori* topos – death the great leveller will render equal Tsars and insignificant clerks (Shapiro: 166), but 'incapable of comprehending these notions in their true magnitude', he 'reduce[s] them to clichés in the Devil-ruled world of *poshlost'*' (ibid., 129-30).

Following on from the pioneering studies of the role of the narrator by Bakhtin, Vinogradov and Chizhevsky, critics have concentrated on two questions: what kind of a character is the narrator, and why has Gogol invented him?

For Judith Oloskey Mills the narrator's 'peculiar' personality determines everything, both language and plot. He is aware, as the plot shows us, that self-assertion is followed by punishment, so after he 'asserts himself' in the passages mocking Akakii Akakievich, he attempts to obviate punishment by the introduction of the pathetic passages; but since these are cynical they do not persuade (Mills: 1106, 1109, 1111). For Sergei Bocharov, Akakii Akakievich is 'measured and entwined' in what (quoting Bely) he calls the 'leitmotifs' of the narrator's 'little words'; language gives him total power over Akakii Akakievich's life and death (Bocharov: 225-6, 235). For Murray Baumgarten he is 'the *picaro*, the rogue, telling his life story' (Baumgarten: 194); for Victor Erlich the 'spoofing bent of the story' with its 'clowning and grimacing' is apparent from the start (Erlich: 146-7); for Charles Bernheimer his successive 'masks of omniscience or skepticism are points of arbitrary arrest in a potentially infinite free play of epistemological perspectives' (Bernheimer: 56). Cathy Popkin makes especially interesting parallels between Akakii Akakievich's inarticulacy and the narrator's discursive problems, suggesting that they are both compulsive collectors, Akakii Akakievich of letters, and the narrator of words (Popkin: 171, 188). She stresses that the narrator never intends 'to accede to the reader's desire for substance', that we never get the point, only words; like Akakii Akakievich 'we are deluged with discourse, one step removed from the things we crave' (ibid., 200, 202). For Donald Fanger most of the entire narration 'appears to be normless, lacking any single implied basis for judgment – which is to say any consistent rationale for the multiplicity of tones and attitudes' (Fanger 1979: 154); and E.A. Vedeniapina unhelpfully suggests that there are actually three narrators, each with a distinct register: the official bureaucratic, the digressive anecdotal, and the intimate, which is connected to Akakii Akakievich's own voice, and each telling only parts of the tale.

Why did Gogol assign such a significant role to his narrator? For Daniel Rancour-Laferriere the *skaz* is a mask, enabling him to introduce material and attitudes that are dangerous and disturbing (Rancour-Laferriere: 19-20). For Robert Maguire, on the other hand all this narrative play is a trick to make the reader feel superior, so that our emotions can then be manipulated 'in ways that are essential to the proper functioning of the story':

> 'The Overcoat' will not work as it should if the reader considers Akaky Akakievich too low and ridiculous a character to become plausibly tragic. To forestall that possibility, Gogol deflects our psychic energies, as it were, by presenting us at the outset with a narrator who launches into a lengthy, elaborate and rambling discourse that sets the scene for Akaky's appearance. Since the narrator is inferior to us in intellect and sophistication, and is laughable to boot, he draws onto himself much of our condescension and mockery, which would otherwise fall directly on Akaky. In this sense he is like a lightning rod.   (Maguire 1994: 196)

For both these critics, in their different ways, the narrator is a disguise for
Gogol's true attitudes. For other critics he is precisely a register of the absence
of consistent attitude, or the relativity of all attitudes. For Bakhtin, in the
essay 'Discourse in the Novel' ('Slovo v romane'), the narrator of 'The
Overcoat' belongs to a group of narrators who manifest themselves as:

> specific and limited verbal ideological points of view, belief
> systems, opposed to the literary expectations and points of view
> that constitute the background needed to perceive them; but
> these narrators are productive precisely *because* of this very
> limitedness and specificity.
>
>   The speech of such narrators is always *another's speech*
> [*chuzhaia rech'*, J.G.] (as regards the real or potential direct
> discourse of the author) and in *another's language* [*na
> chuzhom iazyke*, J.G.] (with regard to that variant of the
> literary language with which the language of the narrator is
> contrasted.)
>
>   Thus we have in this case "nondirect speaking" – not *in*
> language, but through language, through the linguistic medium
> of another – and consequently a refraction of authorial
> intentions.   (Bakhtin 1981: 313, amended)

Behind this narrator is the author, behind the narrator's story the author's
story, and the reader is acutely aware of these two levels:

> We puzzle out the author's emphases that overlie the subject
> of the story, while we puzzle out the story itself and the figure
> of the narrator as he is revealed in the process of telling his
> tale. If one fails to sense this second level, the intentions and
> accents of the author himself, then one has failed to under-
> stand the work.   (ibid., 314)

He concludes that the use of this narratorial form frees the author from a
'unitary and singular language' and offers 'the possibility of never having
to define oneself in language' (ibid., 314-15).

  However as well as being an authorial mask, the narrator is a reporter of
and reactor to Akakii Akakievich's sufferings. In this he can surely stand,
particularly in the inconstancy of his pity, as a representative of the reader,
and of the instability of all our responses to tales of woe. Most importantly
of all, he is a source of literary pleasure – and in this profound sense all his vices,
his forgetfulness, his absurdities, his digressions, are alchemically trans-
muted into the virtues of a supreme comic turn, a 'satisfyingly dissatisfying'
narrative and linguistic performance.

Akakii Akakievich

The very first thing the narrator tells us about his hero is that 'you could not say that he was very remarkable' (*nel'zia skazat' chtoby ochen' zame-chatel'nyi*, 3: 141), and this negation is immediately followed by a sequence of intensifying negatives and diminutives, 'of rather low height, a little pockmarked-ish, a little reddish-haired, a little even, to look at, short-sighted-ish, with a little bald patch on his forehead' (*nizen'kogo rosta, neskol'ko riabovat, neskol'ko ryzhevat, neskol'ko dazhe na-vid podslepovat, s nebol'shoi lysinoi na lbu*, 3: 141; again the repeated negatives and diminutives are more apparent and more elegant in the Russian) that amounts more to an erasure than to an introduction.[20] He tells us other unflattering things about him before he proceeds to tell us his name.

That naming is of fundamental importance to the narrator is already apparent. On the opening page of the story he has used the verb to name (*nazyvat'*) four times: in the first *line* of the story, he opines that it is best not to *name* the department; later he decides to *name* it 'a certain depart-ment'; then he *names* his hero's complexion 'haemorrhoidal' (*chto nazy-vaetsia gemoroidal'nym*) and tells us that he had the rank that is named (*chto nazyvaiut*) 'eternal titular councillor'. So before the child acquires the name 'Bashmachkin, Akakii Akakievich' at his birth and his christening, he has already been given the name 'haemorrhoidal eternal titular councillor' by the narrator.

Names and naming will continue to preoccupy the narrator – he tells us that the godfather is Ivan Ivanovich Eroshkin, and the godmother Arina Semenovna Belobriushkova, and that the landlady's ex-servant is called Anna. Paradoxically, he does not tell us the names of either Akakii Akakie-vich's mother or the landlady. He tells us that the assistant desk-head is having a name-day party at which it will be possible to 'wet the head' (*vsprysnut'*, 3: 157) of the overcoat, as if it were a child; but the names – and therefore the identities – of the two other leading characters in the story are left uncertain. The tailor was Grigorii, who renamed himself Petrovich (3: 148), and the important personage is either Ivan Abramovich or Stepan Varlamovich (but not both, 3: 165).

And so, the hero's name is Bashmachkin (3: 142): not that the narrator is actually very interested in it. According to an eloquent chart produced by David Sloane (Sloane: 476), the narrator is spectacularly more prone to invoke the name of his hero than are the narrators of the other Petersburg tales, but his overwhelming preference is for the first name and patronymic (to which we shall return). Bashmachkin is used just *three times* (putting in on a par with 'haemorrhoidal' and 'eternal titular councillor'). Nevertheless the narrator's ever inquiring mind alerts us that it 'evidently' came from the word *bashmak* (shoe), an etymology that has, of course, been seized upon by critics as additional proof of his incompetence. For Vetlovskaia it clearly comes rather from the diminutive *bashmachok* and is further evidence of Akakii Akakievich's childishness (Vetlovskaia 1988: 51). This interpretation had, however, already been rejected by Karlinsky, who insisted that *bashmachok* would yield Bashmachkov and that 'Bashmachkin can only come from the non-existent feminine form *bashmachka*, which would mean either "contemptible female shoe" (not a woman's shoe, but a shoe that is itself of feminine gender) or, even less probably, "a woman involved with shoes"' (Karlinsky: 303). Clearly the root of the word was important to Gogol: in the drafts his hero had previously been Bashmakevich or Bashmakov (3: 547, 686), and this has led critics to ponder further on its significance. They have noted its lowness, its nearness to the ground: Akakii Akakievich is associated with the pavement, (3: 152, 154) and almost falls to the floor (3: 167); the fact that the *bashmak* is an article of clothing worn by women, rather than men, who wear boots (*sapogi*); and the presence of the word, and the article, at crucial points in the text, being removed by the woman in the painting in which Akakii Akakievich takes an erotic interest (3: 159) and having been removed by the housekeeper, who lets him in wearing only one (3: 162). James Woodward has reminded us that in 'Ivan Fedorovich Shponka and His Aunt' ('Ivan Fedorovich Shpon'ka i ego tetushka', a story whose links to 'The Overcoat' will be discussed below) a *bashmak* is used for killing flies, an image that is itself applied to Akakii Akakievich. (Woodward 1982: 91, alluding to PSS, 1: 305; the fly image is on 3: 143 and 3: 169).

A further reason can be adduced for Gogol's choice of this surname for his hero. While his colleagues all go out enjoying themselves in the evenings, he stays at home working (3: 146). He wears a ragged old coat that is an object of mockery (3: 147). Through the intervention of a (travestied, demonic – see below) 'fairy godmother' he acquires a splendid article of clothing: 'he wanted to try the sleeves: Petrovich helped him put his arms into the sleeves – it turned out that it was good in the sleeves too' (3: 156, in a word 'It fits!'), and he, too, can go to the (name-day) ball. Brightly painted carriages go past him, but he himself goes on foot (3: 158).[21] On the way he sees a picture of a woman *taking off a shoe* (*bashmak*, 3: 159). He arrives and sees 'entire rows of galoshes on the floor' (3: 159). He has a good time at the party, but 'he absolutely could not forget that it was already twelve o'clock and that it was long since time for him to go home' (3: 160). Picking up his overcoat, which to his distress is 'lying on the floor', he leaves in a hurry (3: 160). Alas, he is robbed of the magic garment which, in this version, is also the love object, and in whose honour the party was being held. When he gets home his landlady is also missing a shoe (*bashmak*, 3: 162). He goes back to wearing his old rags (3: 163). He does get the beloved object back ('It's your overcoat I need', 3: 172), but only after his death. Thus Mr *Bashmachkin*, Mr 'female shoe', is a travestied Cinderella. The fairy-tale known in Western Europe mainly in Charles Perrault's version of 1697 circulated in Russia in various versions in the early nineteenth century and one of those collected by Afanasev was called 'The Little Golden Shoe' ('*Zolotoi bashmachok*', Afanas'ev, 2: 316-17, 445).[22]

The narrator then proceeds to describe the christening. This too is replete with negatives ('nikak ne iskali...nikak nel'zia bylo...nikogda i ne slykhivala...', 3: 142). First the narrator mentions the ten names that Akakii Akakievich will not be given. The whole process is initially presented as a kind of riddle, with the mother three times offered a group of names from which to choose.[23] Critics have lingered over the implications of these names, and the ominous tone is adumbrated by the fact that the only one described in any way is 'the martyr Khozdazat' (3: 142).[24] The outcome of the process is also given a definite sense of inevitability both by the mother's invocation of fate, and by the quadruple use of the word 'happened' (*proizoshla/ proizoshlo/ proizoshel/ proizoshlo*) applied to the surname, the christening, 'Akakii Akakievich' and 'all this' (3: 142-3).

The name finally chosen, is, of course, Akakii Akakievich. The narrator is much more taken with this name than with Bashmachkin – he uses Akakii 92 times and Akakievich 90 times (Sloane: 476) – and so are the critics. Interpretation of the name falls into three main areas. For some critics the crucial factor is that he shares the name of the holy martyr St Acacius, a name derived, as Alissandratos and many others remind us, from the Greek *akakios*, meaning 'lacking, or, by extension, even incapable of evil' (Alissandratos: 28-9). This is clearly consistent with the hero's character and behaviour, and has led to the hagiographical investigations discussed earlier.

A second approach to the name is to consider it phonetically. As was discussed in Part One, Eikhenbaum considered the name a 'particular sound combination' (*opredelennyi zvukovoi podbor*), providing the opportunity for semantic play. He reminds us that in an earlier draft Gogol drew overt attention to the sound semantics by suggesting: 'Of course they could somehow have avoided the frequent drawing together of the letter 'k', but circumstances were such that it was absolutely impossible to do this' (3; 522). He concludes that Akakii plus Akakievich sounds like a nickname (*prozvishche*), producing 'a special kind of articulatory mimicry, a sound gesture' (Eikhenbaum 1969: 313-14). Bely too notes Gogol's penchant for 'constructing names on the principle of sound repetition' (Belyi 1982: 233), while for Bakhtin:

> Gogol. A world without names, in it there are only nick-
> names and aliases of various kinds. The names of things are
> also nicknames. Not from the thing to the word, but from the
> word to the thing, the word gives birth to the thing. It equally
> justifies both destruction and birth.... The boundary between
> the ordinary and the fantastic is erased...Akakii Akakievich
> – the ghost which steals overcoats.   (Bakhtin 1979: 358)

Among recent critics, David Sloane is particularly attentive to the phonetic implications of the name, which he considers a 'phonetic "icon" for a whole range of verbal behaviour', including not only Akakii Akakievich's hesitation and stuttering, but also the narrator's digressiveness and the communication difficulties of the important personage (Sloane: 475). Certainly there is punning stuttering of this particle when Akakii Akakievich becomes excited at the prospect of the new overcoat:

> S etikh por *kak* budto samoe sushchestvovanie ego sdelalos' *kak*-to polnee, *kak* budto by on zhenilsia, *kak* budto *kak*oi-to drugoi chelovek prisutstvoval s nim, *kak* budto on byl ne odin, a *kak*aia-to priatnaia podruga zhizni soglasilas' s nim prokhodit' vmeste zhiznennuiu dorogu.... [From that time it was as if his whole existence became somehow fuller, as if he had got married, as if some other person was present with him, as if he was not alone, but some pleasant life's companion had agreed to pass along life's road together with him...,
> 3: 154][25]

For, as Sergei Bocharov and Charles Bernheimer note, Akakii himself is a copying (*perepisanie*), a phonetic repetition of his own father (Bocharov: 231, Bernheimer: 56), and the name emerges after a process of page turning (3: 142) that prophetically parodies Akakii's life's work.

The third major area of interpretation, which finds in the name the children's word *kaka*, meaning excrement, was first alluded to in print by Kruchenykh and Ermakov in the immediate post-revolutionary years (see Part One).[26] It, too, has been much discussed by critics, who link it to the hero's haemorrhoidal complexion (3: 141), to the haemorrhoids he 'earns' from years of sitting at a desk (3: 144), and to the 'tail-coat the colour of a cowpat', of the first version of the story (3: 446). It has been most vigorously elaborated by Daniel Rancour-Laferriere, for whom Akakii's birth is 'a defecation' and Akakii himself is a 'classic anal personality' and (at least in part) 'the most disgusting hero in all of Russian literature...a piece of feces' (Rancour-Laferriere: 93-9, 213, 195; see below, pp. 106-7, 'Psychological and psychoanalytical readings').

After describing the christening, the narrator proceeds to detail Akakii Akakievich's life, at work and at home, and his treatment by those around him. Certain key characteristics emerge.

Above all, as Tishkevich, the surname he acquired in the Vienna draft, implies, he is quiet and meek, a man of few words. When he does speak, according to the narrator, he 'expressed himself for the most part through prepositions, adverbs, and, finally, the sort of particles which are decidedly lacking in any meaning' (3: 149). When he learns the cost of the new overcoat he 'shrieks, perhaps for the first time in his life, for he was always distinguished by the quietness of his voice', and he leaves, 'completely destroyed' by Petrovich's words (3: 151). He is likewise 'not in a state to say a single word' when he returns home after his verbal 'thrashing' by the important personage (3: 167).

His speech defects, particularly the use of the tic-word *togo* (which in English might be rendered *er*) are discussed by several critics. For Fanger he is 'practically a speaking mute, an unparalleled and untranslatable triumph of the inarticulate put into words and yet left miraculously intact' (Fanger 1967: 117). Rancour-Laferriere produces a useful survey of the six different kinds of speech problem he manifests and refers to his speech defect as 'verbal castration' (Rancour-Laferriere: 106-10; 114); but he also points out that 'Akakii Akakievich is not *always* tongue-tied' (ibid., 104), and that his speech impediments manifest themselves in the stress of his encounters with Petrovich and the important personage. Indeed, at other times he seems to speak quite uninhibitedly and assertively, both in direct speech (3: 143, 145, 172) and in his reported threats to the police inspector's clerks (3: 163).

In general, though, his life is marked by asceticism. He has no pastimes and does not go out in the evening (3: 146, 158); he has no interest in clothes or in food (3: 145). What he does love is his work (*on sluzhil s liubov'iu*, 3: 144), and most of all copying his 'favourite' letters. The physiological manifestation of this pleasure – 'he giggled and he winked, and he helped with his lips' (3: 144) – is, of course, the behaviour of a child. The sense that he is still a child is underlined by his precipitous removal from christening to departmental desk (3: 143), and the word *rebenok* is used of him by the narrator when in 'the almost wheedling voice of a child' he asks why Petrovich cannot mend his old coat (3: 150). Several commentators discuss him in these terms, most notably Krivonos, who finds his infantilism echoed in the type of the 'child-hero' throughout Gogol's Petersburg tales (Krivonos 1996b).[27] This dependency is also echoed by the fact that his fate is repeatedly decided by the advice of others. It is Petrovich who pronounces 'decisively' (*reshitel'no*) that the old overcoat cannot be mended and that he must have a new one (3: 151); his colleagues decide that he must celebrate its purchase (3: 157); the sentry on duty tells him to go to the sergeant, but the landlady decides (*takoe reshenie*) that he should see the inspector (3: 162); and 'one someone' decides (*reshilsia*) to advise him to go to the important personage (3: 163). Of course none of this advice does him much good: nor does it help if he himself 'decides' to do things. He 'decides' (*reshil*, 3: 147) to take his old coat to Petrovich and 'decides' (*reshilsia*, 3: 163) to visit the important personage, two actions that have disastrous consequences. Things work out much better when he speaks directly, without prior deliberation ('No, it's better if I copy something', 3: 145; 'Now give me yours!', 3: 172).

The other salient factor about Akakii Akakievich is that he is delivered from the world of eternality and *experiences change*. His initial reaction to this, when he is told by Petrovich that he must replace his overcoat, is an acute attack of what Rancour-Laferriere calls 'neophobia' (Rancour-Laferriere: 83): 'At the word "new" Akakii Akakievich's eyes went all murky' (3: 151), but his behaviour rapidly begins to alter. The thought of the new coat removes his doubt and indecisiveness (*nereshitel'nost'*), brings fire to his eyes and 'the most bold and daring thoughts' to his head. He almost makes a mistake in his copying (3: 155). Before the name-day party he even spends time 'sybaritically' (*posibaritstvoval*) on his bed (3: 158). After he loses it he 'uniquely' misses a day's work (3: 163). As Andrew Barratt points out, while there is critical consensus that this transformation is fundamental to the meaning of the text, there is radical diversity in the interpretation of its significance (Barratt 1979: 5-6; see also Fanger 1979: 158-9). These different interpretations will be discussed in Section 3.

Crucially, the change in Akakii Akakievich wrought by the overcoat involves the discovery of eros. At the start of the text his innocence is mocked by his colleagues with the suggestion that he is beaten by his aged housekeeper: they ask when he is to marry her and shower him in confetti of papers (3: 143). But when Akakii Akakievich is starving himself to pay for the coat he imagines it as 'some pleasant life's companion [*podruga zhizni*, who] has agreed to pass along life's road together with him' (3: 154). On the way to the name-day party he smirks at the picture of a pretty lady removing her shoe (3: 159), a point that is underlined in the drafts by the presence of a second picture, 'which, it seemed, served as a continuation of the first, in which was depicted an equally beautiful lady who was already undressed and in bed' (3: 538).[28] On the way back he is on the point of following a real lady, one who speeds past like lightning, 'every part of her body full of unusual motion' (3: 160). However, the loss of the overcoat brings a vertiginous fall to earth: he is first of all greeted by the ancient landlady in a pose of modesty that parodically rhymes her with the lady in the painting (3: 162), and then accused by the inspector of visiting a 'disorderly house' (3: 163).

For Chizhevsky the 'almost erotic' relationship with the overcoat is consistent with the image of Akakii Akakievich as romantic lover and a sustained line of romantic parody in the story (Chizhevskii 1976: 388). This very suggestion discountenances Heinz Wisssemann, who insists, unpersuasively:

> Closer examination of the quoted passage on which this interpretation is based shows that the hero's mental attitude to the overcoat he desires is not portrayed as an erotic experience, but only *compared* to an erotic experience. The *four times repeated* "kak-budto" (as if, like) shows quite unequivocally that the elements of erotic experience mentioned are not *real*, but are the subjects of a comparison.
>
> (Wissemann: 97)

Conversely, for Erik Egeberg erotic elements are present, even before the introduction of the overcoat, in the descriptions of the 'love' and 'delight' Akakii Akakievich experiences in his copying work (Egeberg: 31; see 3: 144); and Peace, comparing the 'eternal' overcoat to the eternal feminine, stresses that the marital theme is also there from the start (Peace 1976: 73, 77). Dilaktorskaia explains the erotic implications of the marten fur (*kunitsa*) that Akakii Akakievich aspires to for his collar, which in Little Russian folk rituals is a symbol of the bride (Dilaktorskaia 1989: 31).[29] Woodward sees the whole tale as a battle between emasculated man and emasculating, powerful women: putting credence in the narrator's reference to Akakii Akakievich's brother-in-law and invoking the proverbial phrase *byt' pod bashmakom u zheny* (to be henpecked, literally to be under one's wife's shoe), Woodward insists (also unpersuasively) that he is, indeed, married to his landlady (Woodward 1982: 91-2).

Commentators have pointed out that the abortive pursuit of a woman is also the fate of the guardsmen who, when they look under the cap of Petrovich's plain wife, 'twitch their moustaches and adopt a certain particular voice' (3: 148); and of the important personage, who sets off in vain to see his mistress Karolina Ivanovna after a party (3; 172). They also note just how many of the women in the story are explicitly of foreign extraction: Petrovich calls his wife a German (3: 148); Karolina Ivanovna is 'of German origin'. (3: 171); the housekeeper's ex-cook is a Finn (3: 162). The lady in the painting is being watched by a man with a 'Spanish beard' and causes Akakii Akakievich to explain 'oh, those Frenchmen!' (3: 159). This foreignness is associated both with inaccessibility and with wrongness, a point stressed by several critics. Alissandratos reminds us that 'the erotic feelings that acquiring the coat arouse in Akakii indicate something is wrong, since eros is a satanically induced feeling, according to the traditional Orthodox monastic ethos that pervades Russian saints' lives' (Alissandratos: 36). In de Lotto's words, he succumbs to the 'devil of concupiscence' (*bes bluda*) with its 'perfidious warmth' (de Lotto: 77; Akakii Akakievich feels it is 'warm' in the overcoat, 3: 157). For Krivonos the 'whore-overcoat' seduces Akakii Akakievich, and the feminised space of Petersburg (the harlot-city, Toporov 1987) is inhabited, in all Gogol's Petersburg tales, by infernal temptress *damy* (Krivonos 1997, Krivonos 1996b: 124). For Ermakov, every erotic impulse in 'The Overcoat' leads to tragedy, and he shows just how frequently sexual attraction brings suffering in Gogol's other texts (Ermakov 1999: 255-6). The same point is made by Karlinsky, who stresses that both Akakii Akakievich and the important personage suffer 'punishment for yielding to a heterosexual amorous impulse' (Karlinsky: 141).

Thus in its specifically erotic aspect the change undergone by Akakii Akakievich would seem to contain the same ambiguous implications and yield as many interpretations as do its other aspects. Of course Akakii Akaievich did not at all intend to undergo change; he had made a habit of taking his old overcoat to be patched, and though this patching was done in an ugly manner and made the collar smaller every year, he visits Petrovich intending a repeat prescription (3: 147, 150).

The instigator of change is the sentence passed on the old overcoat by the tailor Petrovich.

Petrovich

The first thing we learn about Petrovich is that he lives 'on the fourth floor by the back stairs (*v chetvertom etazhe, po chernoi lestnitse*, 3: 148), and for Toby Clyman both the sound instrumentation and the semantics of this phrase point to Petrovich's determining feature, the fact that he is a representative of the devil (*chert*). He notes that the number four (*chetyre*) is ominous in occult literature, and reports that there are eleven instances of the use of the word four or its derivatives in the tale. He points to the link of the colour black to evil spirits. He finds further evidence of play on the sound *chert* in the description of Petrovich's toenail as 'like a tortoise's shell' (*kak u cherepakhi cherep*, 3: 149) (Clyman: 604-05). The word *chert* itself is also repeatedly invoked during Akakii's visits to the tailor, who charges 'the devil knows [*chort znaet*] what prices' (3: 149, 153), 'as if the devil had pushed him' (*kak budto ego chort tolknul*, 3: 153). His very wife says that the evil spirit (*nelegkaia*) makes him charge such a large amount (3: 153) and even calls him a 'one-eyed devil' (*odnoglazyi chort,* 3: 149).[30]

This deformity, along with the damaged nail of his big toe (3: 149) and the fact that he is boss-eyed (*krivoi glaz*) and pock-marked (3:148), is a key feature identifying him as a devil. In popular belief devils are commonly thought to suffer from the absence or deformation of a prominent bodily organ (Clyman: 602-03). Several of the demonic figures in Gogol's other stories are similarly deformed (Graffy 2000: 252). In a further continuation of the conceit, he owns a tobacco tin with a picture of a faceless general on it, but 'the place where the face had been' has been covered by a square (*chetverougol'nym*) scrap of paper (3: 150). Chizhevsky identifies the picture as a 'satanic icon', consistent with another popular belief, that the devil has no face (Chizhevskii: 393). It is ominously the only thing which Akakii Akakievich can see clearly when his eyes cloud over at the prospect of the new coat (3: 151). The motif is still present at the end of the story when the 'slanting' (*kosee*) nature of his writing marks out the new clerk who is found sitting in Akakii Akakievich's place at the department the very day after they find out about his death as another demonic disciple (3: 169).

Demons in folklore are also commonly believed to be 'of another faith' (*inovertsy*) or 'of another land' (*inozemtsy*).[31] Petrovich abuses his wife as a German (3: 148) and his needle as a barbarian (*varvarka*, 3: 149). He accuses the Germans of inventing stockings only as a means of making more money, for, in the narrator's words, he 'loved to make a dig at Germans when he got the chance' (3: 151); but this may just be part of his demonic smoke screen, for he himself shows 'barbarian calm' (3: 151) and his heavy drinking takes place 'on any church feasts where there is a cross in the calendar' (3: 148). Petrovich is also described as sitting 'with his legs under him like a Turkish pasha'. (3: 149) This pose is also adopted by other 'demonic tempters' in the 'Petersburg Tales' (Graffy 2000: 252-3).

We recall that Petrovich's heavy drinking began when he was freed from serfdom and changed his name from Grigorii (3: 148). Clyman tells us that Grigorii is another name of Greek origin and that it means 'watcher'. In the Slavonic version of the apocryphal story of Enoch, 'watchers' was the name given to the angels who rebelled against God: thus the change of name is an attempt to disguise his demonic role (Clyman: 602). For Priscilla Meyer Petrovich is therefore a pretender (*samozvanets*, literally 'self-namer'), and she reminds us that the pretender to the Russian throne, the 'False Dmitrii', was also a Grigorii, the unfrocked monk Grishka Otrepev (Meyer: 69).[32] But the name he adopts, Petrovich, is really no disguise: it explicitly makes him a son of Peter, and a son of the city he built, whose demonic features are only too apparent and have been discussed earlier.[33]

Petrovich's demonism was first discussed in detail by Chizhevsky, who concluded that 'Gogol clearly wishes the whole adventure with the overcoat to be understood as a "temptation" of Akaky Akakievich by the devil' who can 'capture man not only with greatness...but also with trivialities' (Chizhevskii: 393, 392). Several later commentators have added to this reading, and Petrovich as devil has attracted the sustained attention of Daniel Rancour-Laferriere, who suggests that: 'Semiotically, the devil is a convenient device whereby those elements which are too unpleasant or dangerous to be openly marked *own* (*svoi*) can be clustered together and defensively marked *alien* (*chuzhoi*)' (Rancour-Laferriere: 63).

His pertinent question as to what particular 'evil' Petrovich represents leads to an extended discussion of the devil/Petrovich's anality. This in turns leads to his association with strong or bad smells, first alluded to by the foul smell on the staircase and the smoke in the kitchen (3: 148), echoed in his suggestion that the old coat is 'completely rotten stuff' (*delo sovsem gniloe*, 3: 150), and most overtly manifested in his double sniffing of tobacco from his tobacco box (3: 150) (ibid., 80-2). Rancour-Laferriere reports the Russian folk belief that tobacco was invented by the devil, and several commentators have noted just how much sniffing of tobacco is associated with the overcoat. The policeman Akakii Akakievich bumps into in the street after his first visit to Petrovich sniffs tobacco (3: 152), as do both the policeman who lets the functionary-dead man escape (3: 170) and his timorous colleague in the story's final paragraph (3: 174).

In a later section of his analysis Rancour-Laferriere suggests that Petrovich is both a positive and a negative father figure for Akakii Akakievich,[34] and several commentators have noted comparisons between the two men. Though Petrovich's sitting barefoot (*Nogi...byli nagishom*, 3: 149) would seem to make him the opposite of Akakii Akakievich, Mr Little Shoe, his pockmarks and bad eyesight (3: 148) were among the first qualities to be associated, though in diminutive form, with Akakii Akakievich (3: 141). The tobacco box with the hole in the top (3: 150) rhymes with the 'little box...with a little hole cut in the top' in which Akakii Akakievich keeps his money (3: 154). The tobacco box 'with the portrait of some general' also links him, of course, to the important personage, who has just been made a general (3: 165), and its importance is acknowledged by the great attention paid to it by Akakii Akakievich (3: 151). A further link is suggested by the fact that Akakii Akakievich visits both Petrovich and the important personage with a request which is turned down with a stern verbal 'thrashing' (Dilaktorskaia 1986: 148; Even-Zohar). As underlined by the repetition of a striking foreign word, both men are highly satisfied with the effect (*effekty*, 3: 151; *effekt*, 3: 167) of their sternness, which in each case is to render the hearer senseless (Bailey: 14-15). Thus Petrovich would seem to be both a distorted double of Akakii Akakievich and an intermediary figure between him and the important personage.

The important personage

The name of the important personage is revealed in passing to be either Ivan Abramovich or Stepan Varlamovich (who in their stress and syllabic patterns are actually doubles of each other, 3: 165), and he is also referred to as a general (3: 165) and, by Akakii Akievich, as 'your excellency' (3: 166), but the appellation he is first given by 'one someone', 'one important personage' (*odno znachitel'noe litso*, 3: 163) is the one the narrator overwhelmingly prefers, using it time and time again, sometimes without the prefatory '*odno*', and frequently italicising it.[35] The preference for this strange appellation in the neuter gender, which in the original Russian means, literally, 'one meaningful face', suggests that it must, itself, be 'important', and there are several crucial plays on the word 'meaningful' and the idea of meaning, not all of which can be preserved in translation.

Some of them form further links with his tyrannical predecessor Petrovich. Petrovich had twice meaningfully (*znachitel'no*) pursed his lips as he told Akakii Akakievich the price of the new overcoat (3: 151), glad that he had not lowered himself (*sebia ne uronil*, literally had not dropped himself, 3: 152); when he brings the overcoat his face takes on an extremely meaningful expression (*V litse ego pokazalos' vyrazhenie takoe znachitel'noe*, 3: 156); and when Akakii Akakievich is walking through the streets in it for the first time, Petrovich runs through a 'crooked [*krivoi*] alley' so as to be able to look at the overcoat 'straight in the face' (*priamo v litso*, 3: 157). Akakii Akakievich's words, on the other hand, 'have no meaning' (*ne imeiut nikakogo znacheniia*, 3: 149).

The important personage has only recently become 'important/meaningful', having previously been 'unimportant/meaningless', (*neznachitel'nym*), and his important/meaningful position is even now not considered meaningful by comparison with those who are still more meaningful (*znachitel'neishimi*) though 'you can always find a circle of people for whom what is meaningless in the eyes of others is already meaningful' (3: 164). He attempts to strengthen his meaning by getting his inferiors to meet him on the stairs, and looking them 'very meaningfully in the face' (*smotrel ochen' znachitel'no v litso*), yet still he is afraid that he may 'drop' his meaning (*uronit...svoego znacheniia*, 3: 165). For Vetlovskaia the important personage is but a shadow (*ten'*) who has emerged from the faceless picture on Petrovich's tobacco tin (Vetlovskaia 1988: 62-5).

The important personage is also fundamentally associated with the bureaucratic hierarchy, the ladder of rank (*chin*). This has brought him rewards, but rewards that are extremely ambiguous. On recently attaining the rank of general (*general'skii chin*) he has 'somehow got confused, lost his way and really did not know what to do'. He finds it impossible to speak to those who are 'even one rank' (*odnim chinom*) lower than him (3: 165). His general's rank puts him at least five rungs above the titular councillor Akakii Akakievich, whose attempt to circumvent the usual bureaucratic channels provokes him to fury (3: 167). Thus his primary role in the story of Akakii Akakievich would seem to be his heartless refusal to help him, and the verbal 'thrashing' that leads indirectly to Akakii Akakievich's death.

However, Akakii Akakievich is himself not entirely oblivious to the question of rank: we learn that if he had been rewarded according to his effort he would perhaps have advanced to the rank of state councillor, and he likes to take copies for himself of documents addressed to 'a new or important personage' (3: 144, 146). The phonetic closeness of the word *chin* (a 'foreign' concept, the Table of Ranks having been introduced by Peter the Great) to the foreign word *shinel'* (overcoat) has led commentators to note just how many parallels can be drawn between Akakii Akakievich, who acquires the perfidious gift of the new *shinel'*, and the important personage with his perfidious new *chin*.

Like Akakii Akakievich, the important personage is 'a good man in his soul', but in society he is silent and his situation arouses sympathy (*zhalost'*); he remains outside lively conversations and circles; he is prone to 'remain eternally [*vechno*] in one and the same [*tom zhe*] silent state, rarely pronouncing only certain monosyllabic sounds, and thus he got the title of the most boring of men' (3: 165; the italicised words are all also used directly of Akakii Akakievich). Indeed, he is soon reduced to silence even in the presence of his old acquaintance and childhood friend (3: 165, 166). Like Akakii Akakievich he attempts to compensate for his taciturnity by the repetition of favourite words, the triply echoed 'severity' (*strogost'*, 3: 164) or the phrases he practised in front of his mirror on being appointed to the new rank (3: 166), in behaviour which Dilaktorskaia shows to echo Akakii Akakievich's trying on of the overcoat (Dilaktorskaia 1986: 145), and which Shapiro sees as another banal reduction of an exalted idea, the *theatrum mundi* topos, favoured by the early church fathers, the sense that man is but an actor on the stage of the world (Shapiro: 130-3).[36] A variant of his stock phrase 'How dare you?' (3: 165) has already been used by Akakii Akakievich to the police inspector's clerks (3: 163). Just as for Akakii Akakievich, his new acquisition has caused him to lose his way.

Most notably of all, as regularly noted by critics, each man attends a party, at which he has a good time and drinks two glasses of champagne, which makes him merry. He leaves the party, goes down the staircase (*lestnitsa*), and instead of going straight home, sets off in pursuit of a woman. He is grabbed by the collar and has his overcoat stolen, gets a terrible shock and starts to shriek. Separated from their '*podruga*' (the overcoat, 3: 154, Karolina Ivanovna, 3: 173) each goes home and spends an uneasy night. (Compare Akakii Akakievich, 3: 160-2 to the important personage, 3: 171-3).[37] But whereas Akakii Akakievich, who had himself given up his pursuit of an illicit liaison and was robbed on his way home, immediately told his landlady about his misfortune, the important personage, whose own illicit liaison had been thwarted through no fault of his own, 'told no one of what had befallen him, nor where he had been, nor whither he had wished to go' (3: 173), in what for Nabokov is 'a parody of a Bible parable' (Nabokov 1961: 147).

Thus the important personage is both tyrant, (like Petrovich), the patron who fails to protect, and himself a victim (unlike Petrovich, but like Akakii Akakievich), who, in the reversed relationship of the fantastic epilogue, shares his own victim's fate, in a vengeance effected by the victim himself. The words of one of the robbers of Akakii, 'But the overcoat is mine!' (3: 161), are echoed in the phrase 'now give me yours!' (3: 172), giving the whole story a pleasing circularity.

It is in his second, less obvious role as victim that the important personage seems to attract more interest both from the narrator and from critics. The loss of his coat is not, however, the end for him, and most critics agree that he is little, if at all, changed by his experience.[38] Just as the shock and 'pangs of conscience' he had felt on learning of Akakii Akakievich's death lasted but a single day and were obliterated by an evening spent in 'orderly society' (3: 171), so the suggestion that the 'strong impression' made on him by the theft of his own overcoat leads him to berate his subordinates far less frequently is immediately capsized by the addition 'or at least not before he had heard what had happened' (3: 173). If Akakii Akakievich experiences fundamental and irreversible change, the important personage reverts to his previous state: he is thus, in a satisfying muddying of the semantic waters, at once his double and his antipode.

The Overcoat

Gogol's excessive concern about his clothes is widely alluded to by scholars, who find evidence both in his correspondence and in the memoirs of his friends. In a letter of 7 July 1840, written from Vienna after he had started work on 'The Overcoat', he asks Sergei Aksakov:

> To buy, or to get Mikhail Semenovich to buy from the best boot-maker some Petersburg worked leather, the softest he can get, for boots, that is to say, just the uppers (you can get them ready cut out, they don't take up any space and they are easy to carry); two pairs, or three. Something awful has happened: all the boots which Take made me have turned out too short. The stubborn German! I kept telling him they'd be too short: but the old boot-tree wouldn't take any notice! and they're too wide, so my feet have swollen up. It would be good if I could get hold of these bits of leather, because they make quite good boots here.   (PSS, 11: 296-7)

This letter is alluded to by Alexander Zholkovsky, who compares Gogol's thrifty boot repairs to the habits of the Bashmachkin family (Zholkovsky: 270). We recall that they 'change their soles only about three times a year' (3: 142), and that Akakii Akakievich plans to economise by 'stepping as lightly and carefully as possible...almost on tiptoe' (3: 154). Another source mentioned by Zholkovsky is the memoirs of L.I. Arnoldi, who insists that Gogol always had three, or even four pairs of boots in his case and that they always looked brand new; he considers it entirely possible that 'alone in his room he would put on a new pair and revel in them [*naslazhdalsia*]...and then later he would laugh at himself' (Veresaev: 455). Arnoldi compares this behaviour to that of the boot-loving captain in *Dead Souls*, another text that is full of lovers of clothes and was being written at the same time as 'The Overcoat', but it is also a feature shared by Akakii Akakievich, who, though he originally 'did not think at all about his clothes' (3: 145), is transformed by his acquisition:

> ...he took off the overcoat and hung it carefully on the wall, once more lost in admiration of the cloth and the lining, and then purposely took out for comparison the old dressing gown [the name mockingly given to the old overcoat, J.G.] which was completely falling apart. He looked at it and himself even started laughing.   (3: 158)

There are foppish characters in several of Gogol's texts, including all the

'Petersburg Tales' (Graffy 2000: 264-5). One of them, the artist Chartkov in 'The Portrait' (in an episode which contains further echoes of the experience of Akakii Akakievich), after the change in his circumstances buys a 'fashionable tail-coat', drinks champagne for the first time and then struts along the Nevsky Prospect 'like a golden-eye [*gogolem*], aiming his lorgnette at everyone' (3: 97). (Here Gogol winningly admits to his own obsession by using his name as a euphemistic rhyme for dandy [*shchegolem*].) Further recognition of the importance Gogol attached to clothes is provided by the many stories written in homage to 'The Overcoat' (and discussed in Part One), including those by Zoshchenko, Alekseev, Vakhtin, Voinovich and Aksenov, which have as their love object an article of clothing, and particularly by Bunin's 'Pan Micholski's Jacket', in which the obsessive fop is Gogol himself.

The narrator of 'The Overcoat' shares his creator's sartorial interests. He tells us of the boots of the Bashmachkins (3: 142) and of Akakii's uniform, which is 'not green, but a sort of reddish-floury colour', with a narrow, low little collar and a tendency to be covered with scraps of hay or threads;[39] and of his hat covered in melon rinds (3: 145); of his old overcoat which is now as thin as sackcloth, which has been repeatedly patched by cutting bits off its collar, and which his colleagues have christened 'the dressing gown' (3: 147), but which Akakii Akakievich hopes might 'still serve a bit longer' (3: 151); of the new trousers, new boot tops, the three shirts and the 'couple of pairs of that linen which it is indelicate to name in print' on which he intends to spend his forthcoming bonus (3: 153); of his existing linen, which in the interests of economy he takes to removing as soon as he gets home, and of his half-cotton dressing gown, which, though ancient, has been 'spared even by time itself' (3: 154); of the marten collar he toys with buying, of the 'best cat' he actually gets, 'which from a distance can always be taken for marten', and of the calico chosen for the lining which is so thick and of such good quality that it is even better and glossier to look at than silk (3: 155); of the double silk stitching on the new garment and of its excellent sleeves (3: 156). He tells us of the 'various trousers and tail-coats' mended by Petrovich and of the little cap his wife wears instead of a kerchief (3: 148); of the footcloths he suggests making from the old overcoat and the stockings invented by Germans which do not warm (3: 151); of the beaver collars of the men in the street and the raspberry velvet caps of the cab drivers (3: 158); of the shoe taken off by the lady in the picture, and the rows of galoshes and the overcoats and cloaks, some of them even with beaver collars or velvet reveres, in the hall of the assistant desk-head (3: 159); of the single shoe and the night-shirt of the landlady (3: 162); and of the red braided collars of the ushers of a titular councillor (3: 164). He tells us that the 'old dressing gown' has become even more lamentable when Akakii Akakievich puts it on again (3: 163); and that his will includes three pairs of socks and two or three buttons from his trousers (3: 168). He tells us of the ghost that stole 'all sorts of overcoats: cat, beaver, quilted ones, marmot, fox and bearskin coats, in a word all sorts of furs and skins' (3: 169); and finally of the important personage's luxurious warm overcoat (3: 172).

The central role in the story is of course played by Akakii Akakievich's new overcoat, as advertised by the replacement of the original title, 'The Tale of the Clerk who Stole Overcoats', by the single word *Shinel'*, a change which transfers agency from the clerk to the coat. Critics have attempted variously to interpret its significance. As Andrew Barratt points out, the overcoat is the 'organising principle' of the entire story and 'serves as a catalyst to each of its plots' (Barratt 1979: 14). In Andrei Bely's words, Akakii Akakievich lives 'in his own distinct universe: not the solar [*solnechnoi*] universe, but the...'overcoat' [*shinel'noi*] one: for him "the overcoat" is the world soul, embracing and warming' (Belyi 1982: 45).

For some it is a positive emblem: Anthony Hippisley, in a religious reading of the story (for which see p. 105 below) reminds us that when he started feeling the cold badly Akakii Akakievich wondered whether 'there might not be some faults [*grekhov*, literally 'sins'] in his [old, J.G.] coat,' which is indeed, immediately afterwards said to be 'on the back and on the shoulders just like sackcloth' (*serpianka*, 3: 147). Akakii Akakievich asks Petrovich to find some new pieces to patch it. Hippisley compares Petrovich's words: 'Well of course I can find patches, patches can be found...but there's nothing to sew it on' (3: 150), to Christ's analogy of the sinner's relationship to God: 'No man also seweth a piece of new cloth on an old garment: else the new piece that filleth it up taketh away from the old, and the rent is made worse' (Mark 2: 21), and concludes that the 'the new overcoat symbolises Christ himself' (Hippisley: 124-5). For the narrator the coat is a 'radiant guest' (*svetlyi gost'*), who 'enlivened his poor life for a moment' (3: 169), an image which Surkov traces back to Zhukovsky's 1824 poem, 'The Mysterious Visitor' ('Tainstvennyi posetitel''), with its lyrical evocation of a brief, mysterious angelic visitation and its sense of the evanescence of happiness, of 'sweet joy for an hour' (Surkov: 67-8: Zhukovskii SS, 1: 368-9).

For Vaiskopf the overcoat is a capacious garment, replacing Bashmachkin's dead mother, while at the same time being a guardian angel, and arousing both his aesthetic and his erotic sense (Vaiskopf 1978: 43-4). For Rancour-Laferriere, too, the coat is both a wife and a mother, and its loss is both a death and a castration (Rancour-Laferriere: 115-29, 192-3). For Woodward, on the other hand, the new coat is 'unequivocally identified as a symbol of defiant masculinity' unfurled from Petrovich's handkerchief with its '"nosological", i.e. masculine implications' (Woodward 1982: 105). The erotic implications connected with calling the coat his 'pleasant life's companion' (3: 154) have already been discussed and, as Karlinsky and others remind us, the association of a wife with 'some sort of woollen fabric' was first made by Gogol in 'Ivan Fedorovich Shponka and His Aunt' in which, in a dream, a cloth merchant asks the hero: 'What material would you like?....

Take wife, it's the most fashionable material! Very hardwearing! everyone is having frock-coats made of it these days' (PSS, 1: 307, cited in Karlinsky: 130).

The maker of the new overcoat is the tailor Petrovich, whose repudiation of the old one, 'No, you can't fix it: it's a bad wardrobe' (3: 150) echoes the words of the Jewish tailor to whom Shponka takes his roll of 'wife': 'No... it's poor quality material! No one has a frock-coat made of it' (PSS, 1: 307). Petrovich's 'ownership' of the new overcoat is later reiterated by the pride he takes in it (3: 156), and by the fact that he makes a rushed detour in the street to take another look at 'his' overcoat (*svoiu shinel'*, 3: 157).

Though Gogol once wrote in a letter to an uncle that he himself was 'a good tailor' (*khoroshii portnoi*, PSS, 10: 133), his vision of hell in the *Selected Passages from Correspondence with Friends* is of a world ruled by seamstresses and tailors (PSS, 8: 415), and he often displayed the devil in his stories as a fop (Graffy 2000: 265). Fashion is thus a demonic temptation, and, as we recall, Petrovich is only too eager to follow fashion (*kak poshla moda*) with a collar fixed by 'little appliquéed silver clasps' (*serebriannye lapki pod aplike* [a foreign word], 3: 153). Rancour-Laferriere discusses the French origin of the word *shinel'* and suggests that at the time the story was written the object as well as the word would be considered 'a European, not a Russian artifice' (Rancour-Laferriere: 47-9). He also points out that just as the 'mighty enemy, the frost' is introduced by the Russian phrase 'vrag etot ne kto drugoi, kak nash severnyi moroz', so the overcoat is presented by the words, 'podruga eta byla ne kto drugaia, kak ta zhe shinel'' (ibid., 121, compare 3: 147 and 3:154).

The new overcoat temporarily brings its owner a measure of worldly acceptance.[40] Yet in a particularly striking passage, the congratulations of his colleagues make Akakii Akakievich feel 'even ashamed' (*stydno*), and when they insist that the purchase must be celebrated he becomes utterly confused, does not know what to say, blushes and even tries to 'insist...that it absolutely isn't a new overcoat, it's just, it's the old overcoat' (3: 157). Later, of course, he himself betrays the old overcoat, laughing at it and 'sniggering whenever he thinks of the state it's in' (3: 158), but this betrayal is quickly punished: he is upset to find the new overcoat lying on the floor after the party. He shakes it and, in explicit contrast with his treatment of its predecessor, 'removes every speck of dust' (3: 160), but alas, he is soon to be parted from it forever. The function of Akakii Akakievich as a travestied Cinderella has been discussed above. The stripping of his social pretensions in this scene through the cry 'The overcoat is mine!' would seem to link him to Hans Christian Andersen's emperor, stripped of his false 'new clothes' and revealed in his true nakedness. He falls to the ground and his 'side, and his chest, and all his trousers' get covered in snow' (3: 162). Katherine Lahti has noted how frequently Chichikov's beautiful clean boots are 'violated by mud' in *Dead Souls*, a novel in which the characters consistently indulge in 'commodity fetishism'. She concludes that 'Overvaluation of the worthless is the prime motivator of the plot of *Dead Souls*, which moves along almost entirely because of the discrepancy between the artificial and real values...' (Lahti: 147-50), and it is instructive to apply her words to 'The Overcoat'. The final stage of Akakii Akakievich's punishment for 'artificial values' is death, and it is difficult not to agree with Paul Waszink, who finds in the blunt diagnosis of the unhelpful doctor that it's 'a definite kaput' (*nepremennyi kaput*, 3: 168, perhaps he, too, is a German) a none too subtle rebuke for his abandonment of his faithful *kapot* (Waszink: 291).

As Vaiskopf notes, the thread (nit') is a symbol of fate in folklore (Vaiskopf 1993: 330). The new overcoat is fortified by Petrovich by double stitching of fine silk, and he tests each seam with his own teeth (3: 156). Despite this, as Cathy Popkin reminds us, 'this coat is most frequently shown to be taken off – first at work, then at home, at the party, at the request of the mustachioed thieves, and, subsequently, from the shoulders of numerous Petersburgians, including the Person of Consequence himself' (Popkin: 202), leading her to conclude that the removal and disappearance of the coat signals the frustrating removal of the material (the *thread*) of the story itself.

3. Readings

'The Overcoat' as social criticism

The conventional social reading of the story concentrates upon the perceived characterisation of, and attitude to Akakii Akakievich, whom it views as a 'little man' and a 'poor clerk'. It is seen as the invention of nineteenth-century civic-minded criticism (and of the appalled Count Stroganov) – though, as was shown in Part One, Belinsky scarcely wrote directly about 'The Overcoat', Chernyshevsky thought that Akakii Akakievich was 'a complete ignoramus and a total idiot', and Lenin used him as a byword for servility. It gained a new hegemony in orthodox Soviet criticism; but for Boris Eikhenbaum such a reading was the nadir of scholarly naïvety, and most Western critics have followed his line. Chizhevsky says that a trawl of the tale for social protest will find it 'strangely absent' and that the problem of 'the defence of the "human rights" of the little man' could not possibly have been of importance to Gogol for whom all men were equal before God (Chizhevskii 1976: 387, 389); while for Setchkarev, 'One can hardly say that Gogol was very skillful in choosing a hero if he wanted to champion the poor members of society who had been deprived of their rights. But nothing was further from his mind' (Setchkarev: 218). Erlich felt that in the case of the social critics, 'the reception of a literary work was shaped less by its essential tenor that by the urgency of the reader's emotional needs and ideological compulsions' (Erlich: 144); while for Karlinsky the work actually argued for 'the desirability of total social stasis' (Karlinsky: 143). Peace's astute financial calculations and a comparison with the expenditure of Gogol's other titular councillors lead him to conclude that 'the poverty of Akakii Akakievich is not credible in real terms' and that he could most certainly afford a new coat! (Peace 1976: 66-8). For Rancour-Laferriere, since 'an important element in the organization of a collective is sublimated or redirected homosexuality', it is striking that all the *chinovniki* in 'The Overcoat' are men and the 'hierarchy of chin [rank, J.G.] depicted in the story...at its repressive worst...consists primarily of dried-out, anally oriented bureaucrats who like to give and take orders' (Rancour-Laferriere: 213-14).

The social and bureaucratic aspects of the tale *are* of great interest to Harold A. McFarlin, who zealously teases out evidence of Akakii Akakievich's position in the very middle of the social scale; of his bureaucratic world view; and of his disdain for his social inferiors. His deep immersion in administrative history leads McFarlin to postulate that Akakii Akakievich entered the service in 1805, and that it was the law of 6 August 1809 that turned him into an 'eternal titular councillor' by introducing educational requirements for promotion to the next rank of collegiate assessor (McFarlin: 246, 249).[41] For Charles Sherry this bureaucratic system is a world of appearance and artifice, in which 'man is a functionary, an operator, whose sole purpose is to appear to fill the space allotted to him on the scale of existence established by the Petersburg hierarchy'. The system produces 'readily recognizable semiotic emblems to define the hierarchical relationships among men: uniforms, offices, degrees, medals, honors, money, and the like', all of which 'through a subtle and pervasive alchemy, are to be understood as real qualities of the person possessing them, and are the only means others have for identifying one another' (Sherry: 7, 9).

Much of the recent interest in the social aspects of the tale, however, has been directed at the attitudes and the allusive hints of the narrator.

The stuttering false start of his story after only two words is caused by his awareness that 'there is nothing angrier than departments, regiments, chancelleries of all kinds, and, in a word, all kinds of official estates' (*dolzhnostnykh soslovii*), who are only too ready to take the criticism of an individual as the criticism of the whole of society (3: 141). His solution for the difficulties this threatens is to avoid specificity: 'it is better not to name in which department'; but the hyper-conscientious observation of his own self-denying ordinance quickly develops into a sly running joke. He tells us of 'one [*odnogo*] police inspector' in 'some [*kakogo-to*] town' who took offence at a romantic work about a person of the same rank with a weakness for drink (3: 141); of 'one [*odin*] functionary' in 'one [*odnom*] department' (3: 141); of 'one young man' who feels sorry for Akakii Akakievich (3: 143); of 'one director' who offers him more challenging work (3: 144); of 'some gentleman' of whom Petrovich had been the serf (3: 148) and of 'some general' on his tobacco tin (3: 150); of 'one of the functionaries, some even assistant desk-head' who decides to hold a name day party (3: 157); of 'some one book or other' (*odnu kakuiu-to knigu*, 3: 163); of 'one someone' (*odin kto-to*, 3: 163) who suggests that Akakii Akakievich visit 'one important personage' (*odno znachitel'noe litso*, repeated and italicised to remind us of the narrator's vow, 3: 163); of 'some titular councillor' who set up 'some ushers' at the doors of his minuscule 'reception room' (3: 164); of 'one recently arrived old acquaintance and childhood comrade' (3: 165); of 'one of the departmental functionaries' who saw the ghost with his own eyes (3: 169-70); of 'the sentry of some block' and of 'some retired musician' (3: 170); and finally of 'one Kolomna policeman' (3: 173). He even, in what Formalist criticism would call 'the laying bare of the device', has the clerk whose name we have already heard dozens of times announced to the important personage as 'some Bashmachkin' (*kakoi-to Bashmachkin*) and 'some functionary' (*kakoi-to chinovnik*, 3: 165). For David Sloane, the narrator's very allusion to the need for self-censorship shows extraordinary political daring, and the 'chatty, seemingly frivolous banter characteristic of his delivery elsewhere' is an effective way of obviating the censor's objections (Sloane: 482-3).

The narrator also knows that 'with us the first thing it is necessary to do is to announce the rank' (*chin*, 3: 141), and his text is consistently alert to gradations of rank and to their social and human consequences. He refers to the councillors 'who give no one any counsel [*sovetniki...kotorye ne daiut nikomu sovetov*], nor do they take it from anyone themselves' (3: 147). He blames 'the rank of general' for confusing the important personage (3: 165) and for very often stopping his good feelings from manifesting themselves (3: 171). He broadens his attack with references to the Russian love of tittle-tattle (3: 146), and to the fact that 'in holy Russia everything is infected with imitation, everyone apes and copies [*draznit i korchit*] his boss' (3: 164). In fact a Russian can think of nothing better than sitting in a sleigh wrapped up in a warm coat not thinking about anything (3: 172). He tells us that Akakii Akakievich's colleagues repeat the 'eternal' (*vechnyi*) anecdote of the docking of the tail of the horse in the statue of the Bronze Horseman (3: 146); and in his most daring comparison he likens the misfortune that befalls Akakii Akakievich to that which befalls 'the Tsars and rulers of the world' (3: 169).[42]

The narrator's concerns are shared by the characters. 'A certain someone' is worried that a policeman might find the lost coat 'to impress the authorities' but then just keep it in the police station (3: 163). Akakii Akakievich himself tries to circumvent the chain of *chin* carefully enunciated by the important personage ('you should have handed in your petition to the chancellery; it would have gone to the desk-head, to the section head, and then would have been handed to the secretary, and then the secretary would have delivered it to me') by daring to suggest that 'secretaries are, er...an unreliable lot' (3: 166). This provokes the important personage's fury and his landlady is horrified that in his deathbed delirium Akakii Akakievich's curses follow directly upon the word 'your excellency' (3: 168).[43] For Bakhtin, this rebellion is consistent with the strain of popular cultural consciousness in the story and an expression of its carnivalising mocking of the collective (Bakhtin 1975: 494). Akakii Akakievich's posthumous vengeance is exacted 'without discriminating over rank or title', 'not just from titular councillors but even from privy councillors themselves' (3: 169, 170), and his lack of respect for authority is then comically echoed in the taller, moustachioed 'ghost' of the story's final paragraph, who shakes his fist and sends the Kolomna policeman packing.

Thus, though argument continues over its motivation, it is clear that the story is indeed deeply imbued with an awareness of rank and its consequences.

Religious readings

For Chizhevsky 'there remains no doubt that the thoughts of a religious and moral nature, which disturbed and tormented him [Gogol, J.G.] at various times in his life, have largely determined his artistic production' (Chizhevskii 1976: 391). He quotes from a long letter Gogol wrote to Danilevsky on 20 June 1843 in which he says:

> But the external life is in itself the opposite of the inner, when man under the influence of passionate enthusiasms is dragged along without struggle by the streams of life, when there is no centre in him, resting on which he might overcome the very sufferings and sadness of life.   (PSS, 12: 196)

Chizhevsky concludes that by the centre, Gogol means God, and offers a religious reading of 'The Overcoat' in which Akakii Akakievich is seduced by the trivial attractions of the world (Chizhevskii 1976: 391-3).

The allusion to the subtext in the *Life* of St Akakii by Driessen spawned the number of readings of the story in the light of hagiography discussed above. For several of these commentators, such as John Schillinger, the relationship of Gogol's text to the hagiographical model was one of travesty; but for others the use of the hagiographical source is entirely serious, and it coincides with a period of greatly increased spiritual interest in Gogol's life.[44] For Hippisley the story 'has a spiritual meaning bearing closely on the author's personal experience [and] symbolizes the sinner's pursuit of salvation represented by the coat itself' (Hippisley: 121). He reminds us how frequently in the bible clothing symbolises righteousness. In this reading Petrovich's relationship to Akakii Akakievich 'recalls that of a priest, possibly even a pope, his name Petrovich suggesting the apostolic succession from St Peter' (ibid., 124; Hippisley stresses Gogol's interest in Roman Catholicism during his Roman period). Thus 'his decision to order a new coat may be compared to the sinner's decision to return to God'. When the Prodigal Son repented, his father said 'Bring forth the best robe and put it on him' (Luke 15: 22), and thus, for Hippisley, the new overcoat symbolises Christ himself (ibid., 125). Hippisley does not seem entirely confident in his reading however, conceding that much of Akakii Akakievich's subsequent behaviour is scarcely righteous, and he himself admits that 'It is possible that Satan...has perpetrated a grand deception on Akakii Akakievich' (ibid., 126).

The most sustained and brilliant reading of the story based upon the premise that Gogol's religious intentions in it are entirely serious is offered by Cinzia de Lotto, whose revelation of the range and depth of the spiritual sources of the text was discussed earlier. For de Lotto, the world of Akakii

Akakievich is the ascetic world of a novice, a world of obedience and humility, without passions (de Lotto: 61). What Rozanov saw as his insignificance is in fact the embodiment of the Christian ideal of simplicity and spiritual poverty and heroic commitment to his 'service' (*sluzhba*). He cries out only when his colleagues interrupt his copying work, which in the monastic tradition is lofty creativity (ibid., 64). Gogol, who often referred to Russia as a 'monastery', 'gives the features of a monk to an ordinary civil servant'. Akakii Akakievich is one of the blessed 'poor in spirit' from the Sermon on the Mount. The world does not appreciate this, and nor did 'the entire generations of readers and critics who had been torn out of the context of Christian culture and did not know how to detect in this image the spiritual searchings of its creator' (ibid., 66-7). The change in Akakii Akakievich, motivated by the world and concern about the body, is a seduction and a fall from his state of grace. This is the meaning of the plot of the story.

> If you read the changes in Akakii Akakievich through a 'normal' gaze, the gaze of this world, then you have to agree, his life becomes brighter, more spiritual. But if you start from the idea that Akakii Akakievich is the ideal of the absence of passion, a zealot (*podvizhnik*) of obedience, then the catastrophic nature of his fall is obvious. 'A man of great humility' has betrayed the 'rule' of his life and replaced all his virtues with vices.   (ibid., 77)

Psychological and psychoanalytical readings

Some attempts were made by early critics to analyse Gogol's motivations in writing the story as he did. For Chernyshevsky Gogol hid Akakii Akakievich's faults, because he would have felt a scoundrel if he had revealed them. For Rozanov, on the other hand, it was precisely a feeling of guilt over the ugly figure that he had created that led him to introduce the 'humane passage' in attempted reparation. For Ivan Ermakov the second half of the story is full of Gogol's personal concerns and the relationship of Akakii Akakievich and the important personage is based upon the humiliations endured by his own father; for Alexis Emerson-Topornin it is an expression of Gogol's own 'double' personality, in which meekness was contrasted with insecure egotism (Emerson-Topornin: 47-51). Peace considers that the story possibly 'derives its compelling power from the fact that it is a reflection of a personal and artistic crisis experienced by the author himself', but also quotes approvingly Driessen's contention that 'no one who knows Gogol somewhat will doubt that he is a masterful psychologist' (Peace 1976: 89, 87, citing Driessen 195).

The most interesting recent examination of the story from a psychoanalytical point of view examines the protagonist, rather than his creator. Julia Alissandratos has drawn attention to the diametrical opposition between what she call the 'medieval hagiographic' and 'most modern psychological' evaluations of Akakii Akakievich and his situation, concluding that 'the former emphasizes selflessness, while the latter stresses self' (Alissandratos: 38-9). What in the religious reading is positively coded as obedience and service, in the psychoanalytical reading is negatively coded as repression. What a religious reading interprets as seduction by the world and betrayal of a lofty calling, the psychoanalytical reading sees as emotional maturation. The readings provided by Rancour-Laferriere's sustained and imaginative use of the tools of psychoanalysis in the assessment of the personality traits exhibited by Akakii Akakievich and of his experience have been incorporated into earlier sections of this study. Rancour-Laferriere quotes Daniel Young's insistence that 'no psychoanalytic critic has ever asserted that the unconscious meaning of Gogol's work is the only meaning' (Rancour-Laferriere: 12-13), himself contending that 'psychoanalytic meaning does not exclude, but co-ordinates and unifies other meanings' (ibid., 89). He finds Akakii Akakievich to manifest an anal personality through the triad of orderliness, parsimoniousness and obstinacy (ibid., 99-103), and traces his abortive journey from anal to genital sexuality through the acquisition of the overcoat. He considers Petrovich as devil and as father figure, the important personage as another authority figure, and the overcoat as both wife and mother. These analyses are informed by close attention to detail and to the language of the text, consistently attentive to questions of reader response, and constantly driven by the desire to establish why *this story* has been told in *this way*.

The 'humane passages'

Particular critical attention has been paid to what have come to be known as the story's 'humane passages'. The first of them is related very near the beginning of the tale. The narrator tells us how Akakii Akakievich's colleagues make fun of him, and of his refusal to react. 'Only if the joke was too unbearable, when they jogged his arm and stopped him getting on with his work, would he say: "Leave me alone, why are you offending me?"' (3: 143). These are the very first words Akakii Akakievich speaks in the story. Both the words themselves, and the tone in which they were spoken, somehow inspired pity (*zhalost'*), and one young man, recently employed but already participating in the mockery, stopped as if pierced through and from then on his whole life changed. The words continued to ring in his ears, but in them reverberated other words, 'I am your brother' (*ia brat tvoi*); and the young man would cover his eyes, convulsed by the realisation that even those who seemed to be worldly, noble and honest could conceal so much violent coarseness.[45]

The young man is not the only person to feel pity for Akakii Akakievich. The director who offers him more challenging work (3: 144), the director who gives him a larger than expected bonus (3: 155), the landlady (3: 162), the person who suggests he go to see the important personage (3: 163), and the important personage himself (3: 171) are all similarly motivated. So, too, is the narrator, in the passage considered earlier which follows on from his report of Akakii Akakievich's death and burial, and which is identified as the second humane passage (3: 169); but immediately after establishing that the young clerk hears the words 'I am your brother', the narrator slily provides Akakii Akakievich with another 'brother', a 'young functionary' (*ego zhe brat, molodoi chinovnik*), walking down the street with a cunning smirk on his face (3: 145).

Neither of the humane passages was included in the original story, which adopted a far more mocking attitude to its clerk hero. This led Rozanov to contend (as discussed in Part One) that Gogol incorporated the 'I am your brother' passage in expiation for what he had done. For Judith Mills it is the *narrator* who 'fears...punishment' for his tendency to cynicism and guiltily inserts his humane passage. For Mills, neither humane passage is 'the result of deeply felt emotion' and therefore they remain unconvincing and senti-mental (Mills: 1109, 1111). For Rancour-Laferriere these 'compensatory reaction formations' against our true feelings for the hero are shared by both the narrator and the reader. 'Our pity is no less real for this. It is just revealed for the initial sadistic impulse that it is' (Rancour-Laferriere: 195).

For Eikhenbaum, on the other hand, there can be absolutely no question of looking for ethical motivation for what is simply an artistic device, motivated by a desire to create a tonal contrast and turn the comic into the grotesque (see Part One). This reading has been profoundly influential, particularly in Western criticism: Setchkarev insists that 'to confuse a com-positionally determined utterance with the contents of the poet's soul is inadmissible from the standpoint of aesthetics, and it shifts the value judg-ment to a level alien to aesthetics' (Setchkarev: 222); for Erlich the 'vastly overquoted "humanitarian passage"' is there to provide contrapuntal tension and interpreting it in any other way is 'to clutch at straws' (Erlich 151-2). For O'Toole what he calls the lyrical digressions 'are not different in kind from the other digressions in *The Overcoat*,' but are rather 'on a par with the other gambits Gogol uses to amuse and distract his readers'; and the 'stylistic mannerisms' which they deploy are not very different from those used elsewhere (O'Toole: 23).

Nevertheless, not all of Eikhenbaum's readers have been persuaded by his interpretations of the motivation for the humane passages. Writing in 1928, P.N. Medvedev insisted that the normal readerly interpretation of the passages in question was a socio-ethical one and described the elision of the ethical dimension as misguided (see Part One). Referring to the line 'I am your brother', Chizhevsky concedes that 'Gogol himself could not have failed to see that none of his readers would have accepted such a brother', but this leads him to the conclusion that the story must contain a deeper 'fundamental idea' and to the religious interpretation discussed earlier

(Chizhevskii 1976: 393). Driessen considers that 'Eikhenbaum's main fault is that he...robs the story of all of its content' (Driessen: 200). He pays particular attention to the rhetoric of the second humane passage which, he feels, has hitherto attracted insufficient attention, and considers that it resolves any doubts left by the first passage about the 'real pity' requested for Akakii Akakievich (ibid., 209). Barratt, in turn, accuses Driessen of careless inattention to context, reminding him that the second passage is preceded by a description of Akakii Akakievich's death that includes such colloquial phrases as 'he gave up the ghost' (*ispustil dukh*) and 'they carted him off' (*svezli*, Barratt 1979: 7-8, citing 3: 168-9). Iurii Lotman also insists on attention to style and to context in a broader philosophical sense:

> It is not by chance that where Gogol consciously presents the
> reader with the truth (for example in the famous words 'I am
> your brother!') these passages seem to fall out of the general
> style of the text. According to Gogol's convictions, man is indeed
> the brother of another man, and this lofty truth comprises the
> humanistic basis both of Christianity and of Gogol's social
> utopianism. But no one believes in this truth, no one is guided
> by it in practical life. The truth for Gogol is always only a
> potential possibility [*potentsial'naia vozmozhnost'*], a pro-
> found basis of life which is just as real as is the Christian
> morality on which life is supported. But it is realised through
> non-realisation.   (Lotman 1996: 30-1)

Thus the range of interpretations of the 'humane passages' reflects, in microcosm, the variety of interpretations of the text as a whole.

The ending

The story gained its epilogue during Gogol's fourth and final period of work on the text in Rome in the spring of 1841. The narrator himself describes it as an unexpectedly 'fantastic ending' (*fantasticheskoe okonchanie*) to events (3: 169), but also as 'the fantastic direction of a nevertheless completely true story' (3: 170). Though it consists of a single paragraph it occupies five pages of text and itself contains several plot developments. First it describes the activities of a 'dead man in the form of a functionary' (*mertvets v vide chinovnika*) who steals overcoats and who is identified by one of the depart- mental clerks as Akakii Akakievich. It then tells of a failed attempt to apprehend 'the dead man...alive or dead' (3: 170). This is followed by the revelation of the important personage's belated remorse; of his going to a party; of the shock of the loss of his overcoat; and of the changes in his subsequent behaviour. At this point the 'functionary-dead man' 'ceased to appear' and the narrator infers that the important personage's overcoat 'must have been just the right size for him' (*prishlas' emu sovershenno po plecham*, literally absolutely suited his shoulders, 3: 173. We recall that when he brought the new overcoat Petrovich had 'thrown it very deftly over Akakii Akakievich's shoulders', 3: 156). There are no further coat-thefts. Yet even this is not the end of the story, since 'many active and thoughtful people' continued to insist that they had seen the 'functionary-dead man' and a policeman saw a ghost (*prividenie*, 3: 173) appear from behind a house. But the ghost, 'which was, however, much taller and wore an absolutely enormous moustache', in the story's final words, 'disappeared completely in the nocturnal darkness' (3: 174).

The ending has been identified by several critics as of crucial importance to the meaning of the entire tale. They note that it is shot through with doublings and reversals of events in the main story, ranging from a general plot similarity involving the loss of an overcoat and its consequences, to specifics of character, behaviour and language (Dilaktorskaia 1986: 169-73; Vetlovskaia 1988: 67-8). Barratt provides a diagram comparing the '"surface" structure' and the '"deep" structure' of the 'realistic' and the 'fantastic' plots, both of which he considers to be inherently paradoxical (Barratt 1979: 12). Dilaktorskaia suggests that the 'fantastic' elements begin far earlier in the story (Dilaktorskaia 1986: 173), and Nilsson points out that it is only in the 'fantastic' epilogue that there is topographical specificity with the mention of the Kalinkin Bridge (3: 169, 170), Kiriushkin Alley (3: 170), Kolomna (3: 173) and the Obukhov Bridge (3: 174) (Nilsson 1975: 8-9).

We also note several detailed point of connection. The thieves who steal Akakii Akakievich's overcoat are moustachioed and raise a huge fist to him (3: 161); while the dead 'Akakii Akakievich' threatens with a single finger (3: 170), the moustachioed ghost of the ending also raises an enormous fist, which leads Vladimir Nabokov to identify him as the very man who stole Akakii Akakievich's overcoat (Nabokov 1961: 148). In life Akakii Akakievich 'appeared' (*iavilsia*, the word is used twice on 3: 165) to the important personage 'at the most inappropriate time, most inopportunely for himself, although by the way opportunely for the important personage', who can thus impress his childhood friend (3: 165). The 'appearance' of Akakii Akakievich in the epilogue is a direct reversal of this. The narrator's suggestion that Akakii Akakievich's several days of noisy life after his death are a sort of reward (*nagradu*, 3: 169) for his unnoticed life echoes the bonus (*nagrazhdenie*, 3: 153) that he gets for his unnoticed work in the department (3: 153) and raises the fundamental question of the 'purpose' of the epilogue, in which Akakii Akakievich turns the fact that he is 'unnoticed' to his own advantage. The narrator also tells us that the important personage 'in real terms was almost the reason for the fantastic turn' of events (3: 170).

This has led several critics to view the ending as Akakii Akakievich's post-humous 'vengeance'. For Innokentii Annensky, the reader shares Akakii Akakievich's sense of injustice from the first page; we 'read and feel offence' (*obidu*), and these feelings must have an outlet. The important personage must be made to sense his wrongness.

> But if Gogol had punished him seriously, we would have a boring, moralising fairy tale. If he had forced him to change it would have come out as a lie. But if he hadn't given him a smack, we would have left the book with a feeling of dissatisfaction.   (Annenskii 1979: 215)

Thus the appearance of the fantastic has a '*punitive* character' in the story (ibid., 216). Felix Oinas compares the Akakii Akakievich of the epilogue to Aristophanes's clothes-snatching Orestes in *The Birds* (Oinas: 30), and for Murray Baumgarten too he 'is given what amounts to a Homeric situation' (Baumgarten: 196). Shklovsky refers to the story's 'somehow fairy-tale, folkloric-prophetic resolution' (Shklovskii 1970: 20), but for Meletinsky this is ironically intended:

> If in the popular fairy-tale the hero who 'arouses no hopes' and is often insulted is compensated by a real transfer into a higher social status (and at the basis of this, of course, there lies a fantasy of compensation), then...in the famous 'Overcoat' the fantastic epilogue is...an illusory compensation for a real social tragedy in ordinary life.   (Meletinskii: 82)

Krivonos, too, finds fairy-tale motifs in the ending in which Akakii Akakievich is re-born from the world of the dead as a parodic saviour and deliverer. His thefts of overcoats are like the thefts of things he needs by the hero of the magic tale (*volshebnaia skazka*), but this, too, is rendered with ironic and problematic uncertainty, and his problematic relationship to the world of the living and the dead (*zhivogo ili mertvogo*, 3: 170) gives him the features of a werewolf (Krivonos 1996a: 52).

Several other critics wonder whether the ending is serious or parodic. Victor Peppard provides a useful survey of earlier interpretations and examines the ending's double encoding in the fantastic and the mundane, which 'gives the reader both a fantastic tale and its parodic denial' (Peppard: 73). For Erlich, Akakii Akakievich's posthumous activities show him still in thrall to 'petty passion' and serve as 'additional posthumous proof of his human inadequacy rather than a belated vindication of his essential humanity' (Erlich: 149, 150). Charles Proffitt insists that there is no fantastic ending and no ghost, merely a play upon the reader's conventional expectations (Proffitt: 37).

For Bernheimer: 'The "fantastic ending" of "The Overcoat" triumphantly asserts literature's independence from the repressive forces of reality and gleefully demonstrates its freedom to play with the realms of matter and

spirit, life and death.' He notes the crafty slide from the word dead man to
the word ghost, and insists that: 'The nonconclusion of the story denies any
notion of factuality and leaves the reader afloat in a fluid world of shifting
metamorphoses' (Bernheimer: 59). For Vaiskopf, 'the plot of "The Overcoat" sinks into fiction', a fiction explained by the fact that 'the "Petersburg" of "The Overcoat" is totally assembled in Gogol's mind, "in the
head" of Gogol' (Vaiskopf 1978: 50). Certainly the figure who disappears
into the nocturnal murk seems to take the story with him, 'resolving itself in
laughter' (Eikhenbaum 1969: 326), and for Priscilla Meyer this 'anticlimax
shows the open-ended potential ascent heavenwards or descent to the bottom
among the moustachioed thugs of the pseudospirit world' (Meyer: 72).

What the ending also does is to write Akakii Akakievich out of the tale. In
life it was his destiny to disappear ('And Petersburg was left without Akakii
Akakievich, as if he had never been in it'), and to be replaced in the last sentence of the main text by someone who was 'much taller' (*gorazdo vyshe
rostom*, 3: 169); in death he again disappears ('from that time the appearance
of the functionary-dead man completely ceased', 3: 173), and is again replaced
by someone who was 'much taller' (*gorazdo vyshe rostom*, 3: 174), this time
in the last sentence of the entire story. It would seem open to question whether
this fateful repetition can really be construed as vengeance.

Language and meaning

Words have exaggerated power in 'The Overcoat'. Petrovich uses words to
'kill off' the old overcoat, and the important personage uses words to annihi-
late Akakii Akakievich; they both then luxuriate in the effects (*effekt*) these
words have had (3: 151, 167). Akakii Akakievich says 'Leave me alone, why
are you offending me?' (3: 143) and a young man's life is changed forever.
A thief says 'the Overcoat is mine' and it is (3: 161); a dead man says 'give
me yours' and he gets it (3: 172-3); a 'ghost' says 'what do you want?' and
a sentry runs off in fright (3: 174).

For many critics from Eikhenbaum onwards the centre of the story's
gravity lies in its extraordinarily inventive use of language, and the valuable
insights gained from their close attention to Gogol's play with various
stylistic layers, from bureaucratese to folk speech, and to his repetitions of
seemingly meaningless filler words have been incorporated throughout this
study. O'Toole has recently tabulated the various occurences of hyperbole,
qualification, anticlimax, incongruity and puns (O'Toole: 31-3); and in a
particularly useful article, Woodward notes Gogol's 'aversion to unquali-
fied designation' and offers aggregates for the number of times the various
words and phrases used to destroy precision, words such as 'but' (*no, a*),
'however' (*odnako, vprochem*), 'although' (*khotia*), 'not without' (*ne bez*),
'some' (*kakoi-to, kakoi-nibud'*), 'somehow' (*kak-to, kak-nibud'*), 'as if'
(*kak-budto, tochno*) occur in the text (Woodward: 1967).

In this world of words, in which the hero has favourite letters which can be read on his face (3: 144), the narrator's verbal preferences are also apparent. His preoccupation with naming (*nazyvat'*) and his plays on the word to mean (*znachit'*, *znachitel'nyi*) have been discussed earlier, and they extend into a concern with knowing (*znat'*), recognizing (*uznat'*) and understanding (*ponimat'*). When Akakii Akakievich goes to the party he 'simply did not know(*on, prosto, ne znal*) what to do, where to put his arms and legs and all his figure' (3: 160). After telling his woes to the police inspector he leaves not knowing (*ne znaia*) whether the man will help him (3: 163). The important personage, whose rhetorical questions to his inferiors include 'do you know (*znaete*) who you are talking to?' and 'do you understand (*ponimaete*) who is standing in front of you?' (3: 165), asks Akakii Akakievich 'don't you know (*ne znaete*) the form?', 'don't you know (*ne znaete*) how things are done?' (3: 166), finally working himself into an interrogative frenzy: 'do you know (*znaete*) who you are saying this to?, do you understand (*ponimaete*) who is standing in front of you? do you understand it? do you understand it? I'm asking you' (3: 167). In his final delirium Akakii Akakievich speaks nonsense (*bessmyslitsu*), so you cannot understand (*poniat'*) a thing, though you could see (*videt'*) that it was all concerned with the overcoat (3: 168). The policemen who catch the sneezing dead man 'did not even know' (*znali*) if they had ever had him in their hands (3: 170).

There is also a constant stress on looking and seeing, expressed through the use of the words *videt'*, *smotret'*, *gliadet'*, *zamechat'*, the adverb *vidno*, the noun *vid* and the words *glaza* (eyes) and *litso* (face).

Akakii Akakievich's fate is decided by the powerful gaze of two of the characters he encounters. Petrovich, though described as a 'one-eyed devil' (3: 149), who repeatedly has to screw up his only eye (3: 149, 150, 153) looks carefully over (*obsmotrel*) the old coat, 'from the collar to the sleeves, the back, the skirts and the buttonholes' and then lays it out on the table and looks it over (*rassmatrival*) again at length (3: 150) before confirming that it will have to be replaced, whereupon he 'takes a sidelong glance' (*pogliadet' iskosa*, 3: 151) to see the effect of his words. When he brings the new overcoat he also looks at it (*posmotrel*, 3: 156) with pride; he repeats this action at length out in the street (*smotrel*), and then rushes through a side alley to look at it again, this time straight in the face (*posmotret'... priamo v litso*, 3: 157). The important personage, too, has a terrifying gaze, with which he looks (*smotrel*) very meaningfully (*znachitel'no*) into the face (*v litso*) of those to whom he is speaking as he repeats the words 'severity, severity and severity,' even though there is actually no reason for doing so since as soon as his inferiors see (*zavidia*) him from a distance they drop everything and stand to attention (3: 164). When he sees Akakii Akakievich's meek air (*uvidevshi smirennyi vid*, 3: 166) he starts to berate him, and then 'takes a sidelong glance' (*iskosa vzglianul*, 3: 167, which links him directly with Petrovich, 3: 151 and with the replacement clerk, 3: 169) at his acquaintance to learn how he looks (*smotrit*) at this performance; he is happy to see (*uvidel*) that it has had the desired effect.

Elsewhere, however, the 'natural' epistemological significance of seeing is consistently called into question. Akakii Akakievich seems to be particularly bad at seeing, and at being seen, or good at seeing things wrongly. He has always been seen (*videli*) in the same place since 'clearly' (*vidno*) he was born there; he 'does not look' (*ne gliadia*) at who is giving him papers to work on (3: 143). In his copying he sees (*videlsia*) his own varied and pleasant world (3: 144). He has never in his life paid attention to anything that happens in the street, though 'his brother, the young functionary', will always look (*posmotrit*), and do so with such a penetrating glance (*vzgliada*) that he will notice (*zametit*) even if the ankle strap has come off someone's trousers; if he does look (*gliadel*) at anything, he sees (*videl*) only his writing, and only if he is breathed over by a horse will he notice (*zamechal*) that he is not in the middle of a line but in the middle of the street (3: 145). 'No one could say that they had ever seen him [*videl*] at some party' (3: 146). When he 'sees what's up' (*uvidevshi v chem delo*, 3: 147), he takes his old coat to Petrovich, under whose wife's cap the guardsmen glance (*zagliadyvali*) but are disappointed (3: 148). There is so much smoke in the kitchen that you could not see (*videt'*) even the cockroaches (3: 148). When Petrovich pronounces the word 'new', a mist comes over Akakii Akakievich's eyes (*zatumanilo v glazakh*) and he 'saw clearly' (*videl iasno*) only the general on the tobacco tin (3: 151). Back out on the street he again fails to notice (*ne zametil*) the people who barge into him, but this eventually forces him to 'look around' (*oglianut'sia*) and when he gets home he 'saw his position in a clear and real way' (*uvidel v iasnom i nastoiashchem vide*, 3: 152). He now 'sees' (*uvidel*) that he cannot do without a new overcoat (3: 153).

He has never yet seen (*nikogda eshche ne vidal*) an expression as meaningful (*znachitel'noe*) as the one on Petrovich's face when he brings the overcoat, but then Petrovich begins to 'throw dust' into his eyes by mentioning the 'powerful' (*sil'nykh*) sums he might have charged (3: 156). When he is wearing the new coat, Akakii Akakievich again does not notice where he is going (*dorogi on ne primetil*), and he suddenly ends up in the department, where he looks over (*osmotrel*) the coat before entrusting it to the porter. Everyone gathers round to look at it (*smotret'*, 3: 157), an action that will be repeated at the party (*vnov' osmotreli*, 3: 159). Sitting at home that evening he looks (*vzglianul*) at the old overcoat and even laughs (3: 158). On the way to the party he looks (*gliadel*) at everything he sees as at something new (3: 158), and pauses to look (*posmotret'*, 3: 159) at the painting of a woman; at the party itself he 'looked' (*smotrel*) at the card game, and 'looked (*zasmatrival*) this person and that in the face', but he soon becomes bored and decides to leave. He sees (*uvidel*) his coat lying on the floor (3: 160).

On his way home the lights become fewer – clearly (*vidno*) there is less oil being supplied – so that he can hardly see (*edva vidnymi*) the houses on the other side of a square which looks(*gliadela*) like a terrible desert. Akakii Akakievich looks back and around (*oglianulsia nazad i po storonam*). He decides it is better not to look at all (*luchshe i ne gliadet'*) and covers (*zakryv*) his eyes. When he opens them he sees (*uvidel*) people with moustaches, but cannot work out (*razlichit'*) who they are, so, once again, exactly as when he heard Petrovich's death sentence on the *old* overcoat, a mist comes over his eyes (*zatumanilo v glazakh*, 3: 161). This is the beginning of the end for Akakii Akakievich, and his eventual death is accompanied by 'visions' (*iavleniia*), in which he sees (*videl*) Petrovich and the important personage (3: 168). Only in death does he see clearly (Oh, there you are at last!, 3: 172).

An inability to see clearly also affects those who might help to find the overcoat. After the theft the policeman on duty looks (*gliadel*, 3: 161) to see 'who the devil' is running towards him: Akakii Akakievich accuses the man of 'not looking, not seeing' (*ne smotrit, ne vidit*), to which the affronted policeman replies that 'he did not see' (*ne vidal*) a thing, that he saw (*videl*) him stopped by two acquaintances. His landlady, 'seeing him in a such a way' (*uvidia v takom vide*) wrings her hands and recommends going to the police inspector, whom she sees (*vidit*) on Sundays and who is evidently (*vidno*) a good man (3: 162). Akakii Akakievich, repeatedly told by the inspector's clerks that he is unavailable, says that he must see (*videt'*) him and threatens to complain about them 'and then they will see' (*uvidiat*, 3: 163); but when he does see the inspector, 'instead of paying attention to the main point' he accuses him of visiting a disorderly house. Nor does Akakii Akakievich's death improve matters. One of his former colleagues insists that he has 'seen with his own eyes' (*videl svoimi glazami*) the 'dead man in the form [*v vide*] of a functionary', and recognised (*uznal*) him as Akakii Akakievich, but adds that he was unable to look at him (*rassmotret'*) properly and saw (*videl*) only his threatening finger (3: 170). Later the dead man sneezes into the eyes of three policemen, and by the time they can see again there is no longer any trace of him (3: 170). And finally, a Kolomna policeman 'saw with his own eyes' (*videl sobstvennymi glazami*) a ghost emerging from behind a building (3: 173), but alas, as he tracked it it looked around (*oglianulos'*) and threatened him (3: 174), before disappearing into the dark.

So the story seems shot through with a concern with naming and meaning, with knowing and understanding, with looking and seeing, but a concern that is constantly thwarted and undermined. The meaning of this frustrated search for meaning has been variously interpreted. For some readers it is a manifestation of Gogol's concern with 'eternal questions', with what Chizhevsky calls 'the problem of man's "own place"' (Chizhevskii 1976: 387). For Peace the entire tale is 'the strange story of the search for content through façade' (Peace 1976: 89); but in the view of Waszink:

> *Learning* and *knowing* are processes which may disturb the
> established order.... The author [whom I have called the
> narrator, J.G.] himself warns us that we should not try to
> know too much.... And indeed – every act of learning in the
> story seems to be punished.   (Waszink: 295)

'The Overcoat' as literary performance

In the view of Cathy Popkin, Gogol's hypertrophic attention to language
turns Akakii Akakievich himself into 'really little more than a verbal arti-
fact.... Even his death throes are linguistic' (Popkin: 199). For Bernheimer,
'Akakii actually becomes a text, a text, however, that can be deciphered not
as a series of significant signs, but only as a succession of discrete letters'
(Bernheimer: 56). A similar position is taken by Stephen Moeller-Sally,
who considers that Akakii Akakievich:

> ...emblematizes the perils of a subjectivity that is invested
> entirely in writing. What begins as a vocation ends in a solip-
> sism so complete that it erases not only the world but the
> writer.... Perhaps the most significant detail in this regard is
> Akaky Akakievich's failure to do so little as change first-
> person forms in a text to the third-person. It speaks of a
> textually grounded identity so all-encompassing as to pre-
> vent the possibility of improvising a new self.
>   (Moeller-Sally: 345)

If Akakii Akakievich is only a textual performance by his author, then it
becomes exceedingly difficult to decide what 'The Overcoat' is 'about'.
Fanger refers to its 'crucial uncertainty of tone' (Fanger 1967: 123), while
Victor Brombert is just one of many critics to conclude that:

> The hard fact is that Gogol is a protean writer whose simul-
> taneity of possible meanings allows for no respite and no
> comfortable univocal message...Gogol delighted in verbal acts
> as a game – a game that implied the autonomy of narrative
> style, a declaration of artistic independence, and a thorough
> deflation of *l'esprit du sérieux*.   (Brombert: 53)

For Bakhtin, the carnivalised collective of the story is 'removed by popular
laughter from "real", "serious", "proper" [*dolzhnoi*] life. There is no point
of view of seriousness to contrast with the laughter. Laughter is "the only
positive hero"' (Bakhtin 1975: 494). This leads Bakhtin on to a discussion
of Gogol's grotesque as 'not simply the violation of the norm, but the denial

of all abstract, immovable norms which aspire to absolute and eternal value' (ibid., 495). Following Eikhenbaum, several other critics also seek to explain Gogol's intentions in the story by the invocation of the term grotesque. For Erlich this is manifested in the text's deployment of incongruity both on a verbal and on a moral level, which leads to the projection of 'a freakish, distorted moral universe in which the normal proportions are drastically reversed' (Erlich: 155-6). Sherry quotes Christoph Wieland's definition of the grotesque as 'complete detachment from reality', but insists that in 'The Overcoat' 'the grotesque has an ontological origin. It is in the perception of the real as unreal, of the true as false, that the grotesque originates for Gogol.' He considers that the grotesque in the story reveals 'a world ruled by whimsicality' and that it is this ontological grotesque that lies beneath the stylistic grotesque analysed by Eikhenbaum (Sherry: 25-7).[46]

Cathy Popkin has written eloquently about the consequent frustration experienced in the process of reading the text:

> The elaborate discourse not only presents a formidable obstacle to 'getting on with the story'; much of it bears no palpable story material at all. 'The Overcoat' exemplifies the problem of reading Gogol for the plot; effusive and overwhelming in the ways we have come to expect from Gogol, it both presents a problem and represents it as a matter of content. The story of 'The Overcoat' along with anything else it pretends to encompass, is the problem of its own discourse.
>
> Gogol's best-known story exhibits all the familiar characteristics – the extraneous detail, the hyperbolic specificity, the accretion and enumeration of things and attributes, the reduplicative language, the fulsome digression, the convulsive syntax.... But the reader is teased into regarding all this verbal profusion as potentially content-bearing by the introduction of themes of genuine significance – poverty, bureaucracy, the inequality of rank, 'man's' proverbial inhumanity to man, and so on...
>
> As readers, we want there to be something behind all these words – a man behind the name, a story behind the discourse – thus the temptation to embrace the thematic 'content.' But our own quest for significance – for something substantial and important – is closely re-enacted in Akakii Akakievich's ill-fated quest for a coat. In his seeking and losing the 'thread,' the meaning and the reason to go on, we recognise our own vain pursuit of sense, significance, and substance. Like the reader, Akakii Akakievich longs for good material (*inventio*) that is well crafted (*dispositio, elocutio*). But as the dismantling of Akakii Akakievich reveals, there is nothing solid to hold onto.   (Popkin: 198-9)

So, for Popkin, 'The story of "The Overcoat" is about its own discourse because it depicts a vain quest for substance in a world of proliferating text' (ibid., 203); and the travails of Akakii Akakievich involve more than the loss of a coat:

> Akakii Akakievich embodies virtually every aspect of the discursive act. He is like the text, both in his wandering and in his essentially verbal constitution. He is like the reader in his insistent need for something besides words. And he is a lot like the author [whom I refer to as the narrator, J.G.] in his copying, his indefatigable reproduction of words with no things attached. He resembles Gogol, too, in his proliferation of words with no direction.   (ibid)

Thus many of Gogol's most sophisticated readers insist that the 'subject' and 'meaning' of the story should be sought only in the pleasure afforded by its own creation and performance.

Reception

Over one hundred and sixty years, 'The Overcoat' has provoked an enormous range of mutually contradictory readings. Some find it motivated by pity for a suffering innocent, while for others it is a heroic indulgence in verbal play in a world bereft of significance. Each group of readers characterises other readers as driven by bias, as finding in the text what they themselves have felt the need to put there. Objectors to the hagiographical reading insist that Akakii Akakievich is not a mediaeval monk; objectors to the psychoanalytical reading that he is not a patient in analysis; objectors to the suggestion that it is all a game cannot accept that the story has no purpose. It is difficult not to agree with Brombert, who spoke of a 'simultaneity of possible meanings' (Brombert: 53) that both do and do not cancel each other out, or with Fanger, who, described the story as a kaleidoscope, and continued:

> The metaphor is only approximate, but to the extent that it is valid it may suggest why those who claim that 'The Overcoat' is *not* about Christian charity and arbitrary authority, meekness and pride, poverty and comfort, justice, bureaucracy, city life, even literature itself – why such readers are as mistaken as those who assert that it *is* about these things. Respecting the peculiar mode of its being, it would be more accurate to say that the story is ultimately about significance and insignificance as such, in literature, no less than in life.
> (Fanger 1979: 162-3)

How you read this elusive but voluminous tale would seem to depend upon who you are and what you wish to find in it. This has been borne out by the broad range of tones deployed in the dozens of re-workings, re-imaginings and appropriations that it has spawned. If this is so, then it will certainly not have surprised its author, who has already programmed a kaleidoscope of reactions to the story of 'poor' Akakii Akakievich, and to 'story' in general into his text. A police inspector in an unknown town reads a romantic work in which another police inspector gets drunk and writes to complain that 'state decrees are perishing' (3: 141). A young man hears Akakii Akakievich's cry and it changes his life (3: 143-4). Petrovich, on the other hand, unmoved by his childlike pleas, insists with 'barbarian calm' that he will have to buy a new coat (3: 151). Told of the theft by Akakii Akakievich a policeman on duty says he didn't see a thing (3: 162). When he tells his landlady what has happened (*rasskazal on, v chem delo*), however, she clasps her hands in dismay and begins to offer advice (3: 162). He tells the same story (*rasskaz*) to a police inspector, who reacts 'somehow extremely strangely' (*kak-to chrezvychaino stranno*), misses the main point (*glavnyi punkt*) and asks why he was out so late at night (3: 163). Though some of his colleagues use the loss of the coat as another reason to mock him, the story (*povestvovanie*) touches (*tronulo*) many; they decide to make a collection, but collect so little that it does not help (3: 163). A certain someone, moved by sympathy (*dvizhimyi sostradaniem*), tells him to go straight to the important personage (3: 163). The important personage hears about the theft and haughtily asks him if he knows the procedures (3: 166). Learning later of Akakii Akakievich's death he feels pangs of conscience (*upreki sovesti*) and is briefly out of sorts, but soon recovers (3: 171). All these responses to Akakii Akakievich make fleeting and generally ineffective appearances, and their instability is echoed in the variety of tones adopted by the narrator himself. So the range, motivation and efficacy of potential reader reactions to the story is already predicted and rehearsed within it.

One of Gogol's most attentive readers, Evgenii Zamiatin, once wrote:

> There are books of the same chemical composition as dyna-
> mite. The only difference is that one piece of dynamite [*odin
> kusok dinamita*] explodes once, but one book [*odna kniga*]
> explodes a thousand times.   (Zamiatin, S, 4: 298)

What better proof can be offered of the aptness of Zamiatin's metaphor than the history of the reception of one such book (*odnoi takoi knigi*), Nikolai Gogol's 'The Overcoat'?

Notes to Part Two

1. There are useful discussions of the evolution of the tale in Rozanov, 'Kak proizoshel tip Akakiia Akakievicha' and in Harper: 175-6. For the crucial changes in Gogol's spiritual outlook during these years, see Smirnova: 144 and de Lotto: 60.

2. For a psychological interpretation of the changes Gogol made to the anecdote, see Ermakov 1999: 245. There is a useful discussion of the problem of subtexts and derivations in Rancour-Laferriere: note 57, pp. 231-2.

3. There is a large critical literature on the relationship of 'The Overcoat' to the poor clerk tale: see especially PSS 3: 688-9; Nilsson 1982; Gippius: 107-10; Peuranen: 123-5. Vaiskopf 1993: 305-14 gives a wide-ranging survey of parallels in Russian and Western European literature. See Vinogradov 1976b, and the discussion of it in Part 1 of this study, for the Gogolian synthesis of the comic and the sentimental.

4. For discussion of the links between 'The Overcoat' and *The Bronze Horseman* see especially Fridman; and Alissandratos: 34, 36.

5. For an overview of the relationship between the two writers, see also Fanger 1967 and Fanger 1972.

6. For a comparison between 'The Overcoat' and a later English-language poor clerk tale, Melville's 'Bartleby the Scrivener', written in the early 1850s, see Hyde.

7. On St John Climacus, see Attwater: 199-200. *Klimax* is the Greek word for ladder. The work appeared in English under the title *The Ladder of Divine Ascent*.

8. See Pavlinov: 60 for Gogol's reverence for the martyrs of Lake Sevan.

9. For religious readings of the story based upon its use of hagiographical material, see p. 105-6 above.

10. For an overview of the use of the *lestnitsa* image in Gogol's writings, see Graffy 2000, pp. 246-7.

11. For a detailed study of the suffusion of the Petersburg Tales with demonic forces, see Graffy 2000.

12. This motif is repeatedly used in Gogol's writings. For sources of popular belief about the devil, see especially Vinogradova and Novichkova, pp. 393-443. For the application of these beliefs in Gogol's writings, see Graffy 2000.

13. The key words here are *chistyi* (clean) and *chernyi* (black). The word *nechist'* is a collective noun meaning evil spirits.

14. This motif is of course also present in 'The Nose', in which the nose is first discovered in a loaf of bread, then encountered walking around St Petersburg in uniform and getting into a carriage and preparing to leave for Riga, before being restored to its rightful place. The attempt by the commentators in N.V. Gogol', *Sobranie sochinenii v 9 tomakh*, volume 3-4 (Russkaia kniga: Moscow, 1994), p. 500, to explain the episode with Petrovich's handkerchief by the suggestion that nineteenth-century handkerchiefs were 'of a considerable size' would seem to be vitiated by the following phrase in Gogol's story...unless nineteenth-century pockets were 'of a considerable size' too....

15. On this idea, see Dilaktorskaia 1986: 153-5.

16. This is exactly the plot of Gogol's earlier story 'Old World Landowners'; see Graffy 1989. On the consequences of the intrusion of time and contingency into 'The Overcoat', see especially Waszink; Bailey: 17; Fanger 1979: 158 ff.

17. According to Toporov, in 1837 only 30% of the inhabitants of Petersburg were women, which led to the enormous percentage of unmarried men in the lower and middle ranks. (Toporov 1984: p. 21, note 24).

18. On the mythopoetic designation of the city as harlot (*bludnitsa*), see Toporov 1987. On imagery of the harlot in 'The Overcoat', see Krivonos 1997.

19. These four paragraphs make up well over half of the text. Translators do not usually have the confidence to replicate this.

20. The device of describing him through negatives will continue throughout the tale. See, for example, 3: 143, 144, 169.

21. His fellow Petersburg bachelor, Piskarev, does go to a ball in a carriage, in 'Nevsky Prospect' (3: 23), but it all turns out to be a dream.

22. For Dostoevsky's later reworking of the Cinderella story in his tale 'Dvoinik' ('The Double'), see Diment.

23. In an earlier draft the mother exclaims 'Such names – and there are no such people' (3: 452), reminding us that Gogol was also at work at this time on *Dead Souls*.

24. For Ermakov, all the rejected names have appropriately demeaning connotations. (Ermakov 1999: 260) See Dilaktorskaia 1986: 168 and Peuranen: 128 for semantic interpretation of these names. For de Lotto: 63-4, on the other hand, the semantics of the rejected names precisely suggests their irrelevance.

25. This sound instrumentation continues on the next page and is by no means the only such passage in the story. As noted in Part One, the pun is surely being extended by Eikhenbaum in the very title of his article '*Kak sdelana Shinel'*', which might be retranslated as '"*Kak!*"'. The Overcoat is Made.'

26. In a draft version of his poem 'The Lay of the Exploits of Gogol' (1943-44) Kruchenykh turns Akakii Akakievich into 'Kakak Kakakievich' (Kruchenykh 1999: 449).

27. On Akakii Akakievich as a child, see, for example, Vetlovskaia 1988: 51-2, and Rancour-Laferriere, passim.

28. Ermakov compares the painting to the one seen by a 'distinguished colonel' in 'The Nose', in which a girl is adjusting her stocking and being observed by a bearded dandy.' (Ermakov 1976: 184 . The source is 3: 72). The multiple layers of voyeurism in these episodes – the reader watches Gogol watching the narrator watching the protagonist watching the figure in the picture watching the woman – are perhaps worthy of note.

29. It also has social implications, since higher ranking civil servants were allowed to wear different collars. (Dilaktorskaia 1989: 29)

30. Vaiskopf 1978: 41, in his useful analysis of Petrovich's demonic qualities, notes that there is only one mention of the devil outside of the Petrovich episode. This occurs when, after the theft, the policeman on duty wonders 'why the devil' Akakii Akakievich is running towards him (3: 161) and is therefore also directly linked to the overcoat itself.

31. On the foreignness of demons and their hatred of the Orthodox, see Novichkova: 605 and Graffy 2000: 252-3

32. On Vetlovskaia's comparison of the 'pretender' Akakii Akakievich to Grishka Otrepev, see above, p. 65-6.

33. In the initial draft, 'The Tale of the Clerk Who Stole Overcoats', the name change had been from *Petr* to Petrovich (3: 449). On other demonic Peters in the *Petersburg Tales*. see Graffy 2000: 253. For a detailed interpretation of the implications of the names Petr and Petrovich and their links to Peter the Great, see also Woodward 1982: 102-03.

34. Rancour-Laferriere's extended analysis of the demonic features of Petrovich is contained mainly on pp. 58-86, 165-77. The examination of him as an ambiguous father figure is on pp. 173-7.

35. For Alexis E. Emerson-Topornin the four 'o's in this phrase are the devils ovals (Emerson-Topornin: 40-6), and he notes that Gogol used the soubriquet OOOO for a work published at the beginning of 1831. For an absorbing reading of this soubriquet, see Moeller-Sally.

36. Shapiro finds the topos repeated in the story of the titular councillor who partitions off a tiny area scarcely big enough for a writing desk as his 'reception room' (Shapiro: 134, see 3: 164).

37. Both Vaiskopf 1978: 49-50 and O'Toole: 26 offer tables of some of the parallels between the two experiences.

38. See, for example, de Lotto: 82. Some critics, however, insist that he does reform. Barratt speaks of his fatalistic attitude to the loss of his overcoat, which he 'himself...threw off' (3: 173) as 'the first essential stage in the transformation of his character. This transformation, unlike the change in Akaky Akakievich's behaviour, signifies a true "resurrection"' (Barratt 1979: 21).

39. We note that in the words of Podkolesin, the hero of Gogol's play 'Marriage', 'a black tail-coat is somehow more solid. Coloured ones are more suitable for secretaries, and titular and other small fry – there's something of the milksop in them' (PSS 5: 10).

40. On the social and symbolic significance of clothing see, for example, Wissemann: 91-2, Tosi: 604.

41. McFarlin includes tables of 'the contemporary office pyramid' (p. 238); of the relationship of rank to salary (p. 242); and of the Table of Ranks itself, p. 253. The Table of Ranks can also be consulted in Nikolai Gogol, *Plays and Petersburg Tales,* translated by Christopher English (Oxford University Press: Oxford and New York, 1995) p. xli.

42. As Vetlovskaia points out, in the first, censored version of the text, this phrase read: 'as it falls on the heads of the powerful of this world!' (Vetlovskaia 1988: 43, citing 3: 549).

43. For a comparison with Pushkin's *The Bronze Horseman* and for the more explicit allusion to rank in the drafts of this passage, see above, pp. 66-7.

44. E.A. Smirnova offers a detailed survey of Gogol's spiritual activities of the period, and this leads her to suggest a slightly later date for some of Gogol's changes to the original manuscript (Smirnova: 139-44).

45. The reaction of the young man has been likened by Rolf-Dietrich Keil to the Damascene revelation of St Paul. (Cited from Vaiskopf 1993: 228).

46. There is a very useful discussion of varying definitions of the 'slippery word', grotesque, in Rancour-Laferriere: 31-4.

Annotated Bibliography

Primary sources

Key editions in Russian

Nikolai Gogol', *Polnoe sobranie sochinenii,* ed. N.L. Meshcheriakov and others (14 volumes, Izdatel'stvo Akademii nauk SSSR: Moscow and Leningrad, 1937-52, volume 3, 'Povesti', 1938). [Text, pp. 139-74; 'Drugie redaktsii', pp. 446-61; 'Varianty', pp. 521-49; 'Kommentarii', pp. 675-90.]

———*Peterburgskie povesti*, with notes by O.G. Dilaktorskaia, *Literaturnye pamiatniki* (Nauka: St Petersburg, 1995). [Text, pp. 88-109; 'Drugie redaktsii i varianty', pp. 194-203; O.G. Dilaktorskaia, 'Khudozhest-vennyi mir peterburgskikh povestei N.V. Gogolia', pp. 207-57: the discussion of 'The Overcoat', pp. 238-48, is based on her 1986 study, see below; 'Primechaniia', pp. 285-9.]

N.V. Gogol, *Shinel'/The Overcoat*, James Forsyth (ed.) (Bristol Classcial Press: London, 1991).

Editions in English

Nikolai Gogol, *Plays and Petersburg Tales*, translated by Christopher English (Oxford University Press: Oxford and New York, 1995). Text pp. 115-45, notes pp. 345-7.

The Complete Tales of Nikolai Gogol, edited and introduced by Leonard J. Kent, translations by Constance Garnett revised by Leonard J. Kent (University of Chicago Press: Chicago, 1964, reprinted 1985) two volumes, Text in volume 2, pp. 304-34.

Nikolai Gogol, *The Diary of a Madman and other stories*, translated by Ronald Wilks (Penguin: Harmondsworth, 1972 etc.). Text pp. 71-108.

Secondary sources

This section includes both studies of 'The Overcoat' and other works used in the text. Where there are extended discussions of 'The Overcoat' in sections of books or in articles in journals they are provided with brief annotations.

[Afanas'ev, A.N.,] *Narodnye russkie skazki A.N. Afanas'eva v trekh tomakh*, ed. L.G. Barag and N.V. Novikov (Nauka: Moscow, 1984-5).

Aizlewood, R., 'Towards an interpretation of Daniil Kharms's Sluchai', in N. Cornwell (ed.) *Daniil Kharms and the Poetics of the Absurd* (Macmillan: London, 1991) pp. 97-123.

Aksenov, V., 'Tri shineli i nos', *Kinostsenarii*, 1995, 1, pp. 137-49.

Alissandratos, J., 'Filling in some holes in Gogol''s not wholly unholy "Over-coat"', *Slavonic and East European Review*, 68, 1990, 1, pp. 22-40 [In 'The Overcoat' Gogol subverts and parodies several features of the encomiastic narrative pattern of Russian Saints' Lives. In so doing he offers a critique both of the hagiographic tradition and its cultural values and of contemporary bureaucratic values.]

Annenkov, P.V., *Literaturnye vospominaniia* (Gosudarstvennoe izdatel'stvo khudozhestvennoi literatury: Moscow, 1960). [For the clerk and rifle anecdote, see pp. 76-7.]

Annenskii, I., 'O formakh fantasticheskogo u Gogolia', first in *Russkaia shkola*, 1890, 10, pp. 93-104; **quoted from** his *Knigi otrazhenii* (Nauka: Moscow, 1979) pp. 207-16.

——'Khudozhestvennyi idealizm Gogolia', first in *Russkaia shkola*, 1902, 2, pp. 114-25; **quoted from** his *Knigi otrazhenii* (Nauka: Moscow, 1979) pp. 216-25.

Attwater, D., *The Penguin Dictionary of Saints* (Penguin: Harmondsworth, 1965).

Bailey, J., 'Some remarks about the structure of Gogol''s "Overcoat"', in J.T. Baer and N.W. Ingham (eds), *Mnemozina: Studia litteraria russica in honorem Vsevolod Setchkarev* (Fink: Munich, 1974) pp. 13-22. [A discussion of the structure of the tale, in particular the role of contrast and opposition, and of its language, stressing the use of key words.]

Bakhtin, M., *Problemy tvorchestva Dostoevskogo* (Priboi: Leningrad, 1929; revised and reprinted as *Problemy poetiki Dostoevskogo*, Sovetskii pisatel': Moscow, 1963; third edition, Khudozhestvennaia literatura: Moscow, 1972). In English as *Problems of Dostoevsky's Poetics*, edited and translated by Caryl Emerson (University of Minnesota Press: Minneapolis and Manchester University Press: Manchester, 1984). Quoted from 1972.

——'Rable i Gogol'' (Iskusstvo slova i narodnaia smekhovaia kul'tura)' [1940/1970], **quoted from** his *Voprosy literatury i estetiki* (Khudozhestvennnaia literatura: Moscow, 1975) pp. 484-95.

——'K pererabotke knigi o Dostoevskom' [1961], first published in *Kontekst-1976*, Moscow, 1977, pp. 296-316; **quoted from** his *Estetika slovesnogo tvorchestva* (Iskusstvo: Moscow, 1979) pp. 308-27.

—— 'Iz zapisei 1970-71 godov', in his *Estetika slovesnogo tvorchestva* (Iskusstvo: Moscow, 1979) pp. 336-60.

——'Slovo v romane' [1934-35], reprinted in his *Voprosy literatury i estetiki*,

Moscow, 1975, pp. 72-233; translated in *The Dialogic Imagination. Four Essays by M.M. Bakhtin*, edited by Michael Holquist, translated by Caryl Emerson and Michael Holquist (University of Texas Press: Austin, Texas and London, 1981) pp. 255-422, **from which quoted.**

Barratt, A., 'Plot as paradox. The case of Gogol's *Shinel'*', *New Zealand Slavonic Journal*, 1979, 2, pp. 1-24. [Both the first plot of 'The Overcoat', that of Akakii Akakievich, and the second, fantastic plot are seen as paradoxical, their surface meaning contradicted by their deeper meaning. The two plots are connected and combined by the central motif of the overcoat, its theft and contrasting reactions to that theft.]

——*Yurii Olesha's Envy*, 'Birmingham Slavonic Monographs', 12 (Department of Russian Language and Literature, University of Birmingham: Birmingham, 1981).

Baumgarten, M., 'Gogol's *The Overcoat* as a picaresque epic', *Dalhousie Review*, 46, 1966, pp. 186-99. [On the relationship of the picaresque world and epic ideas in the story.]

Belinskii, V., *Polnoe sobranie sochinenii*, 13 volumes (Izdatel'stvo Akademii nauk: Moscow, 1953-59).

Belyi, A., 'Gogol'', first in *Vesy*, 1909, 4, pp. 69-83; reprinted in his *Lug zelenyi*, Moscow, 1910, pp. 93-121; and in his *Simvolizm kak miroponimanie* (Respublika: Moscow, 1994) pp. 361-71; translated in *Russian Literature Triquarterly*, 4, 1972, pp. 131-43, and, in an amended translation, in Victor Erlich (ed.), *Twentieth-Century Russian Literary Criticism* (Yale University Press: New Haven and London, 1975) pp. 33-50. **Quoted from 1994.**

——*Masterstvo Gogolia* (Gosudarstvennoe izdatel'stvo khudozhestvennoi literatury: Moscow-Leningrad, 1934; reprinted, Fink: Munich, 1969; Ardis: Ann Arbor, Michigan, 1982). **Quoted from 1982.**

——'Neponiatyi Gogol'', *Sovetskoe iskusstvo*, 20 January 1933; reprinted in *Voprosy filosofii*, 1990, 11, pp. 94-9.

Bem, A.L., '"Shinel'" i "Bednye liudi"', in A.L. Bem (ed.), *O Dostoevskom*, 3 (Petropolis: Prague, 1936) pp. 127-38. [One can talk of the influence of 'The Overcoat' on Dostoevsky's *Poor Folk*, but it is an 'influence of rejection'. Close parallels of style, plot and composition are noted, but Dostoevsky's polemical attitude is always apparent. His hero, Makar Devushkin, speaks of writing a formal protest against the cruelty of 'The Overcoat'. *Poor Folk* is that protest.]

Berdiaev, N., 'Dukhi russkoi revoliutsii', first in *Russkaia mysl'*, May-June 1918; reprinted in *Iz glubiny. Sbornik statei o russkoi revoliutsii*, Moscow-Petrograd, 1918; and in *Novyi zhurnal*, 79, 1965, pp. 211-52; **quoted from** *Literaturnaia ucheba*, 1990, 2, pp. 123-40, introd, pp. 119-23.

Bernheimer, C., 'Cloaking the self: the literary space of Gogol''s "Overcoat"', *Publications of the Modern Language Association of America*,

90, 1975, 1, pp. 53-61. [Gogol's extremely secretive personality is expressed through the narrative technique of this story which dissolves all traces of an authorial voice. Akakii Akakievich, who originally has no identity, gains it, but this makes him vulnerable and leads to his demise. The fantastic ending is the triumphal reassertion of literature's independence from life.]

Berliner, G.O., 'Chernyshevskii i Gogol'', in Gippius 1970, pp. 472-533.

Bocharov, S., 'Pushkin i Gogol': ("Stantsionnyi smotritel'" i "Shinel'")', in N.L. Stepanov and U.R. Focht (eds) *Problemy tipologii russkogo realizma* (Nauka: Moscow, 1969) pp. 210-40. [Dostoevsky's Makar Devushkin reacts very differently to his reading of Pushkin's 'The Station Master' and 'The Overcoat'. On the basis of a detailed analysis of their narrative method, the differences between the two stories are exposed.]

Bocharov, S. and Mann, Iu., '"Vse my vyshli iz gogolevskoi 'Shineli'"', *Voprosy literatury*, 1968, 6, pp. 183-5. [A response to Reiser, 1968, below. De Vogüé in fact reiterated and developed the words in his speech at the Gogol centenary celebrations of 1909. He always used the words in the context of Dostoevsky, which is very close to ascribing them to him.]

Boiadzhiev, G., '"Shinel'" v Parizhe', *Literaturnaia gazeta*, 31 March 1959, p. 3.

Briusov, V., 'Rech' V.Ia. Briusova', *Gogolevskie dni v Moskve* (Obshchestvo liubitelei slovesnosti: Moscow, 1909) pp. 157-80; reprinted as 'Ispepelennyi', *Vesy*, 1909, 4, pp. 100-20; in English as 'Burnt to Ashes' in Maguire 1976, pp. 103-31.

Brombert, V., 'Meanings and indeterminacy in Gogol's *The Overcoat*' in A. Toumayan (ed.) *Literary Generations: a Festschrift in Honor of Edward D. Sullivan by his Friends, Colleagues and Former Students* (French Forum: Lexington, Kentucky, 1992) pp. 48-54. [On the multiplicity of simultaneous and conflicting readings the text provokes.]

Brown, C., 'The not quite realised transit of Gogol' in J.T. Baer and N.W. Ingham (eds), *Mnemozina: Studia litteraria russica in honorem Vsevolod Setchkarev* (Fink: Munich, 1974) pp. 41-5.

Bryner, C., 'Gogol's *The Overcoat* in World literature', *Slavonic and East European Review*, 32, 1954, no. 79, pp. 499-509. [On the representation of 'The Overcoat' in English-language anthologies, and the usually erroneous interpretations of it in guides to world literature up to the middle of the twentieth century.]

Bulgakov, M., *Sobranie sochinenii v piati tomakh* (Khudozhestvennaia literatura: Moscow, 1989-90).

Bunin, I., 'Zhilet Pana Mikhol'skogo', *Poslednie novosti*, Paris, No. 3945, 10 January 1932; reprinted in his *Sobranie sochinenii v deviati tomakh* (Khudozhestvennaia literatura: Moscow, 1965-67) volume 7, 1966, pp. 288-91, **from which quoted.**

128 Gogol's *The Overcoat*

Chekhov, A. P., *Polnoe sobranie sochinenii i pisem v tridtsati tomakh* (Nauka: Moscow, 1974-83).

Chernevich, M.N., 'Gogol' i gogolevskie obrazy v sochineniiakh V.I. Lenina (ukazatel')' in Gippius 1970, pp. 573-91.

Chernyshevskii, N., 'Ne nachalo li peremeny?' [1861] in his *Literaturnaia kritika v dvukh tomakh* (Khudozhestvennaia literatura: Moscow, 1981, volume 2, pp. 212-55, notes pp. 317-22.

Chizevskii [Tschizewskij], D., 'Zur Komposition von Gogols "Mantel"', *Zeitschrift für Slavische Philologie*, 14, 1937, pp. 63-94; reprinted, with additions, in Busch, U., Gerigk, H.-J., Hock, E. and Chizhevskii, D., *Gogol - Turgenev - Dostoevskij - Tolstoj, ed. D. Tschizewskij*, *Forum Slavicum*, 12 (Fink: Munich, 1966) pp. 100-26; this version appeared in English as 'The composition of Gogol's "Overcoat"', in *Russian Literature Triquarterly*, 14, 1976, pp. 378-401; and in Trahan, pp. 37-60. The piece was first published in Russian in an amended version not approved by Chizhevsky as 'O "Shineli" Gogolia', *Sovremennye zapiski*, Paris, 67, 1938, pp. 172-95; this version appeared in English as 'About Gogol's "Overcoat"', in Maguire 1976, pp. 293-322; and as 'On Gogol's "The Overcoat"' in Meyer and Rudy, pp. 137-60. [The word 'even' (*dazhe*) is used 73 times in the story, and clusters of it occur at crucial passages. Study of its use reveals much about Gogol's intentions: it is used to indicate oral narration, for humour, but also to indicate the poverty of the moral universe of the protagonists and to bring the reader closer to the hero's sensibility. Gogol was not motivated by social concern but by the philosophical problem of 'man's place'. Akakii Akakievich's enthusiasm for the overcoat is a demonic temptation.] **Quoted from the *Russian Literature Triquarterly*, 1976 translation.**

Chudakova, M.O., 'Bulgakov i Gogol'', *Russkaia rech'*, 1979, 2, pp. 38-48; 3, pp. 55-9.

——'M.A. Bulgakov - chitatel'', *Kniga*, 40, 1980, pp. 164-85.

——'Gogol' i Bulgakov', in V.V. Kozhinov, E.I. Osetrov and P.G. Palamar-chuk (eds) *Gogol': istoriia i sovremennost'* (Sovetskaia Rossiia: Moscow, 1985) pp. 360-88.

Clyman, T.W., 'The hidden demons in Gogol''s Overcoat', *Russian Literature*, 7, 1979, 6, pp. 601-10 [Expanding upon the work of Chizhevsky and others on demonic elements in the story, this piece finds them to be concentrated around the figure of Petrovich, around the number four (*chetyre*) and in the bad winter weather.]

Collins, C., *Evgenij Zamjatin. An Interpretive Study* (Mouton: The Hague and Paris, 1973).

Connolly, J., 'Boris Vakhtin's "The Sheepskin Coat" and Nikolai Gogol's "The Overcoat"' in J. Connolly and S. Ketchian (eds) *Studies in Russian Literature in Honor of Vsevolod Setchkarev* (Slavica:

Columbus, Ohio, 1987) pp. 74-86. [A detailed comparison of style, plot and themes. Vakhtin is found to be much more concerned with specific satirising of contemporary life, and his text has a more positive ending.]

Cuddon, J.A., *The Penguin Dictionary of Literary Terms and Literary Theory*, third edition (Penguin: Harmondsworth, 1992).

Danilevskii, A.A., 'Mutato nomine de te fabula narratur', *Blokovskii sbornik*, 7, *Uchenye zapiski Tartuskogo gosudarstvennogo universiteta*, 735, Tartu, 1986, pp. 137-49.

Danilov, S.S., 'Gogol' v instsenirovkakh' in Gippius 1970, pp. 423-72.

Debreczeny, P., *Nikolay Gogol and his contemporary critics, Transactions of the American Philosophical Society*, 56, No. 3 (The American Philosophical Society: Philadelphia, 1966). [For contemporary reactions to 'The Overcoat', see pp. 9, 29, 36, 37.]

de Lotto, C., 'Lestvitsa "Shineli"', *Voprosy filosofii*, 1993, 8, pp. 58-83. [At the time of writing 'The Overcoat' Gogol was embarking upon a period of sustained spiritual reading. In particular the *Lestvitsa* (Heavenly Ladder) of St John Climacus and the Rule of monastic life of Nil Sorskii are shown to be reflected in enormous detail in the story of Akakii Akakievich and his temptation by the Overcoat. This is the most sustained and persuasive of the readings of the religious influences on the story.]

Dickens, C., *Sketches by Boz Illustrative of Every-day Life and Every-day People* (first published in 1833-36; repr. Oxford University Press: London, New York and Toronto, 1957) **quoted from this edition.**

Dilaktorskaia, O.G., *Fantasticheskoe v "Peterburgskikh povestiakh" N.V. Gogolia* (Izdatel'stvo Dal'nevostochnogo universiteta: Vladivostok, 1986. [On 'The Overcoat', see pp. 142-78, and notes pp. 199-205. The fantastic informs the entire story, not just the epilogue. It is examined here through the treatment of the imagery of the overcoat itself, the cold and time; through an analysis of the links of the tale with the Lives of the Saints; and through a discussion of the epilogue.]

——'Chto znachit "kunitsa" v "Shineli" N.V. Gogolia?', *Russkaia rech'*, 1989, 2, pp. 29-31. [A collar lined with marten (*kunitsa*) has not only implications of social advancement for Akakii Akakievich, but also erotic ones, since in folk rituals and songs the *kunitsa* is also the bride.]

——'Khudozhestvennyi mir peterburgskikh povestei N.V. Gogolia', in Gogol', N. *Peterburgskie povesti*, with notes by O.G. Dilaktorskaia, *Literaturnye pamiatniki* (Nauka: St Petersburg, 1995) pp. 207-57.

——'Gogolevskaia tema v "Dvoinike"', in her *Peterburg-skaia povest' Dostoevskogo* (Dmitrii Bulanin: St Petersburg, 1999) pp. 186-203.

Diment, G., 'Goliadkin as Cinderella, or the case of the lost galosh', *Russian Review*, 56, 1997, 3, pp. 440-4.

Dolotova, L., 'Dostoevskii ili Turgenev?', *Voprosy literatury*, 1972, 11, pp. 186-92. [A response to the Reiser/Bocharov and Mann polemic. Dostoevsky is psychologically extremely unlikely to have used these words. The case for Turgenev saying them is reiterated.]

Dostoevskii, F., *Polnoe sobranie sochinenii v tridtsati tomakh* (Nauka: Leningrad, 1972-90).

Driessen, F.C., 'The Overcoat', in his *Gogol as a Short-Story Writer. A study of his technique of composition* (Mouton: Paris, The Hague, London, 1965) pp. 182-214. [The first half of this piece assesses previous studies, especially the work of Rozanov, Bem, Eikhenbaum and Chizhevsky. The second half offers Driessen's own reading, which stresses the role of the ending, which is closely linked to all the rest of the tale, and the symbolic significance of the overcoat itself. This is also the first study to invoke the Life of St Acacius, but Driessen makes little of his discovery.]

Egeberg, E., 'Filantropicheskoe i eroticheskoe v *Shineli* Gogolia', *Scandoslavica*, 34, 1988, pp. 29-40. [An attempt to relate the erotic implications and the 'humane passages' of the tale, and a reiteration that all readings must be tentative and incomplete.]

Eikhenbaum, B., 'Illiuziia skaza', *Knizhnyi ugol*, 1918, 2, pp. 10-13; reprinted in his *Skvoz' literaturu. Sbornik statei* (Academia: Leningrad, 1924) pp. 152-6 (itself reprinted, Mouton: The Hague, 1962); translated as 'The illusion of *skaz*', *Russian Literature Triquarterly*, 12, 1975, pp. 233-6. **Quoted from 1924.**

——'Kak sdelana "Shinel'"', in *Poetika. Sborniki po teorii poeticheskogo iazyka* (18 Gosudarstvennaia tipografiia: Petrograd, 1919) pp. 151-65; reprinted as 'Kak sdelana "Shinel'" Gogolia', in his *Skvoz' literaturu. Sbornik statei* (Academia: Leningrad, 1924) pp. 171-95 (itself reprinted, Mouton: The Hague, 1962); in his *Literatura. Teoriia. Kritika. Polemika* (Priboi: Leningrad, 1927) pp. 149-65; his *O proze* (Khudozhestvennaia literatura: Leningrad, 1969) pp. 306-26; his *O proze. O poezii* (Khudozhestvennaia literatura: Leningrad, 1986) pp. 45-63; In English as 'How Gogol's "Overcoat" is made', *Russian Review*, 20, 1963, 4, pp. 377-99; in Maguire 1976, pp. 267-91; in Meyer and Rudy, pp. 119-35; and in Trahan, pp. 21-36. [Crucial to the composition of a novella is the role of the personal authorial tone. At the basis of a Gogolian text is *skaz*, a stylised oral narration. In 'The Overcoat' puns of various kinds are of major importance, including puns in the names of the hero. There is no neutral level of language, merely the performance of a variety of tones, the comic and the sentimental-melodramatic. The famous 'humane passage' is merely an artistic device – the mix of tones creates the grotesque. The fantastic ending is another artistic device of the same order. The grotesque style of the whole work makes it possible for Gogol to play with reality in his own newly constructed world. Critics who have thought otherwise are naïve.] **Quotations in the text translated from the 1969 edition.**

Emerson-Topornin, A.E., 'Sinel. The devil's ovals. Motif of the doubles', *Forum at Iowa on Russian Literature*, 1, 1976, 1, pp. 34-56. [The demonic elements in the tale, particularly those associated with Petrovich, are traced. There follows a suggestion that Akakii Akakievich and the Important Personage represents the two sides of Gogol's split personality.]

Epshtein, M., 'Kniaz' Myshkin i Akakii Bashmachkin (k obrazu perepischika)', in his *Paradoksy novizny. O literaturnom razvitii XIX-XX vekov* (Sovetskii pisatel': Moscow, 1988) pp. 65-80. [First as 'O znachenii detali v strukture obraza ("Perepischiki" u Gogolia i Dostoevskogo)', *Voprosy literatury*, 1984, 12, pp. 134-45. A comparison of Bashmachkin and Myshkin as copyists, and as contrasting variants of the hero of a Saint's Life. On Dostoevsky's move from Bashmachkin via the heroes of *Poor Folk* and 'A Faint Heart' to a new kind of hero in Myshkin.]

Epstein Matveyev, R., 'Textuality and intertextuality in Dostoevsky's *Poor Folk*', *Slavic and East European Journal*, 39, 1995, 4, pp. 535-51.

Erlich, V., 'The pitfalls of petty passions', in his *Gogol* (Yale University Press: New Haven and London, 1969) pp. 142-57. [The myopic humanitarian critics are probably motivated by the urgency of their own emotional needs and ideological compulsions. The meaning of 'The Overcoat' lies in the style and the narrative play. The whole tale should be read as an example of the grotesque.]

Ermakov, I.D., 'Nos' [1922], first in his *Ocherki po analizu tvorchestva N.V. Gogolia* (Gosudarstvennoe izdatel'stvo: Moscow-Petrograd, 1924); reprinted in his *Psikhoanaliz literatury. Pushkin. Gogol'. Dostoevskii* (Novoe literaturnoe obozrenie: Moscow, 1999) pp. 262-95; translated as Ivan Yermakov, 'The Nose' in Maguire 1976, pp. 155-98, **from which quoted.**

————'Shinel' Gogolia kak organicheskoe tseloe', [1922], first in his *Ocherki po analizu tvorchestva N.V. Gogolia* (Gosudarstvennoe izdatel'stvo: Moscow-Petrograd, 1924); **quoted from** his *Psikhoanaliz literatury. Pushkin. Gogol'. Dostoevskii* (Novoe literaturnoe obozrenie: Moscow, 1999) pp. 241-61. [Gogol's literary works are personal confessions. He uses the *skaz* form to combine confession and concealment. Despite this contention, which is much repeated, the actual study of 'The Overcoat' here is dull and conventional. Ermakov's main psychological contention is that all sexual desire is punished in the story.]

Erofeev, V., 'Rozanov protiv Gogolia', *Voprosy literatury*, 1987, 8, pp. 146-75; reprinted in his *V labirinte prokliatykh voprosov* (Sovetskii pisatel': Moscow, 1990) pp. 102-37.

Evdokimov, O.V., 'Kto zhe "voshel" v gogolevskuiu "Shinel'"?', *Nachalo. Zhurnal Instituta bogosloviia i filosofii*, 2, St Petersburg, 1995, 2. [I have not been able to trace this source, which compares Akakii Akakievich to the nineteenth-century Kievan Holy Fool (*iurodivyi*) Ivan Grigorevich Bosoi, but it is illuminatingly discussed in Vet-lovskaia, 1999, pp. 29-31.]

Even-Zohar, I., 'The tailor Petrovic pronounces the verdict of Akakij. A note on a stylised scene and a pragmatic connective', *Slavica Hierosolimi-tana*, 3, 1978, pp. 1-7. [On the stylistic and narrative purposes of the use of the words 'da' and 'net' in the key scene of the story in which Petrovich announces that Akakii Akakievich must buy a new overcoat.]

Fanger, D., *Dostoevsky and Romantic Realism* (Harvard University Press: Cambridge, Massachusetts, 1967).

———'Dickens and Gogol: energies of the word' in H. Levin (ed.) *Veins of Humor* (Harvard University Press: Cambridge, Massachusetts, 1972) pp. 131-45.

———*The Creation of Nikolai Gogol* (Harvard University Press: Cambridge, Massachusetts, 1979). [On 'The Overcoat' pp. 153-63. Central to the effect of the tale is the elusive and shifting narrative performance, which makes it impossible to find a single basis for judgement. All assertions are blurred by qualification, even the changes to Akakii Akakievich can be read either positively or negatively. The role of the reader is highlighted since the tale contains a multiplicity of potential 'meanings' and is ultimately about significance and insig-nificance as such.]

Fridman, N.V., 'Vliianie "Mednogo vsadnika" Pushkina v "Shineli" Go-golia', in K.V. Pigarev (ed.) *Iskusstvo slova. Sbornik statei k 80-letiiu chlena-korrespondenta AN SSSR Dmitriia Dmitrievicha Blagogo* (Nauka: Moscow, 1973) pp. 170-6. [Both works tell the story of a poor clerk, who loses his dream and plunges into madness and rebellion against men of power. Both contain fantastic scenes. The case is made for the direct influence of Pushkin's work on 'The Overcoat'.]

Fusso, S. and Meyer, P. (eds), *Essays on Gogol. Logos and the Russian Word* (Northwestern University Press: Evanston, Illinois, 1992).

Gertsen, A.I., *Byloe i dumy*, 3 volumes (Khudozhestvennaia literatura: Moscow, 1967).

Gippius, V., *Gogol'*, Leningrad, 1924; translated by Robert A. Maguire (Ardis: Ann Arbor, Michigan, 1981; repr. Duke University Press: Durham, North Carolina, 1989). **Quoted from 1981.**

Gippius, V. (ed.), *N.V. Gogol'. Materialy i issledovaniia*, [2 volumes] *Literaturnyi arkhiv* (Izdatel'stvo Akademii nauk SSSR: Moscow and Leningrad, 1936; volume 2 reprinted, Brücken: Düsseldorf and Europe-Printing: Vaduz, 1970). **Quoted from 1970.**

Gogolevskie dni v Moskve (Obshchestvo liubitelei slovesnosti: Moscow, 1909).

Goncharov, I.A., 'Luchshe pozdno, chem nikogda (Kriticheskie zametki)' [1879], in his *Sobranie sochinenii v vos'mi tomakh* (Gosudarstvennoe izdatel'stvo khudozhestvennoi literatury: Moscow, 1952-55) vol. 8, 1955, pp. 64-114.

Graffy, J., 'Passion versus habit in Old World Landowners' in J. Grayson and F. Wigzell (eds), *Nikolay Gogol: Text and Context* (Macmillan: London, 1989) pp. 34-49.

———'Zamyatin's "Friendship" with Gogol', *Scottish Slavonic Review*, 14, 1990, pp. 139-80.

———'The Devil is in the Detail: Demonic Features of Gogol's Petersburg' in Pamela Davidson (ed.), *Russian Literature and its Demons* (Berghahn: New York and Oxford, 2000) pp. 241-77.

Grigor'ev, A., 'Russkaia literatura v 1851 godu', first in *Moskvitianin*, 1852, Nos 1-4, **quoted from** his *Sobranie sochinenii* (Kushnerev: Moscow), volume 9, 1916, pp. 1-51.

———'Gogol' i ego posledniaia kniga', first in *Moskovskii gorodskoi listok*, 1847, Nos 56, 62, 63 and 64, **quoted from** Kantor and Ospovat, pp. 106-25.

———'Vzgliad na russkuiu literaturu so smerti Pushkina. Stat'ia pervaia. Pushkin. Griboedov. Gogol'. Lermontov', first in *Russkoe slovo*, 1859, Nos 2-3, **quoted from** his *Sochineniia v dvukh tomakh* (Khudozhestvennaia literatura: Moscow, 1990) volume 2, pp. 48-124.

Gukovskii, G., *Realizm Gogolia* (Gosudarstvennoe izdatel'stvo khudozhestvennoi literatury, Moscow and Leningrad, 1959).

Harper K., 'Dickens and Gogol's "Sinel'"', in W.E. Harkins (ed.), *American Contributions to the Sixth International Congress of Slavists, Prague, 1968, August 7-13*, vol. 2, *Literary Contributions* (Mouton: The Hague and Paris, 1968) pp. 165-80. [Gogol is said in Buslaev's memoir to have been reading Dickens in Rome in 1840. He had a wide knowledge of Western European culture and languages. It is not known what Dickens he may have read, but two 'Sketches by Boz' were translated into Russian in 1839, and parallels are drawn between them and 'The Overcoat'.]

Hippisley, A., 'Gogol's "The Overcoat": a further interpretation', *Slavic and East European Journal*, 20, 1976, 2, pp. 121-29. [Following on from Schillinger's article, this piece examines Gogol's religious views of around 1840 and uses biblical references to clothing to suggest that 'the new overcoat symbolises Christ himself', though it then concedes that it may also be a Satanic delusion.]

Holquist, J.M., 'The devil in mufti: the *Märchenwelt* in Gogol's short stories', *Publications of the Modern Language Association of America*, 82, 1967, 5, pp. 352-62.

Hyde, G., 'Melville's *Bartleby* and Gogol's *The Overcoat*', *Essays in Poetics*,

1, 1976, 1, pp. 32-47. [Both writers try to deliver their clerk heroes from an ideological illusion. Gogol, through his anarchic *skaz* narration, creates an atmosphere of liberty and carnival. For Melville ideological and narrative hierarchies are inescapable.]

Ivanov, V., 'Dostoevskii i roman-tragediia', first in *Russkaia mysl'*, May-June 1911; reprinted in his *Borozdy i mezhi* (Moscow, 1916, repr. Bradda: Letchworth, 1971) pp. 3-60. **Quoted from 1971 edition.**

Jackson, R.L., 'Two views of Gogol and the critical synthesis. Belinskij, Rozanov and Dostoevskij . An essay in literary-historical criticism', *Russian Literature*, 15, 1984, 2, pp. 223-42; reprinted as 'Unbearable questions. Two views of Gogol and the critical synthesis', in his *Dialogues with Dostoevsky. The Overwhelming Questions* (Stanford University Press: Stanford, 1993) pp. 188-207, 324-25, **from which quoted**. [A comparison of the readings of Gogol and 'The Overcoat' of Belinsky and Rozanov, and of the sophisticated interpretation offered by Dostoevsky in *Poor Folk*.]

Kantor, V.K. and Ospovat, A.L. (eds), *Russkaia estetika i kritika 40-50-kh godov XIX veka* (Iskusstvo: Moscow, 1982).

Karlinsky, S., *The Sexual Labyrinth of Nikolai Gogol* (Harvard University Press: Cambridge, Massachusetts, 1976; repr. University of Chicago Press: Chicago, 1992). [On 'The Overcoat', pp. 135-44. The tale is a love story. It addresses two key Gogolian themes: the lethal nature of love, which particularly involves the punishment of heterosexual males; and the destructive nature of change. It also engages pioneeringly with the theme of urban alienation.]

Katarskii, I., 'Gogol' i Dikkens', in his *Dikkens v Rossii. Seredina XIX veka* (Nauka: Moscow, 1966) pp. 67-78.

Kaverin. V., 'Zametki o dramaturgii Bulgakova', in Bulgakov, M., *Dramy i komedii* (Iskusstvo: Moscow, 1965) pp. 5-15.

Keldysh, V., 'Na rubezhe khudozhestvennykh epokh (O russkoi literature kontsa XIX-nachala XX veka)', *Voprosy literatury*, 1993, 2, pp. 92-105.

[Kharms, D.,] 'Dnevnikovye zapisi Daniila Kharmsa', published by A. Ustinov and A. Kobrinskii, *Minuvshee*, 11, 1991, pp. 417-583.

Kharms, D., *Polnoe sobranie sochinenii* (Akademicheskii proekt: St Petersburg, 1997).

Kireev, R., 'Vechnyi tituliarnyi sovetnik', *Znamia*, 1992, 11, pp. 234-9. [An overview of readings of the story by nineteenth-century Russian writers, especially Dostoevsky.]

Knudsen, B., 'Illusion and Reality. Nikolaj Gogol's *Overcoat* in a literary critical perspective', *Scandoslavica*, 41, 1995, pp. 41-53. [A brief discussion of Eikhenbaum's 'Kak sdelana shinel' Gogolia' followed by a detailed reponse to the formal and ideological/religious postulates informing Chizhevsky's work on the story.]

Kozintsev, G., 'The Cloak' [1966] in I. Christie and J. Gillett (eds), *Futurism. Formalism. Feks. Eccentrism and Soviet Cinema 1918-1936* (BFI: London, 1978) pp. 24-7.

——Prostranstvo tragedii (Iskusstvo: Leningrad, 1973); reprinted in his *Sobranie sochinenii v piati tomakh* (Iskusstvo: Leningrad, 1982-86) volume 4, 1984, pp. 6-265.

——'Gogoliada', in his *Sobranie sochinenii v piati tomakh* (Iskusstvo: Leningrad, 1982-86) volume 5, 1986, pp. 174-305.

Kreitser, A.V., '"Shinel'" N.V. Gogolia i "Bednye liudi" F.M. Dostoevskogo. Ob odnom paralleli.' in S.A. Goncharov (ed.), *N.V. Gogol': problemy tvorchestva. Mezhvuzovskii sbornik nauchnykh trudov* (Obrazovanie: St Petersburg, 1992) pp. 102-13. [A comparison is made between the visit of Akakii Akaievich to the important personage and that of Makar Devushkin to the general. The Dostoevskian general is much more humane since Gogol's text manifests features of the mediaeval culture of shame and Dostoevsky's those of the modern culture of guilt.]

Krivonos, V. Sh., 'Fol'klorno-mifologicheskie motivy v "Peterburgskikh povestiakh" Gogolia', *Izvestiia RAN. Seriia literatury i iazyka*, 55, 1996, 1, pp. 44-54, **quoted as 1996a.**

——'Infantilizm i infantil'nyi geroi v "Peterburgskikh povestiakh" N.V. Gogolia', *Russian Studies*, 2, 1996, 3, pp. 111-30, **quoted as 1996b.**

——'Shinel'-bludnitsa. (Vokrug "Shineli" Gogolia)', in E.I. Annenkova and V.D. Denisov (eds), *Tvorchestvo N.V. Gogolia: Istoki, poetika, kontekst* (Rossiiskii gosudarstvennyi gidrometeorologicheskii institut, St Petersburg, 1997) pp. 30-5. [Akakii Akakievich, a child-like figure, is seduced by the whorish Overcoat and turns into a profane anti-child with links with the Other World.]

Kruchenykh, A., *Izbrannoe* (Fink: Munich, 1973).

[Kruchenykh, A.,] *Pamiat' teper' mnogoe razvorachivaet: Iz literaturnogo naslediia Kruchenykh*, ed. N. Gur'ianova (Berkeley Slavic Specialties: Berkeley, California, 1999).

Lahti, K. 'Artificiality and nature in Gogol's *Dead Souls*' in Fusso and Meyer, pp. 143-57, 264-7.

Lampl, H. 'Political satire of Remizov and Zamjatin on the pages of *Prostaja gazeta*' in Greta N. Slobin (ed.), *Aleksey Remizov. Approaches to a Protean Writer* (Slavica: Columbus, Ohio, 1987) pp. 245-59.

Linetskii, V., 'Shinel' strukturalizma', *Novoe literaturnoe obozrenie*, 5, 1993, pp. 38-44. [A polemic with the work of Derrida and with Eikhenbaum's interpretation of his own findings in his famous essay. The genre through which to look at 'The Overcoat' is not the anecdote but the exemplum.]

Lotman, Iu., 'Problema khudozhestvennogo prostranstva v proze Gogolia', *Uchenye zapiski Tartuskogo gosudarstvennogo universiteta*, 209,

Trudy po russkoi i slavianskoi filologii, 11, Tartu, 1968, pp. 5-50.

Lotman, Iu.,'O "realizme" Gogolia', *Trudy po russkoi i slavianskoi filologii, Literaturovedenie*, 2 (*Novaia seriia*) Tartu, 1996, pp. 11-35.

McFarlin, H.A., '"The Overcoat" as a civil service episode', *Canadian-American Slavic Studies*, 13, 1979, 3, pp. 235-53. [Akakii Akakievich's rank of Titular Councillor makes him a middle-ranking civil servant. Discussion of the changes in civil service rules in the early nineteenth-century as background to the tale.]

Mackrell. J., 'Stiff competition', *The Independent*, 31 August 1990.

Maguire, R. (ed.), *Gogol from the Twentieth Century. Eleven Essays* (Princeton University Press: Princeton, 1974; corrected edition, 1976).

Maguire, R., 'The legacy of criticism', in Maguire 1976, pp. 3-54.

———'The Formalists on Gogol', in Robert Louis Jackson and Stephen Rudy (eds), *Russian Formalism: A Retrospective Glance. A Festschrift in Honor of Victor Erlich* (Yale Center for International and Area Studies: New Haven, 1985) pp. 213-30.

———*Exploring Gogol* (Stanford University Press: Stanford, California, 1994).

Markov, V., *Russian Futurism* (MacGibbon and Kee: London, 1969).

Medvedev, P.N., *Formal'nyi metod v literaturovedenii. Kriticheskoe vvedenie v sotsiologicheskuiu poetiku* (Priboi: Leningrad, 1928); in English as Medvedev, P.N./Bakhtin, M.M., *The Formal Method in Literary Scholarship. A Critical Introduction to Sociological Poetics*, translated by Albert J. Wehrle (The Johns Hopkins University Press: Baltimore and London, 1978) **from which quoted.**

Mei, L., 'Grivennik', in A.L. Ospovat (ed.), *Proza russkikh poetov XIX veka* (Sovetskaia Rossiia: Moscow, 1982) pp. 264-85.

Meletinskii, E.M., *O literaturnykh arkhetipakh* (Rossiiskii gosudarstvennyi gumanitarnyi universitet: Moscow, 1994).

Merezhkovskii, D.S., 'Gogol' i chert', first Moscow, 1906; translated in Maguire 1976, pp. 55-102.

———'Gogol'. Tvorchestvo, zhizn' i religiia', in his *Polnoe sobranie sochinenii* (Tvorchestvo M.O. Vol'f: St Petersburg and Moscow) vol. 10, 1911, pp. 163-286; reprinted in his *Izbrannye stat'i. Simvolizm, Gogol', Lermontov* (Fink: Munich, 1972) pp. 163-286. **Quoted from 1972.**

Meyer, P., 'False pretenders and the spiritual city: "A May Night" and "The Overcoat"' in Fusso and Meyer, pp. 63-74, 253-4. [A comparison of 'The Overcoat' with Gogol's earlier story 'A May Night' in the context of their treatment of the supernatural and their use of the theme of the 'pretender'.]

Meyer, P. and Rudy, S. (eds), *Dostoevsky and Gogol. Texts and Criticism* (Ardis: Ann Arbor, Michigan, 1979).

Mills, J., 'Gogol's "Overcoat": the Pathetic Passages reconsidered', *Publications of the Modern Language Association of America*, 89, 1974, pp. 1106-11. [The plot of 'The Overcoat' asserts the moral principle that self-assertion is punished. The narrator is aware of this principle and his fear of punishment leads him to 'reverse' his passages of mockery of Akakii by the 'compensatory' pathetic passages. Thus both the plot and the tone are determined by the narrator's personality and the insincerity of the pathetic passages makes them unpersuasive.]

Milne, L., 'Gogol and Mikhail Bulgakov' in J. Grayson and F. Wigzell (eds), *Nikolay Gogol: Text and Context* (Macmillan: London, 1989) pp. 109-26.

Mirsky, D.S., *A History of Russian Literature from its Beginnings to 1900* (Knopf: New York, 1949; reprinted, Vintage: New York, 1958) **from which quoted.**

——*Uncollected Writings on Russian Literature*, edited, with and introduction and bibliography by G.S. Smith (Berkeley Slavic Studies: Berkeley, California, 1989).

Moeller-Sally, S., 'OOOO; or, The sign of the subject in Gogol's Petersburg' in M. Greenleaf and S. Moeller-Sally (eds), *Russian Subjects. Empire, Nation and the Culture of the Golden Age* (Northwestern University Press: Evanston, Illinois, 1998) pp. 325-41, 438-41.

Nabokov, V., 'The apotheosis of a mask', chapter five of his *Nikolai Gogol* (New Directions: Norfolk, Virginia, 1944; revised edition, New York, 1961, pp. 139-50; reprinted Oxford University Press: Oxford, 1985; reprinted as '"The Overcoat" 1842', in his *Lectures on Russian literature*, ed. and introd. Fredson Bowers, Weidenfeld and Nicolson: London, 1982) pp. 54-61. [In 'The Overcoat', the whole world is absurd and futile. The real plot of Gogol's works always lies in the style. Gogol has no ideas, facts or messages.] **Quoted from 1961.**

Nagornaia, N.M., 'Gogolevskie traditsii v proze Chekhova (Preemstvennost' povestvovatel'nykh sistem)' in G.V. Samoilenko (ed.), *Gogol' i sovremennost'. Tvorcheskoe nasledie pisatelia v dvizhenii epokh* (Vishcha shkola: Kiev, 1983) pp. 62-8.

Nechkina, M.V., 'Gogol' u Lenina', in Gippius 1970, pp. 534-72.

Nemzer, A., 'Sovremennyi dialog s Gogolem', *Novyi mir*, 1994, 5, pp. 208-25.

Nikitaev, A., '"Pushkin i Gogol'". Ob istochnike siuzheta', *Literaturnoe obozrenie*, 1994, 9-10, pp. 49-51.

Nikol'skaia, T.L. 'Vtoraia "vtoraia proza"' in W. Weststeijn, D. Rizzzi and T.V. Tsiv'ian (eds), *"Vtoraia proza". Russkaia proza 20-kh – 30-kh godov XX veka, Labirinti. Collana del Dipartimento di Scienze Filologiche e Storiche*, 18 (Università degli Studi di Trento: Trento. 1995) pp. 277-84.

Nilsson, N.Å., 'Gogol''s *The Overcoat* and the topography of Petersburg', *Scandoslavica*, 21, 1975, pp. 5-18. [The main body of the text of 'The Overcoat', unlike Gogol's earlier 'Petersurg Tales', contains no specific names of Petersburg streets, districts and buildings. They are, however, present in the epilogue. An explanation of this is sought in Gogol's parodic attitude to the fashionable sketches of city life.]

Nilsson, N.Å., 'On the origin of Gogol's "Overcoat"' [1954], in Trahan, pp. 61-72. [An examination of possible sources for the story in Russian and European sentimental city sketches and tales of poor clerks.]

Norshtein, Iu., 'Snimal i "Shinel'"', *Ogonek*, 1988, 43, pp. 17-18.

——'Ia prosto sdelal kino...', *Literaturnoe obozrenie*, 1992, 3-4, pp. 90-100.

——'Tainy animatsii, ili Kak delaetsia "Shinel'"', *Kinovedcheskie zapiski*, 41, 1999, pp. 106-25, **quoted as 1999a.**

——'Sneg na trave', *Iskusstvo kino*, 1999, 9, pp. 102-10; 10, pp. 98-109, **quoted as 1999b**

Novichkova, T.A. (ed.), *Russkii demonologicheskii slovar'* (Peterburgskii pisatel': St. Petersburg, 1995).

Odoevskii, V.F., 'Brigadir', first in *Al'manakh Novosel'e*, Part 1, St Petersburg, 1833, pp. 501-17; **quoted from his** *Sochineniia v dvukh tomakh* (Khudozhestvennaia literatura: Moscow, 1981) volume 1, pp. 69-76.

Oinas, F.J., 'Akakij Akakievic's ghost and the hero Orestes', *Slavic and East European Journal*, 20, 1976, 1, pp. 27-33. [Discussion of the fantastic ending, and in particular links to the characterisation of Orestes as 'clothes-snatcher' in Greek popular belief and by Aristophanes, for whom Gogol's admiration is attested.]

O'Toole, L.M., 'Narrative structure. Leskov: *The Man on Sentry Duty*. Gogol. *The Overcoat*', in his *Structure, Style and Interpretation in the Russian Short Story* (Yale University Press: New Haven and London, 1982) pp. 11-36. [The digressions are of fundamental importance to the meaning of the story, downgrading plot, narrative structure and characterisation. The relationship of the important personage with both Petrovich and Akakii Akakievich is crucial and is discussed in detail. Linguistic play is also fundamental to the story and the article looks at hyperbole, qualification, anticlimax, incongruity and puns.]

Pakhlevska, O., 'Evgen Malaniuk: interpretatsiia Gogolia (v kontekste russkoi antigogolevskoi polemiki)', *Russica Romana*, 4, 1997, pp. 91-138.

Pavlinov, S.A., 'Prekrasnaia dusha i absoliutnaia svoboda', in his *Filosofskie pritchi Gogolia. Peterburgskie povesti* (Authorial publication: Moscow, 1997) pp. 59-69. [The story is closely compared with Hegel's ideas in *The Phenomenology of Spirit*.]

Peace, R., 'Gogol and psychological realism: Shinel'' in R. Freeborn, R.R. Milner-Gulland and C.A. Ward (eds), *Russian and Slavic Literature* (Slavica: Columbus, Ohio, 1976) pp. 63-91. [To identify the devices in 'The Overcoat' is not enough, their purpose must be analysed. The character of Akakii Akakievich is examined through the recurrent contrast of facade and content in the story and through the establishment of motifs, such as those of 'wife', 'significance/insignificance', 'alive/dead' through verbal play. Gogol's 'non-rational approach to the portrayal of psychology' influenced later Russian writers.]

Peace, R., *The Enigma of Gogol* (Cambridge University Press: Cambridge, 1981). [On 'The Overcoat', pp. 141-50, 325-7. Verbal formulae and verbal play are used repeatedly in the story. The use of *skaz* enables Gogol to mock the reader and his expectations.]

Peppard, V. 'Who stole whose overcoat and whose text is it?', *South Atlantic Review*, 55, 1990, 1, pp. 63-80. [An examination of the 'double en-coding' of the ending of 'The Overcoat' as both fantastic story and parody thereof in the context of the varying degrees of seriousness encountered in the genre of the supernatural tale.]

Pereverzev, V.F., *Tvorchestvo Gogolia*, first 1914; reprinted in his *Gogol'. Dostoevskii, Issledovaniia* (Sovetskii pisatel': Moscow, 1982) pp. 40-186.

Peuranen, E., 'Akakii Akakievich Bashmachkin i Sviatoi Akakii', *Studia Slavica Finlandensia*, 1, 1984, pp. 122-33. [Prototypes for Akakii Akakievich are sought both in the poor clerk tales of the 1830s and in the Lives of The Saints, specifically of St Acacius of Sevan, who is linked to Akakii Akakievich by martyrdom through cold, a key motif in the story, and St Acacius of Sinai, whose life closely models his. 'The Overcoat' integrates the genres of short story and saint's life.]

Poliakova, S., '"Shinel'" Gogolia i "Egipetskaia marka" Mandel'shtama' [first 1991], in her *Oleinikov i ob Oleinikove i drugie raboty po russkoi literature* (Inapress, St Petersburg, 1997) pp. 286-8. [The episode of the theft of Akakii Akakievich's Overcoat is echoed in two thefts of clothes in *Egipetskaia marka* from the hero Parnok, who also has traits of physiology and character in common with Akakii Akakievich.]

Popkin, C., *The Pragmatics of Insignificance: Chekhov, Zoshchenko, Gogol* (Stanford University Press: Stanford, 1993). [On 'The Overcoat', pp. 197-205. The story of 'The Overcoat' is the problem of its own discourse. Parallels are drawn between Akakii Akakievich and the reader, both in search of something material and solid to hold on to; and also between Akakii Akakievich, the text, the reader, the narrator and Gogol himself.]

Proffitt, E., 'Gogol's "perfectly true" tale: "The Overcoat" and its mode of closure', *Studies in Short Fiction*, 14, 1977, pp. 35-40. [There is no fantastic ending and no ghost. Gogol is mocking the reader's con-ventional hope for poetic justice for Akakii Akakievich.]

Pushkin, A.S., *Polnoe sobranie sochinenii v sem'nadtsati tomakh* (Akademiia nauk SSSR: Moscow, 1937-59).

———*Polnoe sobranie sochinenii v desiati tomakh*, third edition (Akademiia nauk SSSR: Moscow, 1962-65).

Pustovoit, P.G., ' Gogolevskoe nachalo v tvorchestve I.S. Turgeneva' in G.V. Samoilenko (ed.), *Gogol i sovremennost'. Tvorcheskoe nasledie pisatelia v dvizhenii epokh* (Vishcha shkola: Kiev, 1983) pp. 41-9.

Rancour-Laferriere, D., *Out from under Gogol's "Overcoat": A Psychoana-lytic Study* (Ardis: Ann Arbor, Michigan, 1982). [This is by far the longest single study of the story, and consists of a long methodo-logical introduction and an analysis comprising 35 sections. Rancour-Laferriere is explicitly not concerned to make a psychoanalytical study of Gogol himself. Rather he analyses the behaviour of the characters, in particular Akakii Akakievich and Petrovich, and the implications of the plot in the light of reader response. To do so he deploys extraordinary erudition in the area of earlier studies of Gogol; psychoanalytical writings; and manifestations of popular consciousness, particularly Russian folklore, including obscene folklore. He is also very alert in his close readings to linguistic and syntactical features of the story. The book is engagingly written and consistently suggestive. Only occasionally does it seem to over-interpret its material or to give too much space to background evidence from psychoanalytical case studies, interesting as these are. Rancour-Laferriere makes no case for the hegemony of a psycho-analytical reading and it is striking how close his interpretations are, *mutatis mutandis*, to those of critics writing from other positions.]

Reiser, S., '"Vse my vyshli iz gogolevskoi 'Shineli'." (Istoriia odnoi legendy)', *Voprosy literatury*, 1968, 2, pp. 184-7. [Dostoevsky never said the words commonly attributed to him 'We all came out of Gogol's "Overcoat"', and the French diplomat and historian of Russian literature de Vogüé did not ascribe them to him but to 'Russian writers' in general. The popularity of the formula is put down to the fact that on the basis of his writings Dostoevsky would have been entirely justified in saying it.]

——'K istorii formuly "Vse my vyshli iz gogolevskoi 'Shineli'"' in M.P. Alekseev (ed.), *Poetika i stilistika russkoi literatury. Pamiati akademika Viktora Vladimirovicha Vinogradova* (Nauka: Leningrad, 1971) pp. 187-9. [Return to the question discussed by Reiser 1968 and Bocharov and Mann 1968. There is no proof that Dostoevsky is the source. The words are also linked to Turgenev and could be linked to any writer associated with the 'Natural School'.]

Remizov, A., *Povest' o Ivane Semenoviche Stratilatove. Neuemnyi buben* (in his *Sochineniia*, volume 1, Shipovnik: Moscow, 1910; repr. Russkoe tvorchestvo: Berlin, 1922), **from which quoted.**

Remizov, A., 'Chainichek', *Russkaia mysl'*, 1915, No. 10; reprinted in his *Sredi mur'ia* (Severnye dni: Moscow, 1917); and in his *Mara. Kniga rasskazov* (Epokha: Berlin, 1922) pp. 1-54.

——'Sabotazh', in his *Vzvikhrennaia Rus'* (Tair: Paris, 1927; third edition, OPI: London, 1990) pp. 236-7, **from which quoted.**

——'Stoiat' – negasimuiu svechu Pamiati Evgeniia Ivanovicha Zamiat-ina' *Sovremennye zapiski*, Paris, 1937, No. 64; reprinted in *Nashe nasledie*, 1989, 1, pp. 117-19 **from which quoted.**

Rozanov, V.V., 'Legenda o Velikom inkvizitore F.M. Dostoevskogo. Opyt kriticheskogo kommentariia', first published in *Russkii vestnik*, 1891, Nos 1-4; reprinted in his *Legenda o Velikom inkvizitore F.M. Dostoevskogo. Opyt kriticheskogo kommentariia. S prilozheniem dvukh etiudov o Gogole* (Nikolaev: St Petersburg, 1894); second edition (Merkushev: Petersburg, 1902); third edition (Pirozhkov: St Petersburg, 1906); reprinted Fink: Munich, 1970, pp. 1-249; and in his *Mysli o literature* (Sovremennik: Moscow, 1989) pp. 41-157, 531-6. **Quoted from 1970.**

——'Pushkin i Gogol'', first published in *Moskovskie vedomosti*, 15 February 1891, as 'Neskol'ko slov o Gogole'; reprinted under this title in the first (Nikolaev: St Petersburg, 1894) and second (Merkushev: Petersburg, 1902) editions of his *Legenda o Velikom inkvizitore F.M. Dostoevskogo. Opyt kriticheskogo kommentariia. S prilozheniem dvukh etiudov o Gogole*; reprinted with the new title in the third edition (Pirozhkov: St Petersburg, 1906); reprinted Fink: Munich, 1970, pp. 253-65; in his *O Gogole* (Prideaux: Letchworth, 1970) pp. 5-17; and in his *Mysli o literature* (Sovremennik: Moscow, 1989) pp. 158-66, 536. **Quoted from 1970.**

——'Kak proizoshel tip Akakiia Akakievicha', first in *Russkii vestnik*, 1894, 3, pp. 161-72; reprinted in his *Legenda o Velikom inkvizitore F.M. Dostoevskogo. Opyt kriticheskogo kommentariia. S prilozheniem dvukh etiudov o Gogole* (Fink: Munich, 1970) pp. 266-82; also in his *O Gogole* (Prideaux: Letchworth, 1970) pp. 18-34; and in his *Mysli o literature* (Sovremennik: Moscow, 1989, pp. 166-76, 536-7; translated as 'How the character Akaky Akakievich originated' in *The Ohio University Review*, 10, 1968, pp. 42-56. [Using the recently published drafts of the story, Rozanov finds that Gogol shuns reality in his writings and that his recurrent impulse is to diminish his characters. The 'lyrical' passages are added later out of pity.] **Quoted from 1970.**

Sadie, S. (ed.), *The New Grove Dictionary of Opera*, 4 volumes (Macmillan: London, 1992).

Saltykov-Shchedrin, M., *Polnoe sobranie sochinenii v 20 tomakh* (Khudozhestvennaia literatura: Moscow, 1965-77).

Scatton, L. Hart, *Mikhail Zoshchenko. Evolution of a Writer* (Cambridge University Press: Cambridge, 1993).

Schillinger, J., 'Gogol''s "The Overcoat" as a travesty of hagiography', *Slavic and East European Journal*, 16, 1972, 1, pp. 36-41. [The plot of 'The Overcoat' as a detailed travesty of the Life of St Acacius of Sinai.]

Seemann, K.D., 'Eine Heiligenlegende als Vorbild von Gogol's "Mantel"', *Zeitschrift für slavische Philologie*, 33, 1967, pp. 7-21. [A discussion of the relevance of the legend of Saint Akakii to 'The Overcoat' and a response to the views of Chizhevsky, Driessen and Wissemann. Seemann suggests that Gogol became aware of the St Acacius story through his reading of the *Lestvitsa* of St John of Sinai.]

Setchkarev, V., *Gogol. His Life and Work*, [first in German, 1953] (Peter Owen: London, 1965) pp. 216-26. [It is amazing that this text could have been read as 'realistic' and 'humanitarian'. There follows an analysis of the narrative tone, of the mixture of styles and of Gogol's linguistic play.]

Shapiro, G., *Nikolai Gogol and the Baroque Cultural Heritage* (The Pennsylvania State University Press: University Park, Pennsylvania, 1993).

Shepard, E., 'Pavlov's "Demon" and Gogol''s "Overcoat"', *Slavic Review*, 33, 1974, 2, pp. 288-301. [A comparison of 'The Overcoat' and N.F. Pavlov's story about a clerk of 1839, which Gogol knew. Close parallels are noted but also differences and it is suggested that 'The Overcoat' may be a polemical riposte to the earlier work.]

Sherry, C., 'The fit of Gogol's "Overcoat": an ontological view of narrative form', *Genre*, 7, 1974, 1, pp. 1-29. [An attempt, using an ontological approach, to combine the ethical and aesthetic planes of the story, hitherto discussed separately by the hostile Belinskian and Eikhenbaumian schools. The grotesque world of Gogol's narrative is arbitrarily and whimsically ordered both in terms of space and in terms of appearances and hierarchies.]

Shklovskii, V., 'Siuzhet i stil'', in his *Khudozhestvennaia proza. Razmyshleniia i razbory* (Sovetskii pisatel': Moscow, 1959) pp. 397-418.

———'"Shinel'"', in his *Povesti o proze. Razmyshleniia i razbory* (Khudozhestvennaia literatura: Moscow, 1966), volume 2, pp. 92-103. [Repeats the parts of Shklovskii 1959 that are on 'The Overcoat'.]

———'Novyi Petrograd i "Shinel'"', in his *Tetiva. O neskhodstve skhodnogo* (Sovetskii pisatel': Moscow, 1970) pp. 19-24.

———*Tret'ia fabrika* (Krug: Moscow 1926; repr. Prideaux: Letchworth, 1978; in English as *The Third Factory*, edited and translated by Richard Sheldon (Ardis: Ann Arbor, Michigan, 1977), **from which quoted.**

———*Khod konia. Sbornik statei* (Gelikon: Moscow and Berlin, 1923; repr. Antiquary: Orange, Connecticutt, 1986), **from which quoted.**

Sicher, E., 'Dialogization and laughter in the dark, or How Gogol's Nose was made: Parody and literary evolution in Bachtin's Theory of the novel', *Russian Literature*, 28, 1990, 2, pp. 211-33.

Sinitskaia, S.V., 'Ob imenakh u Gogolia', *Russkaia literatura*, 1998, 3, pp. 272-3.

Sloane, D., 'The name as phonetic icon: a reconsideration of onomastic significance in Gogol's "The Overcoat"', *Slavic and East European Journal*, 35, 1991, 4, pp. 473-88. [An investigation of the phonetic implications of the name Akakii Akakievich, as a key to the stuttering, hesitancy and disjointedness that characterise the text on all levels.]

Slobin, G. Nachtailer, 'Writing as possession: the case of Remizov's "Poor Clerk"' in N.Å. Nilsson (ed.), *Studies in Twentieth-Century Prose, Stockholm Studies in Russian Literature*, 14, Stockholm, 1982, pp. 59-79.

Slonimskii, A.L., *Tekhnika komicheskogo u Gogolia* (Academia: Leningrad, 1923; repr., Brown University Press: Providence, Rhode Island, 1963); translated in Maguire 1976, pp. 323-73. **Quoted from 1976.**

Smirnova, E.S., *Poema Gogolia "Mertvye dushi"* (Nauka: Leningrad, 1987).

Sokolianskii, A., '"Shinel'" ot pervogo litsa. Aleksandr Feklistov v roli Akakiia Akakievicha. Antrepriza "Bogis"', *Moskovskii nabliudatel'*, 1994, 3-4, pp. 18-23.

Sologub, F., *Sobranie sochinenii*, volume 1, *Rasskazy (1894-1908)*, compiled by Ulrich Steltner (Sagner: Munich, 1992).

Sosa, M., 'Gogol from the 1920s: Tynjanov's scenario for "Sinel'", *Slavic and East European Journal*, 30, 1986, pp. 553-58.

Stilman [Shtil'man] L., 'Gogol's Overcoat - thematic patterns and origins', *American Slavic and East European Review* [*Slavic Review*], 11, 1952, 2, pp. 138-48. [A structure of yearning, possession and frustration recurs in Gogol's writings. Though the direct triggers of the tale may have been the anecdote related in Annenkov's memoirs and a Pushkin diary entry, they were only suggestive to Gogol in the context of his own concerns.]

Surkov, E.A., 'Tip geroia i zhanrovoe svoeobrazie povesti N.V. Gogolia "Shinel'"' in N.V. Tamarchenko (ed.), *Tipologicheskii analiz literaturnogo proizvedeniia* (Kemerovskii gosudarstvennyi universitet: Kemerovo, 1982) pp. 67-74. [Akakii Akakievich is compared to the hero of Romanticism, specifically to Hoffmann's Anselm in *The Golden Pot*, and then to the hagiographical tradition, specifically to the Life of St Feodosii Pecherskii (St Theodosius of the Caves).]

Tikhvinskaia, L., *Kabare i teatry miniatiur v Rossii, 1908-1917* (RIK 'Kul'tura': Moscow, 1995).

Toporov, V.N., 'Peterburg i peterburgskii tekst russkoi literatury', *Uchenye zapiski Tartuskogo gosudarstvennogo universiteta*, 664, *Trudy po znakovym sistemam*, 18, Tartu, 1984, pp. 4-29.

——'Tekst goroda-devy i goroda-bludnitsy v mifologicheskom aspekte', *Struktura teksta-81: tezisy simpoziuma*, Moscow, 1981, pp. 53-8; reprinted in T.V. Tsiv'ian (ed.), *Issledovaniia po strukture teksta* (Nauka: Moscow, 1987) pp. 121-32. **Quoted from 1987.**

Tosi, A., 'Andrei Kropotov's "Istoriia o smurom kaftane": a thematic source for Gogol''s "Shinel'"?', *Slavonic and East European Review*, 76, 1998, 4, pp. 601-13. [There are close parallels of plot, characterisation and narrative tone between Kropotov's 1809 story and 'The Overcoat', though the former does not have a fantastic ending. The case for influence is considered.]

Trahan, E. (ed.), *Gogol' 's 'Overcoat': An Anthology of Critical Essays* (Ardis: Ann Arbor, Michigan, 1982).

———'Introduction' in Trahan, pp. 7-19. [A brief overview of criticism of the tale, culminating in the five pieces translated in the book, all of them written before 1960 and discussed in this bibliography.]

Tschizewskij, D.: see Chizhevskii, D., above.

Tsiv'ian, Iu. G., 'Paleogrammy v fil'me "Shinel'"' in M.O. Chudakova (ed.), *Tynianovskii sbornik*, 2 (Zinatne: Riga, 1986) pp. 14-27.

Turgenev, I.S., *Polnoe sobranie sochinenii i pisem v dvadtsati vos'mi tomakh* (Izdatel'stvo Akademii nauk SSSR, Moscow and Leningrad, 1960-8).

Turitsyn, V., 'Tri ekranizatsii "Shineli" N.V. Gogolia', *Kino i vremia*, 4, 1965, pp. 103-28. [The article considers three film adaptations of 'The Overcoat', those by Kozintsev and Trauberg, Alberto Lattuada and Aleksei Batalov, and, interpreting Gogol in traditional Soviet post-Belinskian fashion as motivated by sympathy for the 'little man', finds all three films wanting.]

Tynianov, Iu. N., 'Libretto kinofil'ma "Shinel'"', *Iz istorii Lenfil'ma*, 3, 1973, pp. 78-91.

———*Dostoevskii i Gogol' (K teorii parodii)* (Opoiaz: Petrograd, 1921); **quoted from** his *Poetika. Istoriia literatury. Kino* (Nauka: Moscow, 1977) pp. 198-226, 483-9.

———'O feksakh', *Sovetskii ekran*, 1929, 14, p. 10; **quoted from** his *Poetika. Istoriia literatury. Kino* (Nauka: Moscow, 1977) pp. 346-8, 557.

Vaiskopf, M., 'Poetika peterburgskikh povestei Gogolia (Problema ob"-ektivizatsii i gipostazirovaniia', *Slavica Hierosolymitana*, 3, 1978, pp. 8-54. [On 'The Overcoat', pp. 35-54. A very wide-ranging and suggestive close reading of the text, covering such features as Akakii Akakievich's christening, Petersburg time and space, the demonic qualities of Petrovich, eros, the simultaneous 'birth' from an idea of the overcoat and the important personage, imagery of light and colour, and the connections between life and death in the tale.]

———*Siuzhet Gogolia: Morfologiia. Ideologiia. Kontekst* (Radiks: Moscow, 1993). [See especially Chapter 7, 'Oblachenie v slovo', pp. 305-62. A further close analysis of the story, in part developing the 1978 study, but adding much new material, particularly in the areas of sources for the tale; the hero's name; and clothes imagery in the story.]

Vakhtin, B., 'Dublenka' in *Metropol'*, Moscow, 1979, pp. 74-80; reprinted in his *Tak slozhilas' zhizn' moia... Povesti i rasskazy* (Sovetskii pisatel': Leningrad, 1990) pp. 156-204; in English in his *The Sheepskin Coat & An Absolutely Happy Village*, translated by Robert Dessaix and Michael Ulman (Ardis: Ann Arbor, Michigan, 1989) pp. 7-79. **Quoted from 1990.**

van der Eng, J., 'Bashmachkin's character: a combination of comic, gro-tesque, tragicomic and tragic elements' [1958] in Trahan, pp. 73-85.

[Drawing upon Driessen's reading this study looks at the relationship of the ending and the two 'humane passages' to the rest of the story. It also considers the mix of the comic, the grotesque, the tragicomic and the tragic in the characterisation of the hero.]

Vedeniapina, E.A., 'Kompozitsionno-rechevye osobennosti povesti N.V. Gogolia "Shinel'"' in A.N. Kozhin (ed.), *Iazyk N.V. Gogolia* (Vysshaia shkola: Moscow, 1991) pp. 47-59. [The article identifies three narrative voices in the story: the first represents officialdom and hierarchy, narrates the story strictly and tends to moralise; the second is associative and conversational, interested in picturesque detail; the third, which is used once Akakii Akakievich comes to life, has a more intimate tone, representing the hero's position. The article then discusses the hero's own language.]

Veresaev, V., *Gogol' v zhizni. Sistematicheskii svod podlinnykh svidetel'stv sovremennikov* (Moskovskii rabochii: Moscow, 1990).

Vetlovskaia, V.E., 'Povest' Gogolia "Shinel'". (Transformatsiia pushkinskikh motivov)', *Russkaia literatura*, 1988, 4, pp. 41-69. [Gogol's admiration for Pushkin's tragedy *Boris Godunov* is attested: on the influence of the tale of the threat to the Tsar's porphyry and the 'cap of Monomakh' on the tale of the poor clerk's loss of his overcoat; on the ways in which Gogol reflected and transformed the Pushkinian motifs. An analysis of the character of Akakii Akakievich and of his relationship with the important personage, a figure at the other end of the hierarchical ladder.]

Vetlovskaia, V.E., 'Tragediia *Shineli*', *Russkaia literatura*, 1998, 3, pp. 11-17. [Returns to ideas of Vetlovskaia 1988. On the links of 'The Overcoat' as the tragedy of the loss of an article of clothing to Pushkin's tragedy 'Boris Godunov', the tragedy of the potential loss of the Tsar's porphyry and the 'cap of Monomakh'. Working in the tradition of European 'costume drama' both Pushkin and Gogol come to momentous conclusions about the fates of individuals and nations.]

——'Zhitiinye istochniki gogolevskoi "Shineli"', *Russkaia literatura*, 1999, 1, pp. 18-35. [A return to the discussion by Driessen, Seemann, Schillinger and others of the relationship of 'The Overcoat' with the Life of St Acacius of Sinai. A consideration of the relevance of other St Acaciuses, and of other Lives of the Saints, particularly that of St Vasilii, whose feast day is celebrated on 22 March, the day of Akakii Akakievich's birth. Gogol does not travesty hagiography in the tale: but Akakii Akakievich does not have saintly qualities.]

Vinogradov, V.V., G*ogol' i natural'naia shkola* (Obrazovanie: Leningrad, 1925); in English as *Gogol' and the Natural School*, translated by D.K. Erikson and R. Parrott (Ardis: Ann Arbor, Michigan, 1987); quoted from his *Izbrannye trudy. Poetika russkoi literatury* (Nauka: Moscow, 1976) pp. 189-227. **Quoted as Vinogradov 1976a.**

Vinogradov, V.V., 'Problema skaza v stilistike', first in *Poetika. Vremennik Otdela slovesnykh iskusstv*, 1 (Academia: Leningrad, 1926) pp. 24-50; translated in *Russian Literature Triquarterly*, 12, 1975, pp. 237-50; **quoted from** his *Izbrannye trudy. O iazyke khudozhestvennoi prozy* (Nauka: Moscow, 1980) pp. 42-54.

——*Evoliutsiia russkogo naturalizma. Gogol' i Dostoevskii* (Academia: Leningrad, 1929); translation of the last section, 'Shkola sentimental'nogo naturalizma' in Meyer and Rudy, pp. 161-228; quoted from his *Izbrannye trudy. Poetika russkoi literatury* (Nauka: Moscow), 1976, pp. 3-187. **Quoted as Vinogradov 1976b.**

Vinogradova, L.N., 'Kalendarnye perekhody nechistoi sily vo vremeni i prostranstve' in T.A. Agapkina (ed.), *Kontsept dvizheniia v iazyke i kul'ture* (Indrik: Moscow, 1996) pp. 166-84.

Voinovich, V., *Shapka* (OPI: London, 1988); reprinted in his *Khochu byt' chestnym* (Moskovskii rabochii: Moscow, 1989) pp. 211-95; translated as *The Fur Hat* (Jonathan Cape: London, 1990).

Voloshinov, V.N., *Marksizm i filosofiia iazyka*, Leningrad, 1929; second edition, Leiningrad, 1930; reprinted (Mouton: The Hague and Paris, 1972); in English as *Marxism and the Philosophy of Language*, translated by Ladislav Matejka and I.R. Titunik (Seminar Press: New York and London, 1973), **from which quoted.**

Voronskii, A., *Izbrannye stat'i o literature* (Khudozhestvennaia literatura: Moscow, 1982).

Voropaev, V. and Vinogradov, I., '"Lestvitsa, vozvodiashchaia na nebo." Neizvestnyi avtograf N.V. Gogolia', *Literaturnaia ucheba*, 1992, 1-3, pp. 172-4. [Presentation of Gogol''s 'O gneve i bezgnevii', ibid., pp. 175-7.]

Waszink, P.M., 'Mythical traits in Gogol''s "The Overcoat"', *Slavic and East European Journal*, 22, 1978, 3, pp. 287-300. [Cassirer's concept of *Konkreszens* and Lévi-Strauss's motif of oblivion are used to examine questions of language and identity in 'The Overcoat'.]

Watson, P., *Nureyev. A Biography* (Hodder and Stoughton: London, 1994).

Weddle, D., 'Deadpan afterlife', *Sight and Sound*, 10, 2000, 4, pp. 18-21.

Wellek, R. and Warren, A., *Theory of Literature*, New York and London, 1949; second edition, London, 1954; third edition (Penguin: Harmondsworth: 1963, reprinted 1966). **Quoted from 1966.**

Wissemann, H., 'The ideational content of Gogol's "Overcoat"' [1959] in Trahan, pp. 86-105. [Developing on and polemicising with Chizhevsky, the article agrees that the story is about the problem of man's place in the world. It suggests that Akakii Akakievich does not succumb to evil passion and that the meaning of the story lies in the failure of the important personage to show compassion.]

Woodward, J., 'The threadbare fabric of Gogol's Overcoat', *Canadian Slavic Studies*, 1, 1967, 1, pp. 95-104. [On the linguistic means which Gogol uses to blur reality and undermine certainty in the tale.]

Woodward, J., *The Symbolic Art of Gogol: Essays on His Short Fiction* (Slavica: Columbus, Ohio, 1982). [Chapter 5, pp. 88-112, is on 'The Overcoat'. The story is interpreted as a densely coded variant of Gogol's regular theme of emasculated men and powerful women. This conflict is further adumbrated in repeated allusions to the conflict between Peter the Great and Catherine the Great.]

Yi, H., 'Kurosawa and Gogol: looking through the lens of metonymy', *Literature / Film Quarterly*, 27, 1999, 3, pp. 210-17.

Zamiatin, E., *Sochineniia* (Neimanis: Munich, volume 1, 1970; volume 2, 1982; volume 3, 1986; volume 4, 1988).

Zholkovsky, A., 'Rereading Gogol's miswritten book: notes on *Selected Passages from Correspondence with Friends*' in Fusso and Meyer, pp. 172-84, 268-74.

Zhukovskii, V., *Sobranie sochinenii v chetyrekh tomakh* (Gosudarstvennoe izdatel'stvo khudozhestvennoi literatury: Moscow, 1959-60).

Zinik, Z. *Russkaia sluzhba* (Sintaksis: Paris, 1983).

Zoshchenko, M., *Sobranie sochinenii v trekh tomakh* (Khudozhestvennaia literatura: Leningrad, 1986-87).

Filmography

Shinel' [The Overcoat], directed by Grigorii Kozintsev and Lev Trauberg, Soviet Union, Leningradkino Studio, 1926.

Ikiru [Living], directed by Akira Kurosawa, Japan 1952.

Il cappotto [The Overcoat], directed by Alberto Lattuada, Italy, 1952.

The Bespoke Overcoat, directed by Jack Clayton, Great Britain, Remus Films, 1956.

Shinel' [The Overcoat], directed by Aleksei Batalov, Soviet Union, Lenfil'm Studio, 1959

Shinel' [The Overcoat], directed by Iurii Norshtein, animation, Russia, in production.

Index

[Numbers in **bold** denote annotated entries in the Bibliography.]

Also available in the series: